Governance of Higher Education

Governance of Higher Education explores the work of traditional and contemporary higher education scholarship worldwide, providing readers with an understanding of the assumptions, historical traditions, and paradigms that have shaped the scholarship on governance. Bringing together the vast and disparate writings that form the higher education governance literature—including frameworks drawn from a range of disciplines and global scholarship—this book synthesizes the significant theoretical, conceptual, and empirical scholarship to advance the research and practice of governance. Coverage includes the structures of governance, cultures and practices, the collegial tradition, the new managed environment of the academy, and the politics and processes of governance. As universities across the globe face a myriad of challenges and multiple stakeholder demands, *Governance of Higher Education* offers scholars, practitioners, and higher education graduate students an essential resource for advancing research and the practice of governance.

Ian Austin is the Deputy Director for Continuing and Professional Education at the University of the West Indies, Open Campus, Barbados.

Glen A. Jones is Ontario Research Chair in Postsecondary Education Policy and Measurement, and Professor of Higher Education at the University of Toronto, Canada.

Governance of Higher Education

Global Perspectives, Theories, and Practices

Ian Austin
Glen A. Jones

Routledge
Taylor & Francis Group

NEW YORK AND LONDON

First published 2016
by Routledge
711 Third Avenue, New York, NY 10017

and by Routledge
2 Park Square, Milton Park, Abingdon, Oxon, OX14 4RN

Routledge is an imprint of the Taylor & Francis Group, an informa business

Library of Congress Cataloging-in-Publication Data
Austin, Ian, 1960–
   Governance of higher education : global perspectives, theories, and practices / Ian Austin, Glen A. Jones.
       pages cm
   1. Education, Higher—United States—Administration.   2. Universities and colleges—United States—Administration.   I. Jones, Glen Alan, 1961–   II. Title.
   LB2341.A758 2016
   378.1′01—dc23
   2015010690

ISBN: 978-0-415-73974-0 (hbk)
ISBN: 978-0-415-73975-7 (pbk)
ISBN: 978-1-315-81640-1 (ebk)

Typeset in Aldine and Helvetica Neue
by Apex CoVantage, LLC

Printed and bound in the United States of America by
Edwards Brothers Malloy on sustainably sourced paper

Brief Contents

Contents

Preface

Governance is at the heart of the functioning of higher education but conceptually it can be somewhat elusive. It occurs at the organizational and institutional levels, at the state-institutional level, at the regional level, and at the level of global governing institutions such as the Organisation for Economic Co-operation and Development (OECD). Higher education scholars have long been interested in understanding and describing the governance of higher education, and the broad reforms to university governance that have taken place in recent decades have intensified the interest in this area of scholarship. In order to advance research in higher education governance, we saw a need to develop a textbook that would review the major theories and concepts that underscore scholarship in this area, suggest new theoretical directions, and synthesize, integrate, and provide commentary on the vast and sometimes disparate writings on higher education governance. In this book, *Governance of Higher Education: Global Perspectives, Theories, and Practices*, we set out to achieve these outcomes in 10 chapters.

AUDIENCE

This book is intended for different audiences. It will be tremendously beneficial to higher education graduate students who are studying governance. Higher education faculty who teach governance can adopt this book as a foundational text for their students. We also believe that the book will be of interest to researchers who are turning their attention to the study of higher education governance for the first time and desire an overview of key concepts and ideas, as well as to faculty members and administrators who are navigating the governing terrain of the academy. Higher education practitioners and policy-makers alike who are interested in issues of governance and seeking alternative perspectives from which to understand and analyze governance will also find this book very useful.

STRUCTURE OF BOOK AND CONTENT FEATURES OF CHAPTERS

Because of the changing environment of higher education, we believe that it is vitally important for a textbook on governance to give maximum coverage to new research findings, along with current practices and perspectives. However, we recognize that it is also equally important for seminal and other earlier scholarly works in the field of higher education governance to receive adequate attention. This volume therefore incorporates the work of both early and more contemporary higher education governance scholars, provides critical analysis of their work, explores new possible explanations of governance issues, and presents them in a coherent and integrated way. To achieve this, we build on the depth, breadth, and scope of previous scholarly work; examine underlying assumptions, historical traditions, and paradigms that have shaped the scholarship on governance; and simultaneously explore other conceptual and theoretical avenues that traditionally have only marginally been explored in the higher education governance literature or not at all.

Chapter 1 serves as an introduction to the remainder of the book. It lays the conceptual groundwork that we feel is pertinent to contextualizing and understanding the chapters that follow. Hence, the chapter focuses on defining governance in higher education, highlights traditions from which governing modes originated, discusses universities as societal institutions, conceptualizes them as operating within institutional fields, and differentiates between internal self-governance, external governance, and market-oriented governance.

To locate this book within a theoretical frame of reference, we devoted two chapters to two streams of theory. Thus, chapters 2 and 3 focus on theories that are taken from the organizational and institutional theory literature but are applicable to higher education governance and provide readers with a deeper understanding and alternative perspectives of governance. Hence, chapter 2 covers theories that focus on the influence of external environment on the governance of higher education institutions. Chapter 3 covers theoretical perspectives that help readers to understand internal institutional governance.

Chapter 4 examines state-university relations and the ways in which governance is changing as a result of shifting state-university relations. By drawing on examples of policies, practices, and governance reforms from around the world, we discuss the theoretical and conceptual underpinnings of state-university governance. Specifically, the chapter focuses on the conceptual foundations and policy issues that shape the balance between state responsibilities and universities' autonomy; type and degree of government control versus university autonomy; and the changing role of the state and its impact on higher education governance.

Chapter 5 examines external/systems governance (using national models drawn from North America, Continental Europe, the UK, and Asia) to understand the variations in structures and practices. The chapter discusses the governing state-university relationship in the USA, the UK, France, Germany, Japan, and China within the context of the traditions from which they came and the changes that have taken place within the last 10 years.

Chapter 6 shifts the focus from external relations with the state and other stake-holders and looks at the concepts and practices of academic self-governance in the academy. It covers issues such as academic freedom, collegiality, the functioning of academic governing bodies, shared governance, the fiduciary responsibility of the board of trustees, faculty unionization, and student participation in institutional governance.

Chapter 7 continues the discussion on internal self-governance but focuses specifically on the processes by which universities are governed. Concepts such as bureaucracy, hierarchy, organized anarchy, and the legitimacy of decisions are discussed along with the garbage can model of decision-making. Because power and politics are so endemic in the academy, extensive treatment is accorded to them, specifically, power and politics and conflict and power, politics and organization-environment relations.

Chapter 8 explores the notion of governing higher education as a managed enterprise. It captures the contemporary context of the academy by discussing issues such as neoliberalism and higher education governance, managerialism, and new public management and the way they are reforming governance in the academy. Essentially, this chapter highlights new paradigms that are at the heart of the new world of a managed enterprise and how tools like quality assurance and strategic planning have become instruments of governance. Along with these changes, the chapter analyzes the shift to a stronger executive leadership model and the challenge of governing in this context.

Chapter 9 addresses new issues and challenges in governance. In the first part of this chapter, we look at governance issues related to risk, trust, information technology, and multi-campus institutional arrangements. In the second half of the chapter we focus on the complex governance issues related to the glonacal, transnational, and regional dimensions of higher education. We believe that a book of this type would be incomplete without a discussion on new and emerging issues in higher education governance.

Chapter 10 provides concluding observations and reflections along with considerations for future research.

At the end of each chapter we include a few discussion questions that are designed to stimulate reflection on key issues.

Acknowledgments

The project was originally Ian's idea, borne out of many discussions with Glen on governance issues in higher education. From its initial conceptualization, Glen readily agreed that a book of this type was needed. We began working on it when Ian was a Visiting Scholar at the Ontario Institute for Studies in Education (OISE) at the University of Toronto, and we were able to complete most of the work during that period.

We would like to acknowledge the support that we have both received from OISE's Department of Leadership, Higher and Adult Education, and the administrative assistance that we received from Karen, Joanne, and Vesna Bajic. A number of Glen's graduate students provided assistance with components of the project: Artur Khoyetsyan conducted a number of important bibliographic searches that supported our early work; Sharon X. Li, Christian Noumi, and Kamaljeet Singh provided feedback on the original book proposal including the first chapter; and Sharon Li and Diane Barbaric provided useful feedback on our coverage of specific national systems. Financial support for component parts of the project was provided by the Ontario Research Chair in Postsecondary Education Policy and Measurement and the Social Sciences and Humanities Research Council of Canada.

We benefitted from a number of leading international scholars who kindly agreed to provide us with feedback and insightful comments on specific chapters. We are very grateful for the comments and helpful suggestions that we received from the following:

Giliberto Capano, Scuola Normale Superiore (Italy)
Joe Christopher, Curtin University of Technology (Australia)
Jay Dee, University of Massachusetts-Boston (USA)
Ruth Hayhoe, University of Toronto (Canada)
James Hearn, University of Georgia (USA)
John Hirt, Virginia Tech (USA)
Jussi Kivisto, University of Tampere (Finland)
Thierry Luescher-Mamashela, University of the Free State (South Africa)
Ka Ho Mok, Hong Kong Institute of Education (Hong Kong)
Christopher Morphew, University of Iowa (USA)

Uwe Schimank, University of Twente (Netherlands)
Peter Scott, Institute of Education (England)
Michael Skolnik, University of Toronto (Canada)
Martina Vukasovic, Ghent University (Belgium)

It is important to us that we get your views, thoughts, and recommendations about the book. We therefore welcome any comments on the coverage and content, particularly highlighting any errors, deficiencies, or oversights. Please email us at ian.austin@open.uwi.edu, iaustin@vt.edu, or gjones@oise.utoronto.ca.

In the final stages of the project Glen was a Visiting Professor at the University of the West Indies (UWI) and he would like to acknowledge the support and assistance that he received at the UWI Open Campus and the UWI Cave Hill Campus in Barbados.

On a more personal note, we wish to thank our families. Ian would like to thank his wife, Rockiel, for her valuable editorial feedback on the chapters as they were being developed and for her moral support throughout the entire venture. Glen wishes to thank his wife, Renee, and son, Samuel, for their love and support—especially for letting him work on this project in Barbados while they were freezing at home in Toronto. Finally, special thanks to Heather Jarrow at Routledge for her patience and understanding.

Ian Austin
Glen A. Jones
February 2015

CHAPTER 1

Conceptualizing Governance in Higher Education

Universities have become one of the most important institutions in our society. They educate the professionals that provide our health care, teach our children, strive for justice in our legal system, and design our buildings, bridges, and technologies. They provide a liberal education that challenges and expands our thinking. They are institutions of knowledge creation that contribute to the social and economic development of our society through new concepts, ideas, applications, and inventions. They play a key role as a safe home for social criticism by identifying key problems and contributing to informed public debates.

Universities are not simple organizations. In fact, given the breadth of their goals and missions, the tremendous expertise and specialization that characterize their basic functions, and the huge diversity of their activities, universities have evolved to become one of the most complex organizational forms that the human species has ever created. They employ hundreds, and in some cases thousands, of highly specialized experts who share their knowledge through teaching and pursue what are frequently unique programs of research. The university's physical plant includes classrooms and laboratories, but it also may include medical centers, restaurants, rental housing, museums, art galleries, spaces for worship, and a plethora of specialized research facilities, ranging from agriculture research lands, to supercomputing facilities, to nuclear reactors.

Given the tremendous importance and complexity of the university, the question of how universities are or should be governed has been a recurring issue in higher education. Who decides what programs a university will offer and who will be admitted to those programs? Who decides who will lead the university? Who hires the professors? What role does the government play in funding, regulating, and steering universities? What role should students, business leaders, community organizations, and professional accrediting bodies play in these governing structures? What sorts of checks and balances are needed to ensure that there is appropriate oversight and that the university is moving in the "right" direction? These are all key themes and issues in higher education governance.

Governance is therefore of vital importance in higher education can be a fairly elusive and abstract concept for many people. The complexity and diversity of higher education systems means that what we see depends in large part on where we look. As Burton Clark

(1983) noted in his classic work on the organization of higher education, there are very different levels of authority within these systems and quite different decisions have been made on the power and authority of actors working at different levels within different institutions and systems. Many scholars have analyzed governance from a system-level perspective by exploring the relationships between universities and governments. How does the "system" make decisions about universities? There is a large body of scholarship describing and comparing system governance focusing on such issues as system planning, accountability, quality assessment, and funding. Others have centered their attention on the internal self-governing structures and practices of universities. How do universities decide? All of these research studies, in different ways, increase our understanding of governance, but given the trends and challenges identified by this research, these works also reinforce the importance of governance in higher education.

The importance of governance has been significantly amplified by the dramatic failures of governance and a series of well-publicized scandals in the private sector over the last few decades. Reforming corporate governance has come to be viewed as an important mechanism for rebuilding trust between the company and its shareholders, strengthening the oversight of financial decisions, and enhancing organizational performance outcomes. This makes the interrogation of traditions, structures, and practices of governance critical in the search for fresh and improved ways to govern organizations and systems. Yet, while higher education governance is regarded as an extremely important issue, there continue to be many theoretical and conceptual gaps in the literature. This concern prompted Tight (2004) and Huisman (2009) to describe the literature on higher education generally, and governance in particular, as atheoretical, descriptive, normative, and short on explicit theoretical frameworks.

This book focuses on the governance of universities. Our objective is to provide a comprehensive analysis of governance in higher education, with a particular focus on the governance of public universities, and address the theoretical limitations associated with the existing literature. One component of this analysis is a systematic, structured review of the literature. The other component draws on theories from sociology, political science, organizational studies, institutional theory, and neo-institutional theory, among others, to create a systematic, theory-based explanation of governance in higher education. The objective of this chapter is to establish the conceptual groundwork for the remainder of the book. The chapter will introduce and discuss key concepts that are foundational to understanding the governance concepts, theories, and practices explored in later sections of the book.

HIGHER EDUCATION GOVERNANCE

Governance is essential to the functioning of higher education at all levels, from the basic academic unit of the department (microlevel), to the level of the organization (mesolevel) and at the level of the higher education system (macrolevel). It is the means by which order is created in the academy to achieve the goals of educating, researching, and providing service to multiple publics. At the micro and meso levels, governance is related to the day-to-day functioning of universities and how they order their affairs through governance instruments that facilitate decision-making authority to ensure desired organizational performance outcomes. At the macrolevel, it is through governance mechanisms that the state attempts to ensure that its higher education system is achieving state-desired goals.

Governance has always been an important topic in the study of higher education, but in recent times it has gained more prominence because public universities are receiving increasing public scrutiny. Prior to the late 20th century, universities had a relatively sheltered existence in an environment in which they served stable national markets and had guaranteed financial support from governments (Parker, 2011). While the timelines vary by country, beginning roughly in the mid-1980s, governments and stakeholders in some jurisdictions have raised concerns about the manner in which the academy functions. They referenced performance challenges such as slow responsiveness, lack of agility and flexibility, operational inefficiency, and ineffectiveness (Kezar, 2004). These shortcomings are often attributed to university governance structures and practices. The claim is that the current structures and practices are no longer appropriate for the new, rapidly changing higher education environment (Currie, DeAngelis, de Boer, Huisman, & Lacotte, 2003).

The new higher education environment has been described by many scholars (e.g., Barnett, 2000; Gumport & Pusser, 1999; Marginson & Considine, 2000) as dynamic, shifting, and turbulent. The new environment in which universities now operate is driven by the philosophical prescriptions of globalization and the new economy. These philosophical prescriptions are mainly advanced by neoliberals and global governing institutions such as the Organisation for Economic Co-operation and Development (OECD), the World Bank, and the World Trade Organization (WTO) and have gained acceptance by many governments. They promote the massification and commodification of higher education with an emphasis on market-like behaviors among universities, with students as customers, significant increases in student enrollment, and international competition for students. Additionally, they advance industry-university relations and the sale of academic research as a diversification of funding sources, a phenomenon that is commonly referred to as academic capitalism (Slaughter & Rhoades, 2004). These global governing organizations position universities as vehicles of economic development, and advocate greater, direct stakeholder involvement in the academy. These environmental conditions are accompanied by demands for greater accountability, quality assurance mechanisms, and calls for professional management. As a result, universities face new expectations from states, provinces, national governments, and their expanded stakeholder base. When these factors are aggregated, university environments may be described as becoming increasingly more complex. Governance structures and practices are being restructured to cope with the complexities of the environment.

But what is governance in higher education? Governance is a complex concept and several definitions have been advanced to define governance in higher education but with little consensus (Currie et al., 2003; Rebora & Turri, 2009). They range from very simple conceptualizations, such as authority and legitimate rule—who has the authority to make decisions in the university—to more mid-range definitions, for example, by John Millett (1978), who conceptualizes university governance as "a structure and process of decision-making, within a college or university, about purposes, policies, programs and procedures" (p. 9). These purposes, policies, and procedures are written in statutes and charters that outline the mechanisms through which day-to-day decision-making is executed in attainment of the higher education mission.

Shattock (2006) attempts to further explain governance by introducing the notion of governance operating at multiple levels in higher education, especially when compared to a traditional company or nonprofit organization. Shattock treats governance as extending from a governing body down through senates and academic boards to faculty boards and departmental meetings. This conceptualization places heavy emphasis on internal governance, but governance is both internal and external, although a strong case may be made for seeing the governing board as external. The importance of the external dimension of governance is further augmented by the world-wide restructuring of higher education in which shifts have occurred and continue to occur in the relationship among universities, the state, and external stakeholders. A definition that better captures the external and internal aspects of governance is advanced by Marginson and Considine (2000). They posit that university governance:

> is concerned with the determination of values inside universities, their systems of decision-making and resource allocation, their mission and purposes, the patterns of authority and hierarchy, and the relationship of universities as institutions to the different academic worlds within and the worlds of government, business and community without.
>
> (p. 7)

In defining governance, Marginson and Considine bring to the fore the relational connections of universities to governments, businesses, and the broader community. In essence, this definition reminds us of the prominence and the expanding base of external stakeholders in governing universities. Here external stakeholders are those individuals, states and nongovernmental agencies, and other entities that legitimately represent the interests of "outsiders" in university governance (Amaral & Magalhaes, 2002). We will have a more detailed discussion of external stakeholders in the chapter on theories of governance and in our discussion of governance and stakeholders.

However the definition is constructed, it must be remembered that to varying degrees, public universities are subject to and guided by the policy direction and the underlying policy ideology of the host government. Triggered by global forces, the dominant ideology shaping public policy and impacting higher education across many countries has been converging towards neoliberalism (Currie et al., 2003). Neoliberalism is a "public policy agenda characterized by a desire to extend market relationships and private ownership to all areas of social and economic activity" (Goedegebuure, Hayden, & Meek, 2009, p. 151). This globalizing trend emphasizes the primacy of the market in structuring institutions (Currie, 1998). Defining contemporary governance structures, practices, and ideological orientations through a public policy lens provides yet another way in which to begin to understand higher education governance.

Through the public administration and public policy lens, Rhodes (1997; 2007) views governance generally as having four important components:

1. Interdependence between organizations in which governance includes the government and also non-state actors. Rhodes notes that when there are shifts in the boundaries of the state, the boundaries between the public, private, and voluntary sectors also shift.

2. A network of members in which there is continued interaction in order to exchange resources and negotiate shared purposes.
3. Interactions negotiated and agreed upon by network participants that are based on trust and regulations.
4. A significant degree of autonomy from the state but with the state having the ability to indirectly and imperfectly steer.

In Rhodes's conceptualization, governance in a contemporary sense is characterized by networks. This approach has also been applied to higher education to further illuminate our understanding of governance (e.g., Padure & Jones, 2009). Padure and Jones argue that the policy networks approach to analyzing governance sheds light on international, regional, and domestic networks in which universities, international organizations, national governments, interest groups, epistemic communities, and individuals are all connected. This conceptualization provides a wide-angle view of governance in which multiple stakeholders form a dynamic network and play a critical role. It also suggests that in addition to the formal structures and mechanisms of governance, decision-making can frequently be influenced by interactions and relationships that are less visible, unstructured, and informal.

The OECD (2008) integrates the internal, external, and network perspectives of higher education/university governance into a more all-embracing and comprehensive definition as:

> the structures, relationships and processes through which, at both national and institutional levels, policies for tertiary education are developed, implemented and reviewed. Governance comprises a complex web including the legislative framework, the characteristics of institutions and how they relate to the whole system, how money is allocated to the institutions and how they are accountable for the way it is spent, as well as less formal structures and relationships which steer and influence behavior.
>
> (p. 28; cf. Vidovich & Currie, 2010)

What we want to highlight here is the extent to which there is fluidity in the concept of governance in higher education as illustrated by the various definitions provided above. Reed, Meek, and Jones (2002) argue that the turbulence in and complexity of the higher education environment renders a single definition of governance as incapable of capturing the multiple dimensions and meanings of governance. It must be pointed out that at the system and national levels, there are forces shaping governance structures and practices, and creating differences in governance models (Rhoades, 1992). Therefore, higher education governance is heavily influenced by cross-national differences.

Clark (1983) distinguishes among three models of university governance as the American, the British, and the continental models. Clark's model delineations, although somewhat dated and oversimplified, demonstrated that there were major differences in governance arrangements by region, but there is now a growing convergence of similar kinds of governance designs worldwide (Currie et al., 2003). Nevertheless, it is worth noting that jurisdictional differences can have a bearing on the structures, processes, and practice of governance. And although there is convergence, there are still contextual differences reflected in structures and practices, and no universal prototypical mode of governance. We will discuss some of these contextual differences in detail in chapter 5.

UNIVERSITIES, HIGHER EDUCATION, AND INSTITUTIONAL FIELDS

Universities are enduring organizations and social actors in the institutional field of higher education. An "institutional field" in this sense is a cluster of organizations that share the same prescriptive boundaries, identities, rules of membership, organizational forms, or configuration designs (Greenwood & Suddaby, 2006; Scott, 2001). Fields are defined as "a community of organizations that partakes of a common meaning system and whose participants interact more frequently and fate-fully with one another than with actors outside the field" (Scott, 1995, p. 56). In other words, as a field, higher education organizations have institutional identity and constitutive rules of appropriate behavior and practices that give meaning to universities as social actors (Olsen, 2007). A "university" is therefore more than simply a name; it implies an identity linked to thousands of other universities, a historical lineage tracing back at least to medieval Europe, and a set of rules and practices that are associated with being a "university," but that might not be associated with being a "hospital" or a "bank."

The institutional field also creates relational spaces that provide interactional opportunities among universities and other higher education entities to develop a collective understanding of their sphere of structure, practice, and action (Wooten & Hoffman, 2008). Thus, as a collective, universities understand the rules that direct and circumscribe their behavior, actions, and value systems. They are also able to decipher their broad heterogeneous environments that make disparate demands on them and impose multiple identities (Kratz & Block, 2008). Universities are therefore enduring organizations with deep histories, longstanding traditions, and a set of "rules of the game" to guide their actions.

As institutions, universities are distinct organizational entities embedded in environments within a country and subject to governmental regulations, professional norms, and cultural-cognitive values, beliefs, and traditions (Clark, 1983). Just like other organizations, universities are influenced by the prevailing societal beliefs and values and are also guided by governmental regulations. The result is a tendency to have institutionalized homogeneous structures and processes, including governance. In more recent times, they have been influenced by transnational, intergovernmental, and supranational processes that function beyond the host nation's jurisdictional boundary (Olsen, 2007). That is, the boundary of environmental influence has shifted. And despite different traditions of higher education defined by different regions' ideas about universities (Bauer, Askling, Marton, & Marton, 1999) and higher education having a local or national component, universities are converging as a global institutional field.

This global convergence is the result of international diffusion agents such as the World Bank, the OECD, and the European Union (Mathiasen, 2005). The result is that boundaries, rules, identities, and organizational forms have begun to reflect both national and global similarities. This convergence to similarity, also referred to as isomorphism (DiMaggio & Powell, 1983; Meyer & Rowan, 1977; Meyer & Scott, 1983), is taking place to varying degrees in different contexts. Institutional theorists argue that the tendency toward institutional isomorphism is a survival mechanism by which a university creates organizational legitimacy or acceptance by its external environment (Deephouse, 1996; DiMaggio & Powell, 1983; Meyer & Rowan, 1977; Pfeffer & Salancik, 1978). This acceptance and survival notion is implicit in the Bauer et al. (1999) assertion that "universities have survived by transforming themselves under the impact of extrinsic pressure and intrinsic virtues, and thereby succeeded in keeping their position as the major higher education institution and the center for developing and transmitting knowledge" (p. 13).

Despite the changes at the field and institutional levels, academics continue to cherish the idea of a university as a unique type of organization (Bauer et al., 1999; Selznick, 1966). This is largely because universities have developed distinctive competences and legitimate built-in mechanisms needed for protection and action and also have a value system that surpasses their technical requirements (Selznick, 1996; Scott, 2003) of teaching and research. In other words, universities' existence is not restricted to teaching and research but extends to a set of values, practices, and structures—governance included— that shape their actions and create identity. Olsen (2007) reminds us that as an institution, the university has a fiduciary responsibility and its members are to be "guardians of its constitutive purposes, principles, rules, and processes. . . . defend its institutional identity and integrity whether the threat comes from outside or inside. . . . [and] third parties are also supposed to enforce rules and sanctions noncompliance of institutionalized codes" (p. 27). The governance of universities is therefore a reflection of the institutional field and its traditions, purpose, practices, and values as they have evolved over the centuries.

GOVERNANCE AND MISSION OF UNIVERSITIES

The mission of an organization defines its purpose. For a university, this mission helps to create meaning. It helps individuals to answer questions such as: Whom do we serve? What is our work? And, how do we accomplish our work? (Kezar & Lester, 2009); all micro- and mesolevel questions. At the macrolevel, it also provides a philosophical direction to guide a higher education system and its educational attainments. Fenske (1980) provides a useful working definition of mission in higher education:

> mission is often used to express the aspirations, often unstated, that society has for institutions of higher education. These aspirations are consensual and represent the most general level of hopes and expectations people in general hold for colleges and universities.
> (pp. 178–179)

Universities' missions are crafted at different times to reflect the need to meet the challenges facing higher education, specifically, and society in general. The mission is also driven by the philosophy of what a university ought to be at the time. The mission of Humboldt's University of Berlin, the first research university, was dramatically different from the teaching mission of its peers in early 19th-century Oxford and Cambridge. The creation of the land-grant universities in the United States in the late 19th century, and later the provincial universities in Western Canada, saw the addition of a strong public service mission, in addition to the goals of teaching and research. In the late 20th century, many universities added an international dimension to their statements of mission as higher education became increasingly global in orientation.

Higher education in the current global era is driven by demands of what is frequently called the new knowledge economy. The emphasis of the knowledge economy is on advanced training for human capital development and technology-driven innovation. Hence, "governments increasingly view higher education as strategic to any long-term vision of [a] country's role in a global economic economy and society" (Rojas & Bernasconi, 2011, p. 33). This is illustrated in the number of reforms of higher education governance that have been seen across the world since the 1980s as governments attempt to align university missions and performance outcomes to the developmental demands of the state. Universities are now adopting more specific missions rather than the generic approach of previous times. Rhodes (2001) contends that higher education institutions with a mission that is more role-specific and niche-oriented will perform much better in the current education environment. Rhodes further suggests that identifying and appropriately refining the terms of an institution's mission, role, and function is perhaps one of the most urgent challenges confronting board members and university leaders.

Governance structures should be designed to help a university accomplish its mission. It is generally believed that the better the governance arrangement, the greater the benefits to be derived from it and the greater the chance of the organization achieving its mission. Governance also reinforces a university's mission as an accountability reference point. The decisions made and the activities pursued by a university are assessed against its mission as a safeguard against mission drift and incongruent activities. Universities in the pursuit of their academic and service missions have always had governance as an integral part of the higher education discourse. At this time in the history of universities, many nation-states are placing greater emphasis on higher education as a driver of social development and human capital formation. In effect, universities now face an expanded mission. Concomitantly, university governance has been criticized and labeled as inappropriate for the present environmental demands. In many countries, higher education governance has been restructured and reformed to better accommodate current state/governmental demands. Hence, to begin to fully grasp the evolution of higher education governance requires some reflection on, and understanding of, the higher education mission, history, traditions, and the role universities have played and continue to play in societies.

GOVERNANCE AND TRADITIONS

The ways in which university governance has evolved to some extent depends on the traditions from which universities in different parts of the world have emerged. These traditions date back to the medieval universities first established in the 12th century in Paris and Bologna. Although there is some similarity between contemporary universities and those of earlier centuries, the medieval universities were guild-like organizations of professors (guild masters) and students (scholars) that focused on teaching (Scott, 2006; Ridder-Symeons, 1992) and were headed by an officer called a rector, a title that is still used in many parts of the world. The guild model that originated in the Middle Ages continues to influence the education of doctoral students and the orientation of junior faculty in many systems, illustrating the continuing importance of traditions in universities (Lohmann, 2004; Kaplan, 2006).

We will discuss governance systems in more detail in chapter 5, but at this point, to demonstrate how forms of governance are shaped by traditions, we will briefly review six different models, four of which are found in the UK. In the UK, specifically, are the Oxbridge, Scottish, Civic, and Higher Education Corporation models. The other two are the US and continental models.

The Continental Model

The continental model has its origins in Europe but did not represent a singular monolithic configuration. For instance, at the University of Bologna, the guild of students was the powerful group and was dominant in all matters except determining the requirements for degrees (Scholz, 1980). In other words, the university was largely governed by the students; the masters (professors) were subject to the authority of students and the rectors to the student guild. As Scholz (1980) points out, this form of governance did not persist in Europe, and by the 14th century, students of the University of Bologna had to surrender some of their authority over university affairs to professors, who then became more deeply involved in the governing of higher education.

The University of Paris was founded by scholars and had a very different governance arrangement than Bologna. The university was governed by the teaching faculty subject to supervision by the church. The chancellor, who was an official of the church, supervised the university and had authority to grant and withdraw licenses to teach. Given this authority, there were frequent tensions between the professors and the chancellor, who was viewed as an outsider. This subsequently led to the formation of a professors' guild. These professors were in the faculties of theology, medicine, canon law, and the arts, with the faculty of arts being the largest. By the mid-13th century, the professors in the faculty of arts were headed by a rector, while the others were headed by deans. Scholz (1980) notes that because the faculty of arts was the largest faculty, the rector became the chief officer of the university. Thus, we see the emergence of rectors, deans to head faculties, and the professorate as a guild.

The Oxbridge Model

The history of governance in the United Kingdom (UK) involved the emergence of four distinct models that were the outcomes of quite different traditions: the Oxbridge model, the Scottish model (medieval in origin), the civic university model, and, more recently, the post-1992 higher education corporation (HEC) model (Shattock, 2006). The Oxbridge model, adopted by Oxford and Cambridge, was based on the Paris model. Although headed by a chancellor, it avoided outside interference and promoted collegiality within. The policymaking activities of the university were the domain of the professors, also called assemblies of masters. Shattock describes the model as "the clearest expression of the primacy of academic self-governance . . . derived from the mediaeval concept of guild of masters" (p. 5). The term "nations" was used to align masters to specific groupings, and each nation was headed by a proctor. Eventually, the nation concept was discarded but the proctors who remained, along with the chancellor, became the officers of the university. Hence, at Oxford there was a chancellor heading the university along with officers. At the University of Paris, the Oxbridge adopted model, there was a rector with jurisdiction over masters and students and with the authority to set rules to guide the interaction between students and masters.

The Scottish Model

The Scottish model was also inspired by the University of Paris and was adopted in the 15th and 16th centuries by the universities of Aberdeen, Edinburgh, Glasgow, and St. Andrews, St. Andrews being the first to adopt the charter granted by the Pope (Shattock, 2006). Glasgow, Aberdeen, and St. Andrews had fairly similar constitutions. Like the Oxbridge universities, the Scottish universities were divided up into "nations," and a rector, nominated by officers of the nation, was granted judicial and disciplinary powers but answered to the chancellor (Shattock, 2006). The University of Edinburgh, a newer institution founded in the late 16th century, was slightly different in that it was answerable to the town council which had brought it into existence; the faculty or the Senatus Academicus shared control over university affairs with the town council (Carter & Withrington, 1992).

Despite Edinburgh having to share control with the town council, Scottish universities generally retained a greater amount of power among the academic staff than academics in England. A royal commission of enquiry which was set up in 1825–26 resulted in the Universities (Scottish) Act of 1858. The Act introduced a court at each university chaired by a rector. The court was constituted with a majority of laypersons whose powers extended to all matters not specifically granted to the faculties (Shattock, 2006). It essentially codified bicameralism in university governance. Shattock argues that this represented a radical shift of power away from academics.

A distinctive characteristic of the Scottish university was in the proclamation that "government had both a right and a duty to 'meddle' in the universities" (Carter & Withrington, 1992, p. 7). This was in stark contrast to the Oxbridge universities, in which state intervention was viewed suspiciously and avoided. Importantly, the Church of Scotland had relatively little control and influence over Scottish universities, but Oxford and Cambridge were very closely tied to the Church of England (Carter & Withrington, 1992).

The Civic Model

The Civic Model of university governance in the UK is associated with universities such as Manchester and Birmingham. Shattock (2006) argues that the real beginning of the English bicameral system was proclaimed in the Constitution of Owens College, Manchester, in which there was a governing court, a council as the executive government body, and an academic senate. The court and the council were predominantly composed of laypersons from outside the university, while the senate was made up solely of academics. This model of governance became dominant in the UK, especially for universities that were established after 1900 but pre-1992, and also for Commonwealth universities (Shattock, 2006).

The Higher Education Corporation Model

The Higher Education Corporation (HEC) model, a more recent UK configuration, was an outcome of the Education Reform Act of 1988. It resulted in independent corporations having authority and control over polytechnics, which were traditionally in the hands of local authority. This was further expanded by the Further and Higher Education Act of 1992 that granted university status to polytechnics and Scottish central institutions (Shattock, 2006). Unlike the Civic, Scottish, and Oxbridge models, the HEC model granted the corporate powers of universities to the governing body exclusively. In other words the governing body was the corporation (Shattock, 2006). The mission, general direction, and policy were all under the purview of the governing body, while the academic boards performed an advisory role on academic matters and resource needs, using the vice chancellor as the means to convey information to the governing board (Shattock, 2006). HECs thus used a unicameral structure rather than the bicameral structures found in Civic and Scottish models. Additionally, HECs did not have a tradition of collegial governance.

The US Model

The model of university governance that emerged within the United States was influenced in part by the Swiss Calvinist governance structure in the Geneva Academy, and in part by the Scottish university approach to governing financial matters (Shattock, 2006). An important aspect of this governance model was the authority vested in trustees, partners, or undertakers, as they were called, who constituted a board which chose a president and oversaw the manner in which the president managed the university. An early example of this is Yale University, which received its founding statute in 1701. Another important aspect of this governance model was the rights and responsibilities that were ceded to the academic community. Shattock concludes that the governance arrangements for American public universities were based on a model in which there was a governing board with unicameral powers, a president representing the board, and a complex academic committee structure, sometimes with a formal senate, with significant influence on decisions made by the board.

In summary, a comparison of the above models shows that the traditions by which universities are influenced have shaped higher education governance. Different regions reflect different traditions and, as is the case of the UK, different origins within the same region can also result in divergences in governance. While there are similarities in governance across traditions, there are also notable differences. These differences are rooted in the assumptions on which the traditions are based and where the domains of power and authority reside within a system. In the UK, for instance, except for HEC universities such as the University of Wolverhampton and the University of Hertfordshire, governance is almost totally bicameral in that academic power and authority reside with the academic senate (internally constituted) while executive authority is the domain of the council (made up of laypersons). In the United States, unicameral power is granted to a governing board, but there is significant influence from the academic senate.

Despite a growing convergence to similarity of structures, systems, and practice of governance in higher education—isomorphism—cross-national distinctions still exist. Even within countries with federal systems of government, such as the United States and Canada, there continue to be differences in governance from one state, province, or region to another. We will return to a more detailed discussion of this in chapter 5, on systems of governance.

INTERNAL SELF-GOVERNANCE

A university is a self-legitimating corporate body with responsibility for the creation, dissemination, and the global governance of knowledge (Delanty, 2001). These

knowledge responsibilities are the purview of departments in universities; the department level being the place where faculty engage with their scholarship and their
students. Linked to these responsibilities are governance mechanisms, particularly
academic self-governance. Academic self-governance is rooted in the tradition that
universities should principally be governed by their academic staff using collegiality
to guide governance interactions among colleagues (Trakman, 2008). This tradition
has persisted over time, based on the argument that academics understand their discipline, how the discipline is linked to the goals and aspirations of the university, are in
the best position to guide the process towards goals and aspirations attainment (Evans,
1999; Trakman, 2008), and are the guardians of knowledge integrity. Heckscher and
Martin-Rios (2013) describe the academy and its ethos of self-governance as operating
based on a series of assumptions:

> We are professional scholars, initiated into complex and obscure mysteries that
> outsiders cannot understand; thus, we can only be held accountable by peers who
> share this understanding. We nonetheless should be trusted with judging ourselves
> because we are committed to exercising our mysterious arts for the good of the
> community and our clients. The commitments on which our professionalism rests
> are sustained by lengthy socialization into the proper values of our craft and by the
> institutions that govern our discipline. We present ourselves therefore as deserv-
> ing our hard-earned autonomy and self-governance, with the implication that we
> should be trusted to exercise wisdom in judging appropriate thought and action.
>
> (p. 1)

The internal self-governance to which they refer is linked to decision-making and
decision-making authority. Authority is granted to the appropriate entity in a university
to make decisions, and accompanying this are explicit hierarchies built into the governance structure (Kaplan, 2006). Therefore, there is hierarchy and there is legitimate
authority. Kaplan notes that a chain of command forms the hierarchy—extending from
the president to the department chairs, including the provost and the deans along the
chain—typical of North American universities. In British universities, for example, the
nomenclature along the chain of command may be slightly different but would represent the same hierarchical structure: the vice chancellor, to the pro-vice chancellors, to
the deans, and to the department heads.

In addition, many universities still use collegiality as the guiding philosophical
practice of governance. Internal decision-making in large universities using the collegial model is done mostly through a committee system. Smaller campuses tend to have
a plenary approach in which the full faculty meets to discuss policy. However, in the
committee system, decision-making authority is delegated to committees whose com-
positions reflect participative and representative organizational democracy. Issues are
placed on the agenda, discussed, debated, and interrogated in the process of coming to
a democratic, collaborative, and consultative decision outcome. In this regard, Kaplan
(2006) describes internal academic governance as a combination of internal hierarchical arrangements and collaborative practices.

In most universities, the responsibility for academic self-governance resides with
the senate, though different terms for this academic council are used in different institutions and systems. In many institutions the senate is the ultimate authority on matters

of an academic nature and represents the legitimacy of academic decision-making. Hence, it is a key apparatus of university governance, although in the current ethos, its usefulness is somewhat under scrutiny (Shattock, 2006). While the senate represents the academic decision-making machinery of the academy, the legislative authority over administrative matters often resides with a corporate governing board, also sometimes referred to as a university council. Both bodies usually include representation from faculty, students, and university administration, but the preponderance of representation on the governing board is lay membership, often appointed by the government. In some countries, the two are kept as distinct entities of governance and in others they are combined. Where the bicameral governance model is used, the senate and governing board are kept separate but are parallel. Almost all of the universities in Canada, for example, have a bicameral governance structure. It is based on the principle of having formal corporate governance mechanisms to balance the public interest and the university's academic interest (Jones, Goyan, & Shanahan, 2004).

EXTERNAL GOVERNANCE—STATE-UNIVERSITY RELATIONS

Central to public administration, public sector management, and public policy is the question of the extent to which the state (the government) should steer, plan, regulate, and control societal institutions such as universities (Huisman, 2009). In many countries the traditional modus operandi for the government was to steer and control institutions; this approach defined the governing ethos of many governments, although to varying degrees. Universities as public entities were included among those institutions that were subject to the approach. The extent and nature of government involvement in universities defines the state-university relationship; this is the external governance of the academy. External governance essentially refers to the system or macrolevel of authority, and the role that the government (state, province, or nation) and other external stakeholders play in governing higher education within their jurisdiction.

An essential element of the nature of the state-university relationship is the authority structure. Authority is distributed across the macro, meso, and micro structure. The nature of the state-university relationship depends on the way the authority is distributed among these levels (Currie et al., 2003). Clark's (1983) analysis of authority distribution across levels yielded three broad classifications or models of higher education systems governance: the Continental European, American, and British models. Capano (2011) summarizes the elements of these three models. The basic elements of the Continental European model are: system-based, strongly hierarchical coordination through state-centered policies; no institutional autonomy; powerful authority of the academic guilds; and faculties and schools constituting confederations of chair-holders. The British model is characterized by substantial institutional autonomy, academic collegiality, and limited state involvement. The American model is based on strong procedural autonomy of universities matched by substantial public monitoring of institutional performance and outcomes, external stakeholder involvement, and academics playing a limited role in determining universities' strategic objectives but having substantially more power and authority over traditional academic matters such as staff recruitment and course content (Capano, 2011). Elements of these three models were often exported through colonization or international influence and played a role in the development of many higher education systems in Africa, the Caribbean, and, to a lesser extent, Asia.

From a policy perspective, Capano (2011) and Pierre and Peters (2000) view the role of the government as one that changes according to the governance structure and is hence a variable rather than a constant. They argue that the government is one of the actors in systemic governance and its role changes according to context. On the other hand, they see governance as the way in which institutional policy actors officially in charge of the decision-making process come together to bring about action, solve problems, and steer in a particular way. Capano notes that government has the responsibility for governing and may choose the manner in which to carry out the function. In higher education the government may decide how involved to be, the levels of authority to exert, and the level and type of institutional autonomy that universities should have—procedural versus substantive autonomy. Thus, the way in which governments choose their level of involvement in the European Continental model, the UK model, or the American model shape the state-university relationship and the distribution of authority across levels.

To further advance our understanding of the variations of government involvement in systems governance, Van Vught (1989) offers two models of the state-university relationship: a state control model and state supervising model. The state control model is similar to the hierarchical and procedural modes of governance described by Capano (2011) and is most often present in European countries. It is characterized by the strong authority of the state apparatus and also a relatively strong academic oligarchy within universities (Braun & Merrien, 1999). In this regard, the state intervention extends to conditions for access, the appointment and remuneration of staff, and curriculum matters, but matters of academic content and research are the purview of the academic community (van Vught, 1994).

The state supervising model is more common in countries with an Anglo-Saxon tradition and the authority of the state bureaucracy is weaker compared to countries with the state control model (Braun & Merrien, 1999). This model uses some mix of steering from a distance and self-governing modes. Authority lies with a strong academic community and university administrators. The state's role is primarily to supervise the higher education system to ensure academic quality and maintain accountability (van Vught, 1994). The extent to which the state supervising model is used depends on the general philosophy of government on intervention—with the state supervising model the government plays a more facilitative role, while with state control model the government plays a more interventionist role (van Vught, 1994).

Braun and Merrien (1999) added the dimension of belief systems as a critical factor to be taken into account when analyzing state-university relations; specifically, cultural-oriented belief systems and utilitarian and service-oriented belief systems. They suggest that countries with cultural-oriented belief systems generally offer a greater degree of freedom to universities than utilitarian and service-oriented belief systems. The cultural-oriented belief system is typical of what is found in the United Kingdom, where the collegium model guarantees significant freedom to act in several areas. Service- and utilitarian-orientation is a feature of the market model found in the United States. Braun and Merrien argue that the addition of belief systems to the analysis refines the notion of state-university relationship. They point out that while the Anglo-Saxon model shows similarities based on procedural and substantive autonomy, differences in belief systems result in nuanced ways of governing not captured in van Vught's model. Thus, they advocate for a three dimensions model—substantive autonomy, procedural autonomy, and belief systems—as a more fine-grained analysis of state-university relations.

While these models offer some insight into state-university relations, they do not address the temporality of the nature of the relations. It has been documented across many jurisdictions that the state-university relationship is a shifting one and over time has shifted from less intrusion to more intrusion, in some places, and in more recent times, from more funding per student to less funding (Trakman, 2008). In other words, the contextual relevance of state-university relations encompasses changes over time periods—the temporality element. Hence, governance arrangements can be construed as in a state of flux (Rhoades, 1992). For example in earlier centuries, the government played less of a role in the governance of universities. Delanty (2002) argues that as knowledge became critical to capitalism and the capitalist societies, and as the nation-state played more of a vital role in the facilitation of the expansion of capitalism, an alliance was fostered between the university and the state whereby, in return for academic autonomy, the university supplied useful knowledge. Hence, Delanty (2002) tells us that the modern university was a knowledge-producing institution which was "one of the primary sites of academic/scientific knowledge, which became more and more useful for the nascent nation-state, providing it with legitimacy and also with instrumentally useful knowledge in the context of the rise of professional society" (p. 187). Therefore, governments to varying degrees across regions, provinces, and state and national boundaries established different mechanisms of governance as universities and higher education became more central to the advancement of nations and societies.

Given that time frames are important considerations in state-university relations, scholars have engaged the notion of globalization as a critical contextual variable of the current era. Neoliberal globalization has brought with it a discourse that reduces the nation-state to a minimalist state and increases the power of market forces (Currie, 1998). The state is now viewed as an evaluative mechanism, steering from a distance and facilitating the rise of markets and quasi-markets (Huisman, 2009). This is a major shift in policy brought about by globalization imperatives that have resulted in the erosion of the power and influence of the nation-state. In the case of Australia, for example, Dudley (1998) notes that the country's integration into the global economy was the principal rationale for reshaping education policy and, by extension, changing state-university relations.

For over 200 years, universities and higher education have been tied to the nation-state. It is therefore important not only to analyze the historical relationships between the university and the nation-state but also the current impact of globalization on the institution of the state (Kwiek, 2006). The globalized economy is dominated by multinational corporations and transnational corporations in borderless market spaces. The state is reduced to maintaining law and order, ensuring the legality of contracts, protecting property rights, and facilitating the functioning of markets; functions all critical to global free trade (Dudley, 1998). Countries are expected to and have changed policies and programs to come more in line with the dominant ideology associated with globalization.

The state-university relationship captures an important element of external governance. Much of the higher education literature in the 20th century analyzed the sector by reference to the extent of state intervention (Ferlie, Musselin, & Andresani, 2008). Through this dominant analytical and normative framework, the state was first conceptualized as an apparatus for ensuring the autonomy of higher education; the Mertonian sociology of sciences. Despite its dependence on public funding, higher education was granted substantial institutional autonomy and insulation from government steering, and individual professors were granted academic freedom over teaching and research. There is ample evidence that this model existed to varying degrees in different countries; the UK being the country where this model was most dominant. However, a subsequent second conception of the state arose in the late 20th century, in which the state was viewed as mediating the interests of society, reshaping the development of higher education, and adopting a more command-and-control orientation (Ferlie et al., 2008). And in the very late 20th century to early 21st century, the state-university relationship was built around the role of the market in higher education governance (Dill, 1996). The higher education governance literature captures the shifts in the nature of the relationship during these periods in terms such as from interventionists to evaluative governance (van Vught, 1995; Neave & van Vught, 1991); from dirigisme to supervision; from ex ante to ex post; and from rules to regulation (Amaral, Meek, & Larsen, 2000).

Ferlie et al. (2008) and others such as Musselin (2010) caution us about the dangers of focusing only on state-university relations in trying to understand higher education systems. They contend that attention has also to be paid to the state and the academic profession, especially when referring to European countries in which the state plays a major role in faculty staffing and can directly impact faculty careers. Ferlie et al. point out that the relationship between the state and representatives of the academic profession may be different from that of the state-institution. This would be especially true in countries like France, influenced by the Napoleonic tradition, and where there is co-management between the ministry and representatives of the profession. Hence, an appropriate description and analysis of the higher education system governance, especially in places like Europe, should include state-university-academic profession. The duality of forces—organizational and professional-based forces—encountered by the state should also be recognized in analyzing higher education systems governance (Ferlie et al., 2008).

MARKET-ORIENTED GOVERNANCE

As mentioned previously, higher education is in an era of markets and quasi-markets. Marketization (Williams, 1995), the increasing influence of market competition on academic life, is the new institutional framework within which universities now operate in many systems. The emphasis on markets and marketization is all part of a larger global economic ideological agenda that promotes the efficiency of allocations of scarce resources through market rules and regulations and the diminution of the role of the nation-state. This ideological stance is an outcome of the hegemonic neoliberal discourse about freedom of commerce and trade across national borders; neoliberalism constituting only one element of globalization, which is the broader worldwide phenomenon. It is therefore virtually impossible to address the market model of governance in higher education without first referencing globalization and the neoliberal ideology.

There is no denying that globalization has impacted higher education in significant ways. From an economic perspective, globalization is about the creation of a world market (Wagner, 2004) in which higher education institutions are among the participants. This new world order is facilitated by the rise of the World Trade Organization (WTO) as a global economic coordinating agency and a global governing institution. Following the declaration by the WTO that education is a tradable service, higher education institutions have become active market players. The market ideology expansion into higher education is reflected in the commodification of education, greater sensitivity to "customer" interests, and a bottom-line orientation among universities (Smith, 2004). The economics of this is that universities are competing more aggressively both nationally and internationally for their share of students in the global higher education market. They also compete for research dollars, faculty, revenue, rankings, prestige, and state/provincial/national funds. It is believed that competition for students and government funds are drivers of quality and efficiency in higher education (OECD, 2008). As Newman, Couturier, and Scurry (2010) put it, the search for truth in the academy is now rivaled by the search for revenue.

The change in the governance needed for the market model of higher education is mainly in the adjustment to the coordinating mechanisms. Central to governing in a market-driven environment is the loosening of controls by the state and the granting of more autonomy to universities to be innovative in competitive markets. Concepts such as steering from a distance or the evaluative state capture the policy orientation associated with market model governing. This aligns with Wagner's (2004) view of an internal and an external hierarchy of authority in higher education. Wagner suggests that the external hierarchy is reduced because of the decline of the nation-state. This is manifested in a shift to a mode of governing that facilitates the regulation of higher education by market mechanisms. Internally, higher education institutions are strengthening the internal hierarchy to enhance governing capacity to act and react in fluid competitive global markets (Wagner, 2004). This new internal approach, it has been argued, interferes with traditional conceptualizations of professional academic autonomy and freedom (Peters, 2011).

Wagner (2004) argues that higher education has always been governed by some legitimate form of market, hierarchy, and community. Community here refers to universities as guilds guided internally by community values and having community-based self-regulating governance. However, the current forces of neoliberal globalization advocate that the market should be the primary basis for governing higher education. Internal collegial governance has traditionally emphasized community (the community of scholars). The diminution of the community in preference to the market has moved governance away from the collegial model to an imitation of the corporate model. This constitutes a transforming of universities' institutional identity and constitutive logic.

As is the case in many other countries, Christopher (2012) points out that public universities in Australia are experiencing transformation to corporate governance. Universities are now being governed in an organizational cultural context characterized by performance evaluations, strategic planning, performance budgeting, performance management, financial management, risk management, and internal auditing. Expressed another way, universities are strengthening their internal hierarchy through the use of these corporate management systems. Christopher found that public universities in Australia have great difficulties practicing the corporate approach at the board or council level and at the operational levels of governance because of tensions that exist between the traditional approach by universities and the new corporate approach. Marginson and Considine (2000) describe this tension as "endemic" in public universities in Australia. The corporate approach, for instance, is known to have a less trusting environment in which there is more monitoring and extrinsic rewards, while the traditional collegial governance is associated with a more trusting environment and intrinsic rewards (Christopher, 2012). The problem is a clash of two cultures: academia, based on a culture and traditions that go back centuries, and a modern economic neoliberal philosophy that touts the market as an efficient means of allocating scarce resources. Higher education faces a governing conundrum. We will revisit many of these concepts in more detail in later chapters.

SUMMARY

Governance is at the heart of higher education and universities' abilities to serve their multiple purposes. Its place of importance dates back several centuries to early university practices and traditions. Many of today's practices have emerged out of those early traditions. In addition, a range of definitions have been used to capture it conceptually. The goal of this chapter was to provide readers with a basic contextual understanding of governance in higher education. We felt this was important for readers to grasp the concepts, theories, and practices in the remainder of the book. To ensure that a conceptual foundation was laid, we provided an extensive discussion on the definition of governance to draw attention to its multiple conceptualizations and highlight its importance at the micro-, meso-, and macrolevels. The micro- and mesolevels of governance are foundational to managing the day-to-day affairs of the academy and the facilitation of decision making authority. The macrolevel is the governance mechanism through which the state attempts to ensure that its higher education system is achieving state-desired goals.

The chapter also examined the conceptual foundation and traditions of governance in higher education in order to historicize today's governance. A substantial portion of the chapter was devoted to models of governance and their historical origins. These broad models were the UK, continental, and US models but it was shown that there is variability in governance configurations even within these three. Hence, the chapter underscores the multiple approaches to governing higher education and the way in which contradictions, tensions, traditions, and contemporary neoliberal philosophical orientations are shaping governance in higher education. Researchers, scholars, policy makers, practitioners, and graduate students must all be fully cognizant of the ways in which these dynamics are shaping higher education governance. The chapter laid the groundwork for this.

The chapter concluded by looking at internal self-governance, market-oriented governance, and external (state-university) governance. We also discussed external governance in the context of shifting state-university relations, highlighting the shifts occurring and the policy tools governments are using to gain compliance. Many of the changes occurring are driven by the broader neoliberal ideological prescriptions that advocate a diminution of the nation-state's role in governing and promoting markets-based governance as enhancing efficiency in the academy. These contextual underpinnings we believe are critical to a deeper understanding of governance in higher education and provide a foundation for the chapters to follow.

DISCUSSION QUESTIONS

1. Why is governance so important to higher education?
2. Why is historicizing governance important to our understanding of contemporary trends?
3. What are some of the tensions and contradictions you see in higher education governance?

REFERENCES

Amaral, A., & Magalhaes, A. (2002). The emergent role of external stakeholders in European higher education governance. In A. Amaral, G. Jones, & B. Karseth (Eds.), *Governing higher education: National perspectives on institutional governance* (pp. 1–20). Dordrecht, The Netherlands: Kluwer.

Amaral, A., Meek, L., & Larsen, I.M. (Eds.). (2000). *The higher education managerial revolution?* Dordrecht, The Netherlands: Kluwer.

Barnett, R. (2000). *Realizing the university in an age of supercomplexity*. Buckingham, England: Society for Research into Higher Education and Open University Press.

Bauer, M., Askling, B., Marton, S.G., & Marton, F. (1999). *Transforming universities: Changing patterns of governance, structure and learning in Swedish higher education*. London, England: Jessica Kingsley.

Braun, D., & Merrien, F-X. (1999). Governance of universities and modernization of the state: Analytical aspects. In D. Braun & F-X. Merrien (Eds.), *Towards a new model of governance for universities? A comparative view* (pp. 9–33). London, England: Jessica Kingsley.

Capano, G. (2011). Government continues to do its job: A comparative study of governance shifts in the higher education sector. *Public Administration, 89*(4), 1622–1642.

Carter, J.J., & Withrington, D.J. (1992). Introduction. In J.J. Carter & D.J. Withrington (Eds.), *Scottish universities: Distinctiveness and diversity* (pp. 1–14). Edinburgh, Scotland: John Donald.

Christopher, J. (2012). Governance paradigms of public universities: An international comparative study. *Tertiary Education and Management, 18*(4), 335–351.

Clark, B. (1983). *The higher education system: Academic organizations in cross-national perspective*. Berkeley, CA: University of California Press.

Currie, J. (1998). Globalization as an analytical concept and local policy responses. In J. Currie & J. Newson (Eds.), *Universities and globalization: Critical perspectives* (pp. 15–20). London, England: Sage.

Currie, J., DeAngelis, R., de Boer, H., Huisman, J., & Lacotte C. (2003). *Globalizing practices and university responses: European and Anglo-American differences*. Westport, CT: Praeger.

Deephouse, D.L. (1996). *Does isomorphism legitimate? Academy of Management Journal, 39*(4), 1024–1039.

Delanty, G. (2001). The university in the knowledge society. *Organization, 8*(2), 149–153.

Delanty, G. (2002). The governance of universities: What is the role of the university in the knowledge society? *Canadian Journal of Sociology, 27*(2), 185–198.

Dill, D. (1996). Higher education markets and public policy. *Higher Education Policy, 10*(3–4), 167–185.

DiMaggio, P.J., & Powell, W.W. (1983). The iron cage revisited: Institutional isomorphism and collective rationality in organizational fields. *American Sociological Review, 48*(2), 147–160.

Dudley, J. (1998). Globalization and education policy in Australia. In J. Currie & J. Newsome (Eds.), *Universities and globalization: Critical perspectives* (pp. 21–43). Beverly Hills, CA: Sage.

Evans, J. P. (1999). Benefits and barriers to shared authority. In M. T. Miller (Ed.), *Responsive academic decision-making: Involving faculty in higher education governance*. Stillwater, OK: New Forums Press.

Fenske, R. H. (1980). Setting institutional goals and objectives. In P. Jedamus & M. W. Peterson (Eds.), *Improving academic management* (pp. 177–199). San Francisco, CA: Jossey-Bass.

Ferlie, E., Musselin, C., & Andresani, G. (2008). The steering of higher education system: A public management perspective. *Higher Education, 56*(3), 325–348.

Goedegebuure, L., Hayden, M., & Meek, L. (2009). Good governance and Australian higher education: An analysis of a neo-liberal decade. In J. Huisman (Ed.), *International perspectives on the governance of higher education: Alternative frameworks for coordination* (pp. 145–160). London, England: Routledge.

Greenwood, R., & Suddaby, R. (2006). Institutional entrepreneurship in mature fields: The big accounting firms. *Academy of Management Journal, 49*(1), 27–48.

Gumport, P., & Pusser, B. (1999). University restructuring: The role of economic and political contexts. In J. C. Smart & W. G. Tierney (Eds.), *Higher education: Handbook of theory and research* (Vol. 14, pp. 146–194). New York, NY: Agathon Press.

Heckscher, C., & Martin-Rios, C. (2013). Looking back, moving forward: Toward collaborative universities. *Journal of Management Inquiry, 22*(1), 136–139.

Huisman, J. (Ed.). (2009). Coming to terms with governance in higher education. *International perspectives on the governance of higher education: Alternative frameworks for coordination* (pp. 1–9). London, England: Routledge.

Jones, G. A., Goyan, P., & Shanahan, T. (2004). The academic senate and university governance in Canada. *The Canadian Journal of Higher Education, 34*(2), 35–68.

Kaplan, G. (2006). Institutions of academic governance and institutional theory: A framework for further research. In J. C. Smart (Ed.), *Higher education: Handbook of theory and research* (Vol. XXI, pp. 213–281). Dordrecht, The Netherlands: Springer.

Kezar, A. (2004). What is more important to effective governance: Relationships, trust, and leadership, or structures and formal processes? In W. G. Tierney & V. M. Lechuga (Eds.), *Restructuring shared governance in higher education* (pp. 35–46, *New Directions for Higher Education, 127*). San Francisco, CA: Jossey-Bass.

Kezar, A., & Lester, J. (2009). *Organizing higher education for collaboration: A guide for campus leaders.* San Francisco, CA: Jossey-Bass.

Kratz, M. S., & Block, E. D. (2008). Organizational implications of institutional pluralism. In R. Greenwood, C. Oliver, R. Suddaby, & K. Sahlin (Eds.), *Organizational institutionalism* (pp. 243–268). Thousand Oaks, CA: Sage.

Kwiek, M. (2006). *The university and the state: A study into global transformations.* Frankfurt am Main: Peter Lang.

Lohmann, S. (2004). Darwinian medicine for the university. In R. G. Ehrenberg (Ed.), *Governing academia* (pp. 71–90). Ithaca, NY: Cornell University Press.

Marginson, S., & Considine, M. (2000). *The enterprise university.* Melbourne, Australia: Cambridge University Press.

Mathiasen, D. (2005). International public management. In E. Ferlie, L. Lynn, & C. Pollitt (Eds.), *The Oxford handbook of public management.* Oxford, England: Oxford University Press.

Meyer, J. W., & Rowan, B. (1977). Institutional organizations: Formal structure as myth and ceremony. *American Journal of Sociology, 83*(2), 340–363.

Meyer, J. W., & Scott, W. R. (1983). Centralization and the legitimacy problems of local government. In J. W. Meyer & W. R. Scott (Eds.), *Organizational environments: Ritual and rationality* (pp. 199–215). Newbury Park, CA: Sage.

Millett, J. D. (1978). *New structures of campus power: Success and failure of emerging forms of institutional governance*. San Francisco, CA: Jossey-Bass.

Musselin, C. (2010). *The market for academics*. London, England: Routledge.

Neave, G., & Van Vught, F. A. (Eds.). (1991). *Prometheus bound: The changing relationship between government and higher education in Western Europe*. Oxford, England: Pergamon Press.

Newman, F., Couturier, L., & Scurry, J. (2010). *The future of higher education. Rhetoric, reality, and the risks of the market*. San Francisco, CA: Jossey-Bass.

OECD. (2008). In P. Santiago, K. Tremblay, E. Basri, & E. Arnal (Eds.), *Tertiary education for the knowledge society* (Vol. 1). Paris: OECD.

Olsen, J. (2007). The institutional dynamics of the European university. In P. Maassen & J. P. Olsen (Eds.), *University dynamics and European integration* (pp. 25–54). Dordrecht, The Netherlands: Springer.

Padure, L., & Jones, G. (2009). Policy networks and research on higher education governance and policy. In J. Huisman (Ed.), *International perspectives on the governance of higher education: Alternative frameworks for coordination* (pp. 107–125). London, England: Routledge.

Parker, L. (2011). University corporatization: Driving definition. *Critical Perspectives on Accounting, 22*(4), 434–450.

Peters, M. (2011). *Neoliberalism and after? Education, social policy and the crisis of Western capitalism*. New York, NY: Peter Lang.

Pfeffer, J., & Salancik, G. R. (1978). *The external control of organizations: A resource dependence perspective*. New York, NY: Harper & Row.

Pierre, J., & Peters, G. (2000) *Governance, politics and the state*. London, England: Macmillan.

Rebora, G., & Turri, M. (2009). Governance in higher education: An analysis of the Italian experience. In J. Huisman (Ed.), *International perspectives on the governance of higher education: Alternative frameworks for coordination* (pp. 13–32). London, England: Routledge.

Reed, M., Meek, L., & Jones, G. (2002). Introduction. In A. Amaral, G. Jones, & B. Karseth (Eds.), *Governing higher education: National perspectives on institutional Governance* (pp. xv–xxxi). Dordrecht, The Netherlands: Kluwer.

Rhoades, G. (1992). Governance: Models. In B. Clark & G. Neave (Eds.), *The encyclopedia of higher education* (Vol. 2, pp. 1376–1384). Oxford, England: Pergamon Press.

Rhodes, F. H. T. (2001). The university at the millennium: Missions and responsibilities of research universities. In W. Z. Hirsch & L. E. Weber (Eds.), *Governance in higher education: The university in a state of flux*. London, England: Economica.

Rhodes, R. A. W. (1997). *Understanding governance*. Buckingham, England: Oxford University Press.

Rhodes, R. A. W. (2007). Understanding governance: Ten years on. *Organization Studies, 28*(8), 1243–1264.

Ridder-Symoens, H. (1992). *A history of the university in Europe: Universities in the Middle Ages*. Cambridge, England: Cambridge University Press.

Rojas, A., & Bernasconi, A. (2011). Governing universities in times of uncertainty and change. In P. Altbach (Ed.), *Leadership for world-class universities: Challenges for developing countries* (pp. 33–51). New York, NY: Routledge.

Scholz, B. (1980). Forward: The evolution of university governance. In E. Rausch (Ed.), *Management in institutions of higher learning* (pp. 141–161). Lexington, KY: Lexington Books.

Scott, J. C. (2006). The mission of the university: Medieval to postmodern transformations. *The Journal of Higher Education, 77*(1), 1–39.

Scott, P. (1995). *The meaning of mass higher education.* Buckingham, England: SRHE/Open University Press.

Scott, R. (2001). *Institutions and organizations.* Thousand Oaks, CA: Sage.

Scott, R. (2003). *Organizations: Rational, natural and open systems.* Upper Saddle River, NJ: Prentice-Hall.

Selznick, P. (1966). *TVA and the grass roots: A study in the sociology of formal organization.* New York, NY: Harper & Row.

Selznick, P. (1996). Institutionalism "old" and "new." *Administrative Science Quarterly, 41*(2), 270–277.

Shattock, M. (2006). *Managing good governance in higher education.* New York, NY: Open University Press.

Slaughter, S., & Rhoades, G. (2004). *Academic capitalism and the new economy: Markets, state, and higher education.* Baltimore, MD: Johns Hopkins University Press.

Smith, C. (2004). Globalization, higher education, and markets. In J. K. Odin & T. Manicas (Eds.), *Globalization and higher education* (pp. 69–81). Honolulu, HI: University of Hawaii Press.

Tight, M. (2004). Research into higher education: An a-theoretical community of practice? *Higher Education Research and Development, 23*(4), 395–411.

Trakman, L. (2008). Modelling university governance. *Higher Education Quarterly, 62*(1), 63–83.

van Vught, F. (1989). *Governmental strategies and innovation in higher education.* London, England: Jessica Kinsley.

van Vught, F. (1995). *Policy models and policy instruments in higher education: The effects of governmental policy-making on the innovative behaviour of higher education institutions* (Series no. 26). Vienna, Austria: Institut fur Hohere Studien.

van Vught, F. A. (1994). Autonomy and accountability in government/university relationships. In J. Salmi & A. M. Verspoor (Eds.), *Revitalizing higher education.* Oxford, England: IAU Press.

Vidovich, L., & Currie, J. (2010). Governance and trust in higher education. *Studies in Higher Education, 36*(1), 43–56.

Wagner, P. (2004). Higher education in an era of globalization: What is at stake? In J. Odin & P. Manicas (Eds.), *Globalization and higher education* (pp. 7–23). Honolulu, HI: University of Hawaii Press.

Williams, G. L. (1995). The "marketization" of higher education: Reforms and potential reforms in higher education finance. In D. D. Dill & B. Sporn (Eds.), *Emerging patterns of social demand and university reform: Through a glass darkly.* Oxford: Pergamon Press and the IAU Press.

Wooten, M., & Hoffman, A. (2008). Organizational fields: Past, present and future. In R. Greenwood, C. Oliver, R. Suddaby, & K. Sahlin (Eds.), *Organizational institutionalism* (pp. 130–143) Los Angeles, CA: Sage.

CHAPTER 2

Theories of Governance
Institutions, Agency, and External Influences

In the academy, theory is like a buzzword. It is a commonly used term in academic research and scholarly work. In social and behavioral sciences, for instance, theories are viewed as vital to understanding human action and behavior (Kouzes & Mico, 1979). They are considered by some as the foundation of any logical explanation of a social or individual phenomenon of interest. Theories help us to organize and describe people's experiences, predict future behaviors, and create the means to control conditions that influence people's lives (Argyris, 1976; Argyris & Schon, 1974; Kouzes & Mico, 1979). What an organization such as a university assumes to be true, what it is, what it does, what it values, and how it is governed can be mapped out through the use of theories (Schon, 1971; Kouzes & Mico, 1979).

Academia views scholarly work to be of superior quality when it is built on a strong theoretical foundation (Kezar, 2006; Sutton & Staw, 1995), and many reviewers and readers of scholarly work in behavioral, psychological, or organization science are suspicious of the value of writings that have no theoretical basis (Sutton & Staw, 1995). Consequently, scholars generally use theory to map out the conceptual landscape undergirding their research and as a guide to shape their intellectual contribution. These discussions of the theories underscoring research are typically captured by labels such as theoretical perspective, theoretical framework, and underlying theory (Tight, 2004).

This is the first of two chapters to address the use of theories in higher education, or more specifically, higher education governance. Although there has been some progress on governance research and some attempts to incorporate theoretical frames from other disciplines, higher education governance remains relatively under-theorized, particularly when compared to corporate governance. There is therefore much room for additional theoretical and paradigmatic improvements. We recognize that there is no grand theory of higher education governance, but there are some leading theories that can help us to interrogate governance from different conceptual angles and decipher its complexities. In this chapter, we discuss five theories that are relevant and pertinent to higher education governance, how their application could enhance the development of governance research, and the ways in which these theories are useful in building the higher education governance knowledge base. The theories discussed are institutional theory (DiMaggio & Powell, 1983; Meyer & Rowan, 1977), agency theory (Jensen & Meckling, 1976), stewardship theory (Davies, Schoorman, & Donaldson, 1997), stakeholder theory (Freeman, 1984), and resource-dependence theory (Pfeffer & Selancik, 2003).

These theories constitute a combination of environmental framed theories and stakeholder/agency monitoring theories drawn from mature bodies of knowledge on corporate, public, and nonprofit governance. Individually, each of these theories provides a reasonable foundation for understanding and analyzing higher education governance. But because each theory provides its own perspective, has its own salience, and may not adequately capture all angles or the wider influencing forces associated with governance, a multi-theoretical approach has been advocated to address the limitations of any single theoretical explanation (Christopher, 2010; Daily, Dalton, & Canella, 2003; Eisenhardt, 1989). When combined using a multi-theory approach, these theories may provide a much richer understanding and a stronger platform for critical analyses of the governance of the academy.

INSTITUTIONAL THEORY

Institutional theory has had a significant influence on the study of structures, processes, and activities in organizations. As such, it has become a dominant perspective in macro-organization theory (Suddaby, 2010). A number of seminal contributions to this body of scholarship came in the late 1970s with the work of Meyer and Rowan (1977) and subsequently DiMaggio and Powell (1983)—although earlier representations may be traced back to the works of Selznick, Marx, Weber, Durkheim, Veblen, and Commons (Kavanagh, 2009). In fact, some argue that Selznick is the grandfather of institutional theory (Hatch, 2006).

From its initial proposition, the theory focused on the effects of the social environment on organizations—the effects of social rules, norms, and expectations. These environmental effects were perceived as constraints on organizations that shaped structures and practices. In other words, institutional theory was, and still is, about organizations and their environment, and it emphasizes that the social rules, expectations, norms, and values within the environment constitute conformity pressure that is experienced by similar organizational types or organizational populations (Pfeffer & Salancik, 2003). For example, research universities would constitute a similar organizational type involving a set of environmental norms, values, and expectations that would shape structures, cause universities to act in prescribed ways, and drive specific practices.

Proponents of the theory contend that this environmental pressure is felt by organizations in two ways. First, it is felt through technical, economic, and physical pressure associated with the sale of goods and services in markets. Second, the pressure is felt through social, cultural, legal, and political expectations of the organization to act in a particular way. Hatch (2006) notes that in environments which emphasize technical, economic, and physical demands, organizations are rewarded for efficiency and effectiveness when they respond to the environment. And, in environments where social, cultural, legal, and political demands are more prevalent, organizations are rewarded for conforming to the expectations of social institutions such as government, religion, and education (Hatch, 2006). Hence, an organization responding favorably or in alignment with external environmental expectations is a key element of institutional theory. The fundamental basis of this conformity lies in the organization's desire for environmental acceptance and legitimacy (DiMaggio & Powell, 1983; Suchman, 1995).

A core premise of organizational conformance is that organizations are more than production systems with a collection of suppliers, consumers, and competitors (Meyer & Rowan, 1977). Meyer and Rowan point out that organizations are also social and cultural systems embedded in an "institutional" context where the state, professional associations, interest groups, and public opinion shape behavior. By highlighting the social context of organizations, Meyer and Rowan contend that organizations within an industry or sector such as universities tend to use the same organizational configuration and adopt similar behaviors and practices. This facilitates order in the sector.

Governance helps to create inter- and intra-organizational order in a sector. This is facilitated through structures and practices. These structures and practices are guided by institutional scripts which convey expected norms, beliefs, and values associated with a particular sector or organizational field; for example the field of higher education. Institutional scripts convey meaning and allow institutions to make sense of their environment in a way that shapes their governance. Hence, institutions adapt their governance structures and practices to environmental pressures and demands such as those created, for instance, by the pressures of competition in a market-driven higher education environment.

DiMaggio and Powell (1983) contend that organizations incorporate institutional rules and practices in their own structures and in the process become more homogeneous and similar to others in the field (the field concept is discussed in more detail in the section on institutional logics). Hence, as the institutional rules of higher education change to accommodate, for instance, a market-driven philosophy or greater stakeholder involvement, shifts occur in governance structures because these new rules are incorporated into the structure. This is the isomorphic process and it is the means through which organizations change and become more similar to others. Organizations conform and homogenize through one or more of three institutional pressures: coercive, mimetic, and normative isomorphism (DiMaggio & Powell, 1983). A university and its governance may become shaped and institutionalized by its environment through one or more than one of these pressures acting simultaneously.

Coercive Isomorphism

Coercive isomorphism refers to external pressure, usually from governmental laws and regulations or other social groups, to conform and adapt. This will occur, for example, in situations where the government enacts laws that require universities to conform to a practice or a preferred set of practices. Universities that receive public funds may be required to conform to specific rules concerning procurement procedures or maintain certain program quality standards—regulations that will mean that publicly supported institutions in the jurisdiction will have similar processes in place because these processes are required in order to obtain government funding. In this regard, governing practices would be similar.

Mimetic Isomorphism

Mimetic isomorphism refers to an organization voluntarily imitating the structures, practices, and processes of other organizations in response to uncertainty in the environment. In other words, when faced with uncertainty, organizations emulate other successful organizations. For instance, some universities have adopted managerial practices from the corporate world. In addition, benchmarking and comparisons between universities have also led to mimetic behaviors as universities adopt successful practices from other universities. The fact that it is becoming increasingly easy to access information on university practices through websites and reports available on the Internet means that it becomes easier to identify organizational practices and emulate "best practices" or successful solutions to common problems.

Normative Isomorphism

Normative isomorphism is professional-based conformance pressure in which key group members internal to the organization or members of an occupational group define the conditions of their work, subscribe to a set of associated values, and have norms that determine what the organization should be like (DiMaggio & Powell, 1983; 1991). Applied to universities, faculty members have a set of professional beliefs through which they create their identity and define the conditions of their work. For instance, key elements of faculty identity are collegiality, academic freedom, and professional autonomy. University governance tends to conform around these professional norms and beliefs; although in recent times coercive and mimetic pressures have been weakening some of the cherished professional values, conditions of work, and driving the refashioning of governance in the academy.

MULTILEVEL INSTITUTIONAL GOVERNANCE

Scott (1995) provides an excellent graphical depiction of institutional theory (see Figure 2.1) showing top-down and bottom-up processes of institutional creation and diffusion consisting of three levels of analysis. At the apex are the societal and global institutions. In higher education, these would include organizations such as UNESCO, the OECD, the World Bank, and the World Trade Organization, which create formal models of what the institutional context of universities should be. They influence what is possible, acceptable, and legitimate and shape governance mechanisms and practices located at the second (middle) level (Judge, Douglas, & Kutan, 2008). At the second level, governance mechanisms consist of organizational fields (higher education) and organizations (such as universities). Universities in this regard are influenced by and also influence their organizational field and institutional context. Social and cultural factors are likely to play a major role at this level and cultural diffusion can be a driver of change (Hartley, Butler, & Benington, 2002). At the organizational level it must be noted that universities vary by function, size, structure, culture, stakeholder interests, and capacity for change and should not be considered as monolithic. For instance, there are large research-intensive universities, liberal arts colleges, private for-profit universities, small universities, and universities where external stakeholders play a significant role. At the lowest level are the actors in institutional settings who may be individuals (such as individual faculty members) or groups (such as faculty committees). These

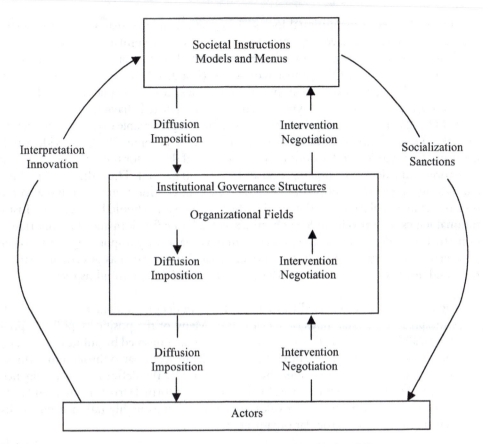

Figure 2.1 Conceptual Model of Institutional Theory and Institutional Forces

Source: Scott (1995)

actors may be constrained or empowered by the forces occurring at the other two levels (Giddens, 1977; Hartley et al., 2002).

INSTITUTIONAL LOGICS AND ORGANIZATIONAL FIELDS

Clusters of particular types of organizations (industry/sector grouping) that are bound by institutional rules are called organizational fields. An organizational field is "a community of organizations that partakes of a common meaning system and whose participants interact more frequently and fatefully with one another than with actors outside the field" (Scott, 1995, p. 56). The field concept captures the idea of a community of organizations, a concept that resonates with universities given the common elements associated with these organizational forms. Through the community of organizations, social and technical influences are placed on members of the community. This influence shapes and/or constrains structures and behaviors of field members and creates conformity to institutionalized expectations, and, as the field matures, structures and practices become increasingly entrenched within organizations (Greenwood & Hinings, 2006). University governance is therefore shaped over time by institutionalized rules and prevailing norms of the higher education organizational field that are legitimated by the social environment (Lynall, Golden, & Hillman, 2003).

Through a set of institutional logics, organizations in a similar sector or industry respond to institutionalized expectations and practices in similar ways. These institutional logics are determined by socially constructed rules, norms, and beliefs to be followed by members of the industry or sector (Friedland, Robert, & Alford, 1991). Institutional logics provide "assumptions and values, usually explicit, about how to interpret organizational reality, what constitutes appropriate behavior, and how to succeed" (Thornton, 2004, p. 70). In other words, these logics enable organizational actors to make sense of situations (Greenwood, Díaz, Li, & Lorente, 2010), provide a link between the cognition and actions of individuals, and define for them the institutional structures and rules of the organization and society in general. Thus, the way in which a university is governed reflects the logics of the higher education sector and also the society's conceptualization of the way in which universities should be governed. Institutional logics may also include such values as academic freedom and the importance of participatory decision-making processes in governance. By responding to the logics of a sector, industry, society, or state, organizational forms such as governance structures and practices are legitimated. Meyer and Rowan (1991) remind us that

> the elements of rationalized formal structure are deeply ingrained in, and reflect, widespread understandings of social reality. Many of the positions, policies, programs, and procedures of modern organizations are enforced by public opinion, by the views of important constituents, by knowledge legitimated through the educational system, by social prestige, by the laws, and by the definitions of negligence and prudence used by the courts. Such elements of formal structure are manifestations of powerful institutional rules which function as highly rationalized myths that are binding on particular organizations.
>
> (p. 44)

It must be pointed out though that organizational fields have multiple and often conflicting logics (Reay & Hinings, 2005) but field members tend to respond to a "dominant logic" (Bettis & Prahalad, 1995). Hence, understanding the tendency for organizations to exhibit similarity in structural forms and organizational practices is linked to a set of logics or a dominant logic specific to the institutional context (Greenwood et al., 2010). This characterization is typical of governance in higher education. Universities generally have similar structures internally, and although there is some variation by region and context, many of the broad parameters of state/university/stakeholder involvement in governance are similar. There is further convergence within subgroupings of universities so that the governance structures of large research universities may be quite similar, but they may be somewhat different from the governance arrangements associated with small liberal arts or religious colleges.

Although there is a dominant logic to which universities converge, this dominant pre-existing logic could become delegitimized as a result of changes occurring within the field (Bettis & Prahalad, 1995; Greenwood & Hinings, 1996). Hence, universities may be governed on principles of autonomy and limited state involvement, and this would constitute the dominant logic that shapes governance structures and practices. However, this could become delegitimized and replaced by the institutionalization of a new dominant logic that suggests less autonomy and greater state and external stakeholder involvement in governance.

INSTITUTIONAL THEORY AND THE ACADEMY

Institutional theory helps to explain some of the governance structures and practices observed in universities—the coming together of isomorphism, legitimacy, and universities' environments. One of the keys to understanding university governance is to examine the institutional environmental forces that impact legitimacy seeking behaviors (Judge et al., 2008). University leaders pursue legitimacy, approval, and funding from their general environment in order to survive (Fogarty, 1996). This is a critical factor in the current higher education context, in which universities have become more open entities resulting in wider external environment influences (we will examine this in more detail in discussing open systems in chapter 3). Suffice it to say at this point that according to systems theory, a university is separated from its environment by its boundary, which provides the university with an identity and acts as a point of contact with other systems in the environment (Bess & Dee, 2008). The more open a system, the more permeable its boundary, and the more it is influenced by the external environment. Because over the last few decades universities have become more open entities, they are now more susceptible to judgments about their practices and behaviors and, by extension, their legitimacy. This has resulted in challenges to existing forms of governance and major shifts in how institutions are governed.

The influences associated with institutional theory are economic, social, and political. Sometimes social and political forces can have an even greater impact on universities than economic forces (Judge et al., 2008; Warren, 2003). For example, the influence of external stakeholder groups has grown significantly over the last decade. Amaral and Magalhaes (2002) note that recent changes occurring in the academy in some jurisdictions have resulted in a shift in the locus of influence from an almost exclusive internal stakeholders' domain to an increasing role for external stakeholders. Some national reforms have led to the creation of new or reconstituted university governing boards which have dramatically increased the role of external stakeholders in determining the strategic direction of universities. These are social and political forces that influence strategic university decisions, including research priorities or the development of new academic programs, domains once the exclusive purview of academics. The economic influence is linked to the expectation of universities to create knowledge and develop workers' skills that are needed for knowledge-based economies and global competitiveness and also to the expectation to produce research that is relevant to the development of national economies (Castells, 1996; Jongbloed, Enders, & Salerno, 2008).

From an institutional theory perspective, universities seek to preserve or enhance their legitimacy by conforming to environmental pressure and are driven to adopt governance structures that fit with societal demands and expectations. Universities are often expected to foster strategic partnerships with external entities, particularly business and industry, and through this interaction, they are creating greater external connectedness, changing the modes of knowledge production, and driving the Mode 2 research approach (Gibbons et al., 1994; Jongbloed et al., 2008). To satisfy these institutional expectations, network type governance models are emerging.

One governing instrument that has been used by governments to encourage institutions to respond to external expectations involves linking performance outcome measures to funding. If a university is not performing at the level expected and according to institutional norms, then its legitimacy is threatened and may result in reduced access to government appropriations. In addition, the degree to which the government trusts that the university is capable of making effective decisions through institutional governing mechanisms may diminish, and the government may take steps to assert more control through regulations and in the process reduce institutional autonomy.

RESOURCE DEPENDENCE THEORY (RDT)

Resource dependence theory has for a long time been a leading and influential theory for understanding organization-environmental relations (Drees & Heugens, 2013) in that it recognizes the influence of the external environment on organizational actions. This environmental interaction is based on the notion that organizations are not self-sufficient and must engage in exchanges with their external environment in order to survive (Scott, 2003). Implicit in this is an open systems framework (which we will discuss in more detail in the next chapter) which addresses exchanges between the organization and its environment. And with these exchanges come issues of power and dependence. Hence, at the organizational level, RDT offers a unified theory of power and interdependence (Casciaro & Piskorski, 2005).

It is important at this point to draw a distinction between institutional theory and resource dependence theory. It is necessary to do this because they both emphasize organizations and their environments. Both theories also connect the external environment to an organization's internal decision-making machinery. RDT is based on the assumption that organizations are dependent on their environment for critical resources and, as a result, organizations are controlled by and vulnerable to their environments (Pfeffer & Salancik, 2003). Basically, organizations need resources to survive and they must interact with those who control the resources. On the other hand, institutional theory emphasizes environmental rules, regulations, and social forces—norms, values, and expectations—imposing constraints on organizations and shaping their structures, processes, and behaviors.

Several higher education scholars have utilized RDT in their research. For instance, Slaughter and her colleagues (Slaughter & Leslie, 1997; Slaughter & Rhoades, 2004) work on *academic capitalism*, considered by many as a significant scholarly contribution, draws heavily on resource dependence theory. A fundamental assumption of resource dependence theory is that organizations as open systems are dependent on the external environment for critical and important resources and are impacted by environmental contingencies (Pfeffer & Salancik, 2003). Resources needed by organizations such as raw materials, labor, capital, equipment, knowledge, and other services are controlled by the environment, and this creates dependence, resource acquisition uncertainty, and organizational vulnerability. It is the nature of this dependence that shapes organizational actions and decisions.

At the heart of this assumption are the actors, both the organization needing the resource and the resource holders. A central tenet of RDT is that the party that controls the resources has power over the party in need of the resources. Power is manifested in two ways: (a) the environment can restrict the access that an organization has to the resources it needs; and (b) the environment can dictate how the resources are used by the organization (Bess & Dee, 2008). Typical of this would be public universities (the organization) relying on the state for funding (the external environment/actor) but the funds are accessed only through satisfactorily adhering to specified conditions, for example, achieving a specified graduation rate or enrolling a percentage of students from a certain population demographic. In some jurisdictions, governments traditionally provided universities with unconditional block grant funding and allowed them significant autonomy over certain types of decisions, but some governments' recent exercise of power through the imposition of conditional funding requirements has eroded institutional autonomy (Ordorika, 2003; Slaughter & Rhoades, 1997).

The extent of the dependency is a function of the criticality and scarcity of the resources needed by the organization (Hatch, 2006). Criticality is the importance of the resource to the organization. It is virtually impossible for an organization to function without access to its very critical resources. Scarcity is about availability of resources. Criticality and scarcity create a high level of dependency by the organization on the environment, and, in the process, the environment gains more power over the organization. Not only is there more power over the focal organization, but unmitigated resource dependence limits organizational autonomy (Drees & Heugens, 2013; Pfeffer & Selancik, 1978). RDT assumes that organizations, through their agents, are active participants with their environments (Scott, 2003). Hence, the greater the dependency challenge is for universities, the more likely they are to restructure their dependencies. Thus, while it is incumbent upon organizations to satisfy dependency conditions, it is also important to establish strategic partnerships with suppliers of critical resources, or cultivate alternative sources of the critical resource in ways that minimize the power dependency factor. Hence, where there is a tendency for high dependency, the organization's actions are directed at survival by creating the ability to cope with environmental contingencies. For example, a university may negotiate exchanges with the state to ensure the continuation of resources (Pfeffer & Selancik, 2003). Negotiations may then lead to an agreement for the university to increase graduation rates or minority student enrollment in exchange for government funding. In such a case, a university builds a strategic partnership with the state in an exchange relationship. Such an exchange relationship constitutes a mode of governing rooted in compliance and accountability.

What constitutes critical and scarce resources is subject to change and redefinition, and, by extension, it changes the power dynamic with resource suppliers. Thus, power may be determined by the definition of an organization's social reality and control over resources (Pfeffer & Selancik, 2003). Pfeffer and Selancik (2003, p. 260) outline eight conditions that facilitate the control of organizations:

1. The possession of some resources by the social actors [in the environment]
2. The importance of the resource to the focal organization; its criticality for the organization's activities and survival
3. The inability of the focal organization to obtain the resources elsewhere
4. The visibility of the behavior or activity being controlled
5. The social actor's discretion in the allocation, access, and use of the critical resources
6. The focal organization's discretion and capability to take the desired action
7. The focal organization's lack of control over resources critical to the social actor
8. The ability of the social actor to make its preferences known to the focal organization

Pfeffer and Salancik note that these conditions can be altered by the actions of the focal organization to avoid exposure to these circumstances, thereby gaining discretion and more control over the dependency situation. For instance, forming new external relationships can enhance autonomy and address power imbalances because of the potential this has for securing critical resources from alternative sources (Hillman, Withers, & Collins, 2009). That is to say, reducing the dependence on a single supplier minimizes the organization's vulnerability to access the resources (Bess & Dee, 2008). For example, when government grants to a university are decreased, it is quite common for the university to try and increase income from other sources, such as placing more emphasis on fund-raising, research contracts, or the sale of goods and services. If the institution is successful in fund-raising and is able to establish a large endowment, it will become less dependent on government resources, and this, in turn, will have implications for the power relationship between the government and the university. Alternatively, if the dependent organization (a university) also has a resource that becomes more important for the resource holder, then dependence power can be reduced. Thus, if a university's role in a society becomes more important to the government, then this could reduce the government's power over the university.

While the environment is the source from which the resources come, environmental actors are the players who affect the organization-environment relationship and thereby support or interfere with the organization's resource exchanges (Hatch, 2006). Therefore, when resources are both scarce and critical, university leaders have to track and manage dependencies more closely. Christopher (2010) argues that tracking and managing dependencies requires directors/trustees and the management of universities to be equipped with the skills, knowledge, and expertise to ensure that an effective external relationship is established with key actors to secure the needed resources. The basic argument here is that the extent to which a university can secure critical and scarce resources from its environment depends on the quality and effectiveness of this governance, specifically its senior management and directors/trustees (Christopher, 2010; Daily & Dalton, 1994). This implies that governance mechanisms are pertinent to managing external environmental influences and reducing uncertainty brought on by resource dependence (Christopher, 2010). In particular, the extent to which the directors/trustees (board of governors or university council members) can intervene on behalf of a university to manage its external environment and resource dependency is considered as "board capital" (Young, Ahlstrom, Bruton, & Chan, 2001) and is an important aspect of managing RDT. The external members can provide advice and counsel, legitimacy, channels for communication between the external and internal stakeholders, and can assist in securing resources and commitments from external entities (Lynall et al., 2003). It can therefore be extrapolated from this that resource dependence theory is a useful tool for understanding the size and composition of governing boards of universities—having the right people on the board who can intervene and negotiate the environment on behalf of a university, co-opt external organizations, and maximize the provision of important external resources.

Through its governance mechanism, a university may also reduce the level of dependency by enacting a new environment for the organization (Bess & Dee, 2008; Scott, 2003). Enacting a new environment means that a university's leadership does not accept its external environment as unchanging, but rather engages in creating an environment that is more favorable to them. The leadership may convince the government to increase operating funding levels, encourage the government to create a new grant to support a university initiative, or seek alternative funding from nongovernmental sources. Hence, the university gains more control over its environment. In essence, managing resource dependence requires environmental monitoring, understanding the environmental context well, and developing countervailing mechanisms to rebalance power (Hatch, 2006). These elements all shape governance in the academy from a RDT perspective.

RESOURCE DEPENDENCY THEORY AND THE ACADEMY

The state oversight and accountability environment for public colleges and universities has evolved over the last few decades. Funding mechanisms have become one governing instrument through which states seek greater accountability from higher education institutions. As resource dependent entities, universities are expected to satisfy state performance funding expectations. Tandberg and Hillman (2014) indicate that states measure "performance" in various ways, including student retention, graduation rates, student scores on licensure exams, job placement rates, faculty productivity, and campus diversity. This approach to governance focuses on measuring performance and accounting for outcomes as opposed to regulatory compliance requirements and accounting for expenditures (Volkwein & Tandberg, 2008). In jurisdictions where this is happening, it highlights the role of resources as an important element of governance.

The state of Virginia in the USA is a case in point that aptly demonstrates how universities attempt to assume greater control of their external environments. In the 1990s, universities in Virginia experienced a decrease in funding appropriations from the state. Because of this decline in resource contribution, the three leading universities in the state (the College of William and Mary, the University of Virginia, and Virginia Tech) sought to gain greater institutional autonomy from the state by pursuing a "Chartered Institutions" status. This status would effectively reshape the governance relationship and redraw the authority lines among these institutions and the state, grant more institutional autonomy, and allow these three universities to assume greater control over the means by which they generate revenue (Pusser, 2008). The chartered status would effectively allow each of the institutions to set its own tuition, enroll more out-of-state students, and assume the status of "political subdivisions of the state" rather than "state agencies" in exchange for a reduction in financial appropriations from the state (Couturier, 2006; Pusser, 2008). After much debate and protracted negotiations, the final legislation did not grant the three universities the chartered status they originally sought.

In the final analysis, the State of Virginia created a multilevel institutional autonomy structure (level I, level II, and level III) in which institutions had to demonstrate their ability, based on financial resources and managerial capacity, to function at levels II and III before they could be granted the desired level of autonomy. What is pertinent about this case is that it shows how a university may seek to shift power dependency by changing the dynamics in its external environment and in its governance relationships. The Virginia Secretary of Education at the time captured the relational dynamics between the three universities and the state in this statement: "the reality is the Commonwealth [State of Virginia] probably needs them more than they need the Commonwealth. It will hurt if we lose some of their leverage" (Burdman, 2004, p. 16; cf. Pusser, 2008). Resource dependence is therefore about understanding and interpreting some of the dynamics of governing in higher education: how universities adjust their governance to accommodate the demands of the external environment, especially in high resource dependent circumstances; how resource holders can force changes to higher education governance; and how universities as resource-dependent entities could shift their environments in ways that change the dependency power dynamics.

AGENCY THEORY

Agency theory (also referred to as principal-agent theory or principal-agency theory) has its roots in economics (Alchian & Demsetz, 1972; Ross, 1973) and finance (Jensen & Meckling, 1976) and has become very influential in organizational theory and strategic management, particularly for explaining governance in the corporate sector. Humans are viewed as rational, opportunistic actors who are seeking to maximize their personal utility (Eisenhardt, 1989; Jensen & Meckling, 1976). Principals and agents, the two key constituents in this theory, are considered to be rational utility maximizers who seek to increase their individual utility (Davis et al., 1997). The principals are the owners (shareholders in the case of a public corporation) and the agents are managers/ executives hired by the principals. The theory purports that a principal-agent relationship is established once owners enter into a contract with a manager to manage their organization, which then results in the delegation of authority to agents and in a moral responsibility on the manager (the agents) to act in the best interest of the principals (Jensen & Meckling, 1976). This constitutes a hierarchical contractual relationship between the principal and agent(s).

Agents view their hiring as an opportunity to maximize their own utility, which may not be in the best interest of principals. In other words, there may be a divergence of interest and utility choices between principals and agents. Given a choice, agents would opt for the one that is more aligned with their interests and would maximize their utility; they would be opportunistic. Opportunism, according to Williamson (1985), "refers to the incomplete or distorted disclosure of information, especially calculated efforts to mislead, distort, disguise, obfuscate, or otherwise confuse" (p. 47). Because of this, when agents are hired by owners, monitoring devices and incentive schemes are used to ensure that these agents do not engage in self-serving utility maximizing behaviors but instead act in the interest of owners. Hence, the magnitude of the divergence of interests is minimized by creating structures to impose control on agents (Davis et al., 1997). Such control devices constitute governing mechanisms used by organizations. The classic example of this is the use of the corporate board of directors to oversee a corporation's affairs, including the work of the chief executive officer. A similar case may be made for university boards, as we will demonstrate shortly.

The misalignment between the utility functions of principals and agents is referred to as the agency problem. The agency problem leads to agency costs, which are incurred as a result of agents maximizing their utility at the expense of principals, principals incurring costs to monitor agents, and principals having incentive schemes to control agents' behavior. There are two sources of agency problems: moral hazard and adverse selection (Arrow, 1985). Pertinent to moral hazard and adverse selection is information asymmetry. The information asymmetry element of agency theory assumes that there is a difference in information held by the principals from that held by agents. The agency problem arises because of these differences.

Principals at the time of hiring agents are not aware *ex ante* which agents would engage in such self-satisfying behaviors, and the problem created by this pre-selection information asymmetry is referred to as adverse selection. Adverse selection arises from the principals' inaccurate knowledge of agents and the agents' future intentions. This can be the result of misrepresentations on the part of the agents about their performance, motivation, and abilities at the point of negotiating and contracting because they possess private information to which the principals are not privy (Bergen, Dutta, & Walker, 1992; Kivisto, 2005).

The postselection or contractual agency problem, also referred to as moral hazard, is also attributed to asymmetric information. After the contract between the agent and principal has been established, the agent may not perform at the level expected or the level the contract specifies, but the agent may distort the portrayal of their performance (Barney & Ouchi, 1986). Because the information is asymmetric, the principals may not know exactly what is correct about the performance or actions of agents. The reason principals enter into contracts with agents in the first place is because principals do not have the time or skills to undertake the day-to-day management of the organization, and so agents would always know more about the day-to-day work of the organization, and their own performance, than would the principals.

Prudence dictates that the principal should take action to limit the agent's utility maximization and the principal's losses (Williamson, 1985). Hence, governance structures are used to minimize the misalignment between the principals' and agents' goals, minimize agency costs, keep agents' self-serving behaviors in check (Davis et al., 1997; Jensen & Meckling, 1976), and ensure that there is more accurate information about the actions of agents. These structures serve as control and monitoring devices, and boards of directors are a good example. Boards represent the interests of principals by discharging their fiduciary responsibility and by communicating principals' objectives and interests to managers to ensure that the interests of principals are pursued. In so doing, boards minimize agency costs. However, agency theory assumes controls are imperfect, and these imperfections create opportunities for agents to still act contrary to principals' interests. Thus, to varying degrees, agents act opportunistically. Agency theorists therefore advocate governance as the means to police the explicit and implicit contracts between principal and agents in order to limit opportunism and conflict of interest (Demsetz, 1983; Fama & Jensen, 1983). Within these contracts, principals use a combination of oversight, compensation (incentives), and punitive approaches to force or encourage the agents to act in the principals' best interest and thereby reduce or minimize the risk factor associated with the agency problem (Davis et al., 1997).

AGENCY THEORY AND THE ACADEMY

Agency theory is still not as widely used in higher education as it is in the corporate governance literature. However, there is a growing group of scholars who have used this theory in research on higher education governance (e.g., Gornitzka, Stensaker, Smeby, & de Boer, 2004; Kivisto, 2005; 2007; 2008; Lane, 2007; Lane & Kivisto, 2008; Leifner, 2003). Some of the studies have used this theory to explain government-university relations and as a conceptual framework or heuristic tool to explain university governance. For example, Kivisto (2005) applies agency theory to higher education governance by examining the interorganizational relationship between government (principal) and publicly funded higher education institutions (agents). Despite an increasing acceptance of agency theory within higher education research, its application still largely remains disjointed (Kivisto, 2008), and the theory has not systematically evolved in higher education (Lane & Kivisto, 2008).

Shattock (2006) raises concerns about its applicability to higher education, noting that the thrust of the theory centers around shareholders needing instruments of governance, such as a board of directors, to monitor managers and executives to ensure compliance and actions in the best interests of shareholders. Shattock distinguishes higher education from corporations by pointing out that public and not-for-profit universities do not have shareholders in the same way, and he argues that higher education institutions do not have the "principal" which is a central tenet of agency theory. Shattock further extends this argument to show that universities, even in the most managerialist context, do not have "managers," largely because the academy functions on the basis of personal autonomy and diversity of objectives.

Despite these concerns, we subscribe to the view that agency theory is applicable to the conceptualization and understanding of governance in higher education. Lane and Kivisto (2008) argue that agency theory

> can be useful for investigating and explaining why universities respond to legislative actions in different ways, the impact of competing demands from different government officials on the decision making of institutional officials, and how bureaucratic governance arrangements can alter policy effectiveness and institutional autonomy.
>
> (p. 142)

What makes it even more compelling to apply agency theory to higher education governance is the shifting nature of government-university relationships being observed worldwide. Macrolevel governance of universities now emphasizes more self-regulation by universities but accompanied by increased accountability to governments (Kivisto, 2008; Gornitzka et al., 2004). This is accompanied by a shift from traditional hierarchical authority-based governance to contractual, exchange-based governance (Kivisto, 2008). Implicit in these arrangements are a desire to ensure compliance, a waning trust of universities' (the agents') interests being aligned with government (the principal), and a perceived need to minimize opportunistic behaviors on the part of universities. These are all fundamental to the principal-agency perspective. Kivisto (2008, p. 342) proposes four possible manifestations of opportunistic behavior by universities as:

1. shirking by individuals;
2. opportunistic pursuit of prestige and opportunistic pursuit of revenues;
3. opportunistic cross subsidization; and
4. distortion of monitoring information.

Again, these are all symptomatic of the agency problem.

Kivisto (2008) suggests that three elements are necessary when considering the government-university relationship from an agency theory perspective.

1. The government delegates tasks such as teaching and research to a university.
2. The government allocates resources to a university for accomplishing the tasks.
3. The government has an interest in governing the accomplishment of these tasks.

Toma (1986) was one of the first to apply agency theory to higher education governance in a study of governing boards. Toma was interested in discovering the factors that influence politicians to select one governing board structure over another. In a later study, Toma (1990) examined the board types and the impacts that different types had on the operational direction of public universities. Following on Toma's work, several other scholars have applied agency theory to investigate governance structures and institutional characteristics (Lane & Kivisto, 2008). Some of the findings suggest that board organization and membership selection impact its effectiveness and interest and that board structure can shape the principal-agent relationship which can be manifested in board priorities and actions (Lane & Kivisto, 2008). All of these studies have used agency theory in ways that make quite useful contributions to the research literature.

Given some level of institutional autonomy, a government would not necessarily know exactly what actions a university may take, and the university may intentionally act in ways that diverge from what is agreed upon in the social contract. The university may pursue its own private interest and actively engage in behaviors to achieve institutional objectives at the expense of government's expected returns on invested funds (Kivisto, 2005). In other words, a university's strategic choices may not be aligned with those of the state. For example, government funds may be intended for a specific use, such as teaching and learning, but may be diverted to research in the interest of building the reputation and prestige of the university. This constitutes an agency problem. Kivisto views this action as a moral hazard in which the agent (the university) engages in self-serving behaviors not aligned with the preferences of the government (the principal). Hence, the divergence is the result of self-interested behaviors, which follows the economic assumption, as opposed to "slippage," in which the divergence is unintentional and could be the result of miscommunication between principal and agent.

To overcome the moral hazard problem, the principal can govern the institution by adopting two different contractual approaches: a behavior-based contract or an outcome-based contract (Kivisto, 2005). With a behavior-based contract, the principal employs monitoring mechanisms to determine the kinds of behaviors exhibited by agents. Examples of these monitoring mechanisms are boards of directors/trustees, detailed reporting systems, budget systems, and other accountability measures. Kivisto argues that government-driven quality assurance systems and evaluation processes are examples of monitoring devices intended to demonstrate efficiency and effectiveness and assure the public of higher education quality attainment. These devices are intended to disclose more of the agents' behaviors and thereby reduce the information asymmetry. Agency theory assumes that universities are less likely to act in self-serving ways and more in the interests of the governments and other stakeholders if such mechanisms are in place.

An outcome-based contract places the onus on the agents for the achievement of outcomes. Universities are rewarded for achieving goals aligned with the government's expectations and desired outcomes. This contractual approach is believed to limit the possibility of universities acting in opportunistic ways because the reward is based on performance outcomes that are aligned with the government's interest (Kivisto, 2005). This leads to goal congruence between universities and government (Eisenhardt, 1989). In other words, the choice of an outcome-based form of governing reduces goal conflict. Outcome indicators might include, for example, student enrollment, completion rates, and the number of advanced degrees awarded. In such cases, the state may tie funding to specified university outcomes. The most recent example of this is some states in the USA and some countries in Europe linking university funding levels to graduate employment rates. The outcome-based approach is more evident in situations where governing models grant more procedural autonomy to institutions but limit their substantive autonomy. In other words, universities have more control over the *"how"* but the state imposes its will on the *"what"* (goals and outcomes).

In choosing between outcome-based or behavior-based models of governing higher education, the challenge for governments is to determine which approach allows them the best contractual conditions—the best set of outcomes at the lowest governing costs. Governing costs refer to the direct costs of implementing and maintaining governing procedures and also the indirect costs associated with a university's divergence from the government's expectation, whether the result of opportunism or simply "slippage" (Lane & Kivisto, 2008). Hence, the government (principal) can adopt the outcome-based governing model and thereby reduce goal conflict but incur the agency costs associated with the outcome-based model, or it may opt for the behavior-based model and thereby reduce information asymmetries but incur the costs associated with behavior-based models (Kivisto, 2007). Whether the governance is premised on an outcome-based or behavior-based philosophy, the bottom line is that the government and other primary stakeholders have these governing mechanisms in place to police the contracts between them and the university. In this regard, the board of trustees at a university has a fiduciary duty to monitor and control the behavior of university agents.

STEWARDSHIP THEORY

Stewardship theory has its origins in psychology and sociology. It assumes that agents/executives want to be good stewards and perform at their best in the interest of the organization (Donaldson & Davis, 1991). The theory is premised on a set of behavioral relationships that run contrary to the individualistic, self-seeking portrayal of executives in agency theory. Rather, it presents a collectivist view of individuals in organizations. According to stewardship theory, agents are pro-organizational and motivated to act in the best interest of the collective and are not inclined to engage in self-serving behaviors. This does not mean that the interests of agents and principals will always be aligned, but simply that agents derive greater utility from cooperative behaviors and act in ways that promote cooperative interests at the expense of their self-interest (Davis, et al., 1997). Hence, the attainment of organizational objectives and the satisfying of principals take priority, resulting in manager-principal convergence of interests and utility maximization for the agents (managers).

Davis et al. (1997) assert that when stewards are contracted by loosely coupled, heterogeneous organizations with multiple competing stakeholders, they tend to act in the best interest of the group by trying to satisfy competing claims. This they believe occurs even in politically charged environments, such as some universities. Because stewardship theory is based on the collectivist notion of managers acting in the best interest of the principals, the stewards' structural environment should reflect this orientation. If principals believe in the idea of the agents' willingness to act in the best interests of the organization rather than in self-serving ways, then there is more trust of stewards, and governing structures would reflect less monitoring and more empowerment (Davis et al., 2007). In other words, governance structures associated with strong pro-organizational actions grant significant authority and discretion to executives/managers or agents (Donaldson & Davis, 1991). As a result, principals incur less agency cost.

STEWARDSHIP THEORY AND THE ACADEMY

Stewardship theory can be very useful in analyzing governance in higher education, in part because the notion of the collectivist steward, as opposed to the self-serving agent, is a conceptualization that seems to resonate with the traditional view of the university as a public institution serving the needs of the broader society. Typical of this model of governing in higher education are situations in which public universities are granted significant autonomy—substantive and procedural—over their strategic and operational priorities and there is limited governmental interference. The assumption in such cases is that the university is a good steward of the government's resources and would act in ways that satisfy the government. Drawing on an example from for-profit organizations, a governance structure found in that sector which is considered facilitative of stewards' pro-organizational actions is the chief executive officer chairing the board of directors (Davis et al., 1997). An example in higher education would be a university president being given significant leeway by the board of trustees in managing the resources, operational priorities, and strategic direction of an institution. It may be argued that in such a case one of the board's primary functions is to support the president's decision-making and to provide advice and counsel to the university's leadership rather than engaging in excessive monitoring behaviors.

It must be pointed out though that the extent to which authority and discretion are granted depends on the risk level of principals. Risk-taking principals are more inclined to subscribe to a stewardship theory prescription of governance while risk-averse principals would be more inclined to have structures associated with agency theory type governance (Davis et al., 1997). Implicit in this assertion is that principals' risk profiles also play an important part in the type of governance structures used in organizations.

Davis et al. (1997) point out that there are two dimensions on which the assumptions of agency theory and stewardship theory differ: psychological and situational. The factors that constitute the psychological dimension are motivation, identification, and use of power. The factors the make up the situational dimensions are management philosophy and culture. In agency theory, agents are motivated by extrinsic rewards such as commodities that can be purchased in the marketplace. The theory assumes that because agents are motivated in this way, control mechanisms are structured around extrinsic motivation—principals may create financial incentives to discourage agents from acting in self-serving ways. This is consistent with the individualistic economic assumption.

Conversely, stewardship theory assumes that stewards are motivated intrinsically and are driven by the need for growth opportunities, achievement, affiliation, and self-actualization (Davis et al., 1997). These growth needs are consistent with the intrinsic motivation underlying stewardship theory. Thus, in a university environment where the philosophical orientation embraces stewardship theory, the governance structures and practices would emphasize self-efficacy (Bandura, 1991), self-leadership (Manz, 1990), and self-determination (Deci, 1980) of stewards and a belief in their capabilities to manage resources. Again, this orientation is associated with greater autonomy for university leaders and administrators to administer the affairs of the institution.

The second psychological factor is identification. When stewards identify with the organization, they take on a membership relationship with the organization that enhances their willingness to pursue its mission, vision, and objectives (Davis et al., 1997; Mael & Ashforth, 1992). In this regard, the satisfaction of stewards resides in the attainment of organizational success as perceived by principals. Because stewards link their success to the success of the organization, they are more willing to take responsibility and engage in corrective behaviors when the need requires. On the other hand, self-serving agents would make every effort to avoid taking responsibility and exacerbate problems by taking action to conceal their shortcomings. The tradition of appointing or electing a university president or rector from within the organization, as found in many systems within Europe and South America, is obviously based on a series of assumptions about the relationship between the individual and the organization, including the individual's role in the community, and their sense of identity with, and loyalty to, the university, assumptions that are obviously related to the notion of stewardship.

The third psychological factor is use of power. Power in this regard is broken down into personal power and institutional power (Gibson, Ivancevich, & Donnelly, 1991). Davis et al. (1997) argue that personal power takes time to develop, does not function through the formal channels of the organization, is relational, and can be sustained for long periods. They point out that personal power is consistent with the principal-steward relationship. Conversely, institutional power is ascribed to principals by virtue of their position. Institutional power is comprised of coercive, legitimate, and reward power. Agency theory is based on reward power and legitimate power. Davis et al. point out that institutional power is the means by which there is influence in the principal-agent relationship. Personal and institutional power are both facilitated by the culture of the institution. A university environment fosters expert and referent power which are characteristic of personal power. While power has been investigated in higher education governance, disaggregating power into institutional and personal power could lead to very interesting theoretical angles from which to analyze governance. For example, researchers could explore whether the application of personal power better explains faculty governance, while institutional power better explains university boards and their governance practices.

The situational dimension constitutes the second set of assumptions that differentiates agency theory from stewardship theory. The factors in this dimension are management philosophy, culture, and power distance. The management philosophy depends significantly on the assumptions about the nature of humankind—individuals as economic beings versus individuals as self-actualizing beings. The notion of the economic model of humankind arises in the work of Cyert and March (1963) and is consistent with agency theory. The self-actualizing model of man is associated with the work of Argyris (1973) who argued for an organizational culture that encourages self-actualization. A management philosophy that encourages self-actualization is consistent with stewardship theory (Davis et al., 1997). Davis and his colleagues point out that a more recent differentiation between management philosophies has been advanced by Lawler (1986; 1992); namely, control-oriented versus involvement-oriented philosophies.

Organizations in which agency theory thinking predominates tend to use a control-oriented philosophy. In this environment, a transactional relationship tends to be dominant and it relies on institutional power (Davis et al., 1997). The principal-agent relationship is a low trust one in which instances of uncertainty cause greater controls to be implemented; it is a control-oriented system. On the other hand, stewardship theory is more applicable in organizations in which there is an involvement-oriented approach. Trust is a major factor in such a setting and the risk-uncertainty factor is addressed through training and empowerment (Davis et al., 1997). Relationships in this context are based on personal power as opposed to institutional power found in control-oriented situations.

The second factor on the situational dimension that can determine the difference between agency and stewardship relationships is culture (Davis et al., 1997). As noted earlier, agency theory assumes individualistic behaviors on the part of the agents while stewardship theory assumes a collectivist culture. In countries where there is a strong individualistic culture, relationships based on agency theory tend to be more prevalent. In countries with collectivist cultures, relationships are based more on stewardship theory. In these situations, group membership and relationship building are important. Hence, the practice of governance in Japan, for example, with a more collectivist culture, would be different from a typical American university because of the individualistic culture of the US.

The third factor on the situational dimension is power distance. Power distance is "the extent to which less powerful members of institutions and organizations within a country expect and accept that power is distributed unequally" (Hofstede, 1991, p. 28; cf. Davis et al., 1997). In high power distance cultures, it is accepted that less powerful individuals will depend on more powerful members of society, and this is usually found in strong class and caste systems (Davis et al., 1997). The reverse is true in low power distance cultures. Inequalities are minimized and the independence of the less powerful is respected. Low power distance is associated with decentralized organization structures in which there is consultation in decision-making, while high power distance organizations are more centralized.

The examination of governance using a power distance conceptualization may help us understand the process by which agency and stewardship relations develop in organizations and hence the structure and practice of governance. Davis et al. (1997) note the conflicting findings between the USA and Japan when power distance is applied to individualism versus collectivism. For example, high power distance is expected to be found more in individualistic cultures where there is a predisposition to agency theory, but the USA is considered an individualistic culture with low power distance while Japan is considered a collectivist society with high power distance. Resolving variances such as these would yield new insights into governance and how such paradoxical differences shape governance practices.

The concept of power distance has obvious implications for higher education; some universities are extremely hierarchical, with major differences in power and influence between senior research professors and junior staff, while in other universities the power structure is relatively flat and junior and senior faculty view each other as equal colleagues regardless of differences in formal rank. These differences in power distance may have important implications for institutional governance, for example, who is allowed to participate in the governance process and at what level.

STAKEHOLDER THEORY

A useful way to begin the discussion of stakeholder theory is to briefly reflect on agency theory. In agency theory, the key players are the principals (shareholders), agents (managers), and the board of directors (who represent the principals). This conceptualization applies primarily to corporate governance and restricts the governance relationship to these three groups. Aguilera, Filatotchev, Gospel, and Jackson (2008) view this approach as narrow and restrictive, noting that governance should incorporate wider interdependencies that capture other groups in both the internal and external environment. Therefore, agency theory, when viewed strictly as an agency-shareholder relationship, is bereft of the full range and complexity of relationships around which governance should be structured (Clarke, 2005). It is advocated that a wider environmental set of claims exists, built around social obligations, and third party interests impact on the governance of organizations (Christopher, 2010). The recognition of this extended group of parties/claimants has led to an emphasis on stakeholders rather than just shareholders.

Executives and managers are now more acutely aware of the importance of stakeholders to organizations. They know that stakeholders can impact the organization negatively or positively and these stakeholder groups have to be managed carefully. Much of this awareness came following Freeman's (1984) landmark book, *Strategic Management: A Stakeholder Approach*. According to Freeman, to manage their organizations effectively, managers must become more aware of the multiple constituents on whose support the organization depends and attempt to satisfy their demands or build relationships with them. The importance of stakeholders to organizations has become a quite commonplace assumption in the management literature.

Freeman (1984) defines a stakeholder as "any group or individual who can affect or is affected by the achievement of the organization's objectives" (p. 46). Stakeholders have a legitimate claim on an organization but are also affected by the organization's actions. These stakeholder groups can be internal, external, or an interface group (Savage, Nix, Whitehead, & Blair, 1991). In a university, the internal stakeholders are faculty and staff. External stakeholders are the government, nongovernmental organizations, students, and private citizens. There are also private enterprises with a legitimate stake in a university, including entities that fund research or make other contributions to the university. An example of an interface group would be a board of directors or, in the case of a university, a board of governors who serve a bridging function between the organization and its external environment. Hence, stakeholder theory helps to define influencing and influenced groups and the extent of accountability that will be recognized and discharged by an entity (Gray, Dey, Owen, Evans, & Zadek, 1997).

STAKEHOLDER THEORY AND THE ACADEMY

Over the last two decades, the relationship between higher education institutions, the state, and society has changed (Amaral & Magalhaes, 2002). External stakeholders now play a greater role in the governance of universities and have wider decision-making influence than in prior decades. A key difference is that external stakeholders are more than just governments that fund public universities. They include individuals from civil society and private organizations. Jongbloed et al. (2008) draw a distinction between stakeholders and lay representatives on university governing boards. Stakeholders have differently defined roles and responsibilities and exercise their relationship with universities in a different way from lay representatives. Stakeholder involvement in university governance is more related to responsiveness to society and the legitimacy of an institution in the eyes of the wider society represented by these multiple stakeholder groups.

A philosophical precept underpinning a more stakeholder-driven governance is the notion that universities are now expected to be more relevant and responsive to their "external world" (Amaral & Magalhaes, 2002). This runs contrary to the traditional role of universities in which universities were expected to be detached from society, reflect on it, rise above immediacy, and be more long-term in their orientation (Neave, 1995). Arguably, this current stakeholder influence model is based on the economic function of universities and their expanded social obligations. To accommodate the new ways of viewing the expectations of universities, the state in many countries has modified university governing mechanisms to allow and encourage third-party intervention.

Expanding stakeholder influence on higher education institutions can lead to a restoration of trust and at the same time it can provide an avenue for accessing important information from the external environment (Harrison, Bosse, & Phillips, 2010; Mayer, Davis, & Schoorman, 1995). Harrison et al. (2010) argue that although trustworthiness is not the only essential element in an organization-stakeholder interaction, it is a very useful means of accessing sensitive information and an important source of knowledge. Hence, one can argue that a university that subscribes to an expanded stakeholder governance structure could enhance its decision-making by virtue of having wider stakeholder involvement and access to additional information. This in turn has been shown to improve the performance of organizations (Hillman & Keim, 2001).

In essence, higher education is shifting to a more collaborative form of governance in which there can be mutually beneficial interaction among stakeholders. With this model of governance, the universities' independence is no longer protected as was the case with the Humboldtian-Newman model. Amaral and Magalhaes (2002) assert that

> the assumption underlying the Humboldtian-Newmanian model was that there was a direct relationship between the university's independence from the material—economic, social and political—interests of the society in which the institution was integrated, and the university's ability to accomplish its mission: the pursuit of knowledge for its own sake, and the preservation and dissemination of knowledge.
>
> (p. 11)

But in the current ethos, this is no longer the case because of the prevailing economic and utilitarian view of higher education.

The bottom line is that a university's governance should facilitate the fostering of quality relationships with its multiple legitimate stakeholders. This view recognizes that a university's numerous external relationships constitute a source of complexity in the functioning of the academy that must be managed to ensure that an institution's opportunities are not hampered (Rojas & Bernasconi, 2011) and its mission is achieved.

THE ROLE OF THEORY AND THE POSSIBILITIES FOR A MULTI-THEORY APPROACH IN THE STUDY OF GOVERNANCE

We have outlined five theories that are useful for conducting research in governance. Higher education researchers and scholars have at different times used theories in different ways. For example, in the 1970s, there was an orientation towards the positivist paradigm when higher education scholars attempted to create a core set of theories or develop a unifying theory (Kezar, 2006). Later, in the 1980s and 1990s, the focus shifted to include the application of established theories from other fields, such as organization science, to provide legitimate explanations to higher education phenomena.

The two most influential theories underpinning governance research, agency theory and stewardship theory, represent two opposite ends of the principal-agent theory spectrum. When considered individually, they do not explain higher education governance completely, but they offer different perspectives of it (Shattock, 2006). For instance, Christopher (2010) argues that agency-oriented governance does not capture the unique wider environmental influencing forces occurring between a university and its external environment—the legal and regulatory issues, social issues, ethical issues, human resources issues, and behavioral issues. These all impact a university and shape the boundaries and constraints under which it is governed. These are not captured under a single theoretical construct.

In addition, universities face an environment of increased social and economic obligations to their communities, along with an expanded stakeholder base. Also, the notion of self-interests vis-à-vis trust of various stakeholders is impacted by sociological, ethical, and cultural values of respective countries and would therefore shape a university's governance and the type of monitoring that would be required (Christopher, 2010).

On the other hand, stewardship theory is based on notions of trust, a high-level of commitment, and a closer alignment of interests between internal and external stakeholders. Thus, it is argued that it recognizes the wider influencing forces and interdependencies in governance. Christopher (2010) suggests that stewardship theory complements agency theory by providing an alternate conceptualization of governance in a way that overcomes some limitations of agency theory. Stakeholder theory recognizes the complexity of wider environmental forces arising from a wider stakeholder base and their impact on higher education. Simmons (2004) contends that the theory identifies and recognizes multiple stakeholder interests by attending to organizational obligations to more disparate groups. Although stakeholder theory can stand on its own in conceptualizing governance, it can also serve to buttress explanations from agency and stewardship theory. Therefore, multiple theories may be needed to fully comprehend governance. The multi-theory approach has been advanced by scholars like Christopher (2010) and Lynall et al. (2003) as a solution to the limitation of any one theory.

Christopher (2010) advocates for combining theories in a way that recognizes the different dimensions of the wider environmental influencing forces. Christopher argues that such an approach would capture the major determinants of good and effective governance by incorporating complementary or groups of theories into the analysis of governance. For instance, the individualized approach of agency theory and the socializing approaches that address the wider stakeholder base to which universities must attend are both accommodated under the multi-theoretical approach (Roberts, 2001). In other words, these theories can have a complementary effect. Christopher further adds that this approach facilitates an analysis of boards of trustees, the operational management, and assurances of compliance and alignment simultaneously. Thus, for example, board capital, a university's access to resources, and expanded stakeholder-based interdependencies are incorporated under resource dependence and stakeholder theory, while levels of trust, monitoring, and compliance are accommodated under agency and stewardship theory.

We are not suggesting that it is a matter of choosing one perspective over the other, but that it is important to identify the conditions under which each is applicable (Lynall et al., 2003. It is also important to recognize that no single theory would suffice to completely explain governance in higher education. Combinations of different theoretical approaches present alternative perspectives which allow a more holistic and comprehensive understanding of the issues.

SUMMARY

This is the first of two chapters focusing on theories that can be used to study higher education governance. In this chapter we focused on five theories: institutional theory, agency theory, stewardship theory, stakeholder theory, and resource-dependence theory. Each represents a unique set of constructs and concepts that can be used as a foundation for higher education research. Each is supported by a mature body of prior research on governance issues in other sectors. Given the unique perspectives and limitations associated with each theory, we have also suggested that there may be possibilities associated with adopting a multi-theory approach. We will continue our review of key theories and paradigms in the next chapter.

DISCUSSION QUESTIONS

1. What are some of the assumptions about the external environment and the relationship between the university and the external environment presumed by each major theory described in the chapter?
2. Choose a specific issue in higher education governance. What are the key factors or elements that you would consider in choosing a theory to use to study that issue?
3. Compare and contrast the ideas and assumptions underscoring agency theory and resource-dependency theory. Can you imagine ways in which the two theories might work together in some form of multi-theory approach?

REFERENCES

Aguilera, R. V., Filatotchev, I., Gospel, H., & Jackson, G. (2008). Costs contingencies and complementarities in corporate governance models. *Organization Science, 19*(3), 475–494.

Alchian, A. A., & Demsetz, H. (1972). Production, information costs, and economic organization. *The American Economic Review, 62*(5), 777–795.

Amaral, A., & Magalhaes, A. (2002). The emergent role of external stakeholders in European higher education governance. In A. Amaral, G. Jones, & B. Karseth (Eds.), *Governing higher education: National perspectives on institutional governance* (pp. 1–20). Dordrecht, The Netherlands: Kluwer.

Argyris, C. (1973). Organization man: Rational and self-actualizing. *Public Administration Review, 33*(4), 354–357.

Argyris, C. (1976). *Increasing leadership effectiveness.* New York, NY: John Wiley.

Argyris, C., & Schon, D. A. (1974). *Theory in practice: Increasing professional effectiveness.* San Francisco, CA: Jossey-Bass.

Arrow, K. (1985). The economics of agency. In J. Pratt, & R. Zeckhauser (Eds.), *Principals and agents: The structure of business* (pp. 37–51). Boston, MA: Harvard Business School Press.

Bandura, A. (1991). Social cognitive theory of self-regulation. *Organizational Behavior and Human Decision Processes, 50,* 248–287.

Barney, J. B., & Ouchi, W. G. (Eds.). (1986). *Organizational economics.* San Francisco, CA: Jossey-Bass.

Bergen, M., Dutta, S., & Walker, O. C., Jr. (1992). Agency relationships in marketing: A review of the implications and applications of agency and related theories. *Journal of Marketing, 56*(3), 1–24.

Bess, J., & Dee, J. (2008). *Understanding college and university organization: Theories for effective policy and practice.* Sterling, VA: Stylus Publishing.

Bettis, R. A., & Prahalad, C. K. (1995). The dominant logic: Retrospective and extension. *Strategic Management Journal, 16*(1), 5–14.

Burdman, P. (2004). Has the state become an albatross? *National CrossTalk, 12*(2), 14–16.

Casciaro, T., & Piskorski, M. J. (2005). Power imbalance, mutual dependence, and constraint absorption: A closer look at resource dependence theory. *Administrative Science Quarterly, 50*(2), 167–199.

Castells, M. (1996). *The rise of the network society: The information age: Economy, society and culture.* (Vol. 1). Oxford, England: Blackwell.

Christopher, J. (2010). Corporate governance—A multi-theoretical approach to recognizing the wider influencing forces impacting on organizations. *Critical Perspectives on Accounting 21*(8), 683–695.

Clarke, T. (2005). Accounting for Enron: Shareholder value and stakeholder interests. *Corporate Governance, 13*(5), 598–612.

Couturier, L. K. (2006). Checks and balances at work: The restructuring of Virginia's public higher education system. *National Center Report #06–3.* San Jose, CA: National Center for Public Policy and Higher Education.

Cyert, R. M., & March, J. G. (1963). *A behavioral theory of the firm.* Englewood Cliffs, NJ: Prentice Hall.

Daily, C., & Dalton, D. (1994). Bankruptcy and corporate governance: The impact of board composition and structure. *Academy of Management Journal, 37*(6), 1603–1617.

Daily, C. M., Dalton, D. R., & Canella, A. A. (2003). Corporate governance: Decades of dialogue and data. *Academy of Management Review, 28*(3), 371–382.

Davis, J., Schoorman, F., & Donaldson, L. (1997). Toward a stewardship theory of management. *Academy of Management Review, 22*(1), 20–47.

Deci, E. L. (1980). *The psychology of self-determination.* Lexington, MA: D.C. Heath.

Demsetz, H. (1983). The structure of corporate ownership and the theory of the firm. *Journal of Law and Economics, 26*(2), 375–389.

DiMaggio, P. J., & Powell, W. W. (1983). The iron cage revisited: Institutional isomorphism and collective rationality in organizational fields. *American Sociological Review, 48*(2), 147–160.

DiMaggio, P. J., & Powell, W. W. (1991). The iron cage revisited: Institutional isomorphism and collective rationality. In W. W. Powell & P. DiMaggio (Eds.). *The new institutionalism in organizational analysis.* Chicago, IL: University of Chicago Press.

Donaldson, L., & Davis, J.H. (1991). Stewardship theory or agency theory: CEO governance and shareholder returns. *Australian Journal of Management Review 16*(1), 49–64.

Drees, J.M., & Heugens, P.P.M.A.R. (2013). Synthesizing and extending resource dependence theory: A meta-analysis. *Journal of Management 39*(6), 1666–1698. doi.10.1177/0149206312471391

Eisenhardt, K. (1989). Agency theory: An assessment and review. *Academy of Management Review 14*(1), 57–74.

Fama, E.F., & Jensen, M.C. (1983). Separation of ownership and control. *Journal of Law and Economics, 26*, 301–325.

Fogarty, T.J. (1996). The imagery and reality of peer review in the US: Insights from institutional theory. *Accounting, Organizations and Society, 21* (2/3), 243–267.

Freeman, R.E. (1984). *Strategic management: A stakeholder approach.* Boston, MA: Pitman.

Friedland, R., Robert R., & Alford, R.R. (1991). Bringing society back in: Symbols, practices, and institutional contradictions. In W.W. Powell, & P.J. DiMaggio (Eds.), *The new institutionalism in organizational analysis* (pp. 232–263). Chicago, IL: University of Chicago Press.

Gibbons, M., Limoges, C., Nowotny, H., Schwartzman, S., Scott, P., & Trow, M. (1994). *The new production of knowledge: The dynamics of science and research in contemporary societies.* Thousand Oaks, CA: Sage.

Gibson, J.L., Ivancevich J.M., & Donnelly, J.H. (1991). *Organizations.* Homewood, IL: Irwin.

Giddens, A. (1977). *Studies in social and political theory*, London, England: Hutchinson.

Gornitzka, A., Stensaker, B., Smeby, J-C., & de Boer, H. (2004). Contract arrangements in the Nordic countries. Solving the efficiency/effectiveness dilemma? *Higher Education in Europe, 29*(1), 87–101.

Gray, R., Dey, C., Owen, D., Evans, R., & Zadek, S. (1997). Struggling with the praxis of social accounting: Stakeholders, accountability, audits and procedures. *Accounting Auditing & Accountability Journal, 10*, 325–364.

Greenwood, R., & Hinings, C.R. (1996). Understanding radical organizational change: Bringing together the old and new institutionalism. *Academy of Management Review, 21*, 1022–1054.

Greenwood, R., Díaz, A.M., Li, S.X., & Lorente, J.C. (2010). The multiplicity of institutional logics and the heterogeneity of organizational responses. *Organization Science, 21*(2), 521–539.

Greenwood, R., & Hinings, C.R. (2006). Understanding strategic change: The contribution of archetypes. *Academy of Management Journal, 36*(5), 1052–1081.

Harrison, J.S., Bosse, D.A., & Phillips, R.A. (2010). Managing for stakeholders, stakeholder utility functions, and competitive advantage. *Strategic Management Journal, 31*, 58–74.

Hartley, J., Butler, M., & Benington, J. (2002). Local government modernization: UK and comparative analysis from an organizational perspective. *Public Management Review, 4*(3), 387–404.

Hatch, M.J. (2006). *Organization theory: Modern symbolic and postmodern perspectives.* Oxford, England: Oxford University Press.

Hillman, A.J., & Keim, G.D. (2001). Shareholder value, stakeholder management, and social issues: what's the bottom line? *Strategic Management Journal, 22*(2), 125–139.

Hillman, A.J., Withers, M.C., & Collins, B.J. (2009). Resource dependence theory: A review. *Journal of Management, 35*(6), 1404–1427. doi.10.1177/0149206309343469

Hofstede, G. (1991). *Cultures and organizations: Software of the mind.* London, England: McGraw-Hill.

Jensen, M.C., & Meckling, W.H. (1976). Theory of the firm: Managerial behavior, agency costs and ownership structure. *Journal of Financial Economics 3*(4), 305–360.

Jongbloed, B., Enders, J., & Salerno, C. (2008). Higher education and its communities: Interconnections, interdependencies and a research agenda. *High Education, 56*, 303–324. doi. 10.1007/s10734-008-9128-2

Judge, W. Q., Douglas, T. J., & Kutan, A. M. (2008). Institutional antecedents of corporate governance legitimacy. *Journal of Management, 34*(4), 765–785.

Kavanagh, D. (2009). Institutional heterogeneity and change: The university as fool. *Organization, 16*, 575–595.

Kezar, A. (2006). To use or not to use theory: Is that the question? In J. C. Smart (Ed.), *Higher education: Handbook of theory and research* (Vol. XXI, pp. 283–344). Dordrecht, The Netherlands: Springer.

Kivisto, J. A. (2005). The government-higher education institution relationship: Theoretical considerations from the perspective of agency theory. *Tertiary Education and Management, 11*(1), 1–17.

Kivisto, J. A. (2007). *Agency theory as a framework for the government-university relationship.* Tampere, Finland: Higher Education Group/Tampere University Press.

Kivisto, J. A. (2008). An assessment of agency theory as a framework for government-university relationship. *Journal of Higher Education Policy and Management, 30*(4), 339–350.

Kouzes, J. M., & Mico, P. R. (1979). Domain theory: An introduction to organizational behavior in human services organizations. *Journal of Applied Behavioral Science, 15*(4), 449–469.

Lane, J. A. (2007). Spider web of oversight: Latent and manifest regulatory controls in higher education. *Journal of Higher Education, 78*(6), 615–644.

Lane, J. A., & Kivisto, J. (2008). Interests, information, and incentives in higher education: Principal-agent theory and its potential applications to the study of higher education governance. In J. C. Smart (Ed.), *Higher education: Handbook of theory and research* (Vol. 23, pp. 141–174). Dordrecht, The Netherlands: Springer.

Lawler, E. E. (1986). *High involvement management.* San Francisco, CA: Jossey-Bass.

Lawler, E. E. (1992). *The ultimate advantage.* San Francisco, CA: Jossey-Bass.

Leifner, I. (2003). Funding, resource allocation, and performance in higher education systems. *Higher Education, 46*(4), 469–489.

Lynall, M. D., Golden, B. R., & Hillman, A. J. (2003). Board composition from adolescence to maturity: A multitheoretic view. *Academy of Management Review, 28*(3), 416–431.

Mael, F., & Ashforth, B. E. (1992). Alumni and their alma mater: A partial test of the reformulated model of organizational identification. *Journal of Organizational Behavior, 13*, 103–123.

Manz, G. G. (1990). Beyond self-managing teams: Toward self-leading teams in the workplace. In R. Woodman & W. Pasmore (Eds.), *Research on organizational change and development* (pp. 273–299). Greenwich, CT: JAI Press.

Mayer, R. C., Davis, J. H., & Schoorman, F. D. (1995). An integrative model of organizational trust. *Academy of Management Review, 20*, 709–734.

Meyer, J. W., & Rowan, B. (1977). Institutionalized organizations: Formal structure as myth and ceremony. *American Journal of Sociology, 83*, 340–363.

Meyer, J. W., & Rowan, B. (1991). Institutionalized organizations: Formal structure as myth and ceremony. In W. W. Powell, & P. J. DiMaggio (Eds.), *The new institutionalism in organizational analysis.* Chicago, IL: University of Chicago Press.

Neave, G. (1995). On visions, short and long. *Higher Education Policy, 8*(4), 9–10.

Ordorika, I. (2003). The limits of university autonomy: Power and politics at the Universidad Nacional Autónoma de México. *Higher Education 46*(3), 361–388.

Pfeffer, J., & Salancik, G. R. (2003). *The external control of organizations: A resource dependence perspective.* New York, NY: Harper and Row.

Pusser, B. (2008). The state, the market and the institutional estate: Revisiting contemporary authority relations in higher education. In J. C. Smart (Ed.), *Higher education: Handbook of theory and research* (pp. 105–139). Dordrecht, The Netherlands: Springer.

Reay, T., & Hinings, C. R. (2005). The recomposition of an organizational field: Health care in Alberta. *Organization Studies, 26*(3), 349–382.

Roberts, J. (2001). Trust and control in Anglo-American systems of corporate governance: The individualizing and socializing effects of processes of accountability. *Human Relations, 54*(12), 1547–1572.

Rojas, A., & Bernasconi, A. (2011). Governing universities in times of uncertainty and change. In P. Altbach (Ed.), *Leadership for world-class universities: Challenges for developing countries* (pp. 33–51). New York, NY: Routledge.

Ross, S. A. (1973). The economic theory of agency: The principal's problem. *American Economic Review, 63*(2), 134–139.

Savage, G. T., Nix, T. W., Whitehead, C. J., & Blair, J. D. (1991). Strategies for assessing and managing organizational stakeholders. *Academy of Management Executives, 5*(2), 61–75.

Scott, W. R. (1995). *Institutions and organizations.* Thousand Oaks, CA: Sage.

Scott, W. R. (2003). *Organizations: Rational, natural and open systems.* Upper Saddle River, NJ: Prentice-Hall.

Schon, D. A. (1971). *Beyond the stable state.* New York, NY: Norton.

Shattock, M. (2006). *Managing good governance in higher education.* New York, NY: Open University Press.

Simmons, J. (2004). Managing in the post-managerialist era: Towards socially responsible corporate governance. *Management Decision, 32*(3/4), 601–611.

Slaughter, S., & Leslie, L. L. (1997). *Academic capitalism: Politics, policies, and the entrepreneurial university.* Baltimore, MD: Johns Hopkins University Press.

Slaughter, S., & Rhoades, G. (2004). *Academic capitalism and the new economy: Markets, state, and higher education.* Baltimore, MD: Johns Hopkins University Press.

Suchman, M. (1995). Managing legitimacy: Strategic and institutional approaches. *Academy of Management Review, 20*(3), 571–610.

Suddaby, R. (2010). Challenges for institutional theory. *Journal of Management Inquiry, 19*(1), 14–20.

Sutton, R., & Staw, B. (1995). What theory is not. *Administrative Science Quarterly, 40*(3), 371–384.

Tandberg, D. A., & Hillman, N. W. (2014). State higher education performance funding: Data, outcomes and policy implications. *Journal of Education Finance, 39*(3), 222–243.

Thornton, P. (2004). *Markets from culture.* Stanford, CA: Stanford University Press.

Tight, M. (2004). Research into higher education: An a-theoretical community of practice? *Higher Education Research and Development, 23*(4), 395–411.

Toma, E. F. (1986). State university boards of trustees: A principal-agent perspective. *Public Choice, 49*, 155–163.

Toma, E. F. (1990). Boards of trustees, agency problems, and university output. *Public Choice, 67*, 1–9.

Volkwein, J. F., & Tandberg, D. A. (2008). Measuring up: Examining the connections among state structural characteristics, regulatory practices, and performance. *Research in Higher Education, 49*(2), 180–197.

Warren, R. (2003). The evolution of business legitimacy. *European Business Review, 15*(3), 153–163.

Williamson, O. E. (1985). *The economic institutions of capitalism. Firms, markets, relational contracting.* New York, NY: Free Press.

Young, M. N., Ahlstrom, D., Bruton, G. D., & Chan, E. S. (2001). The resource dependence, service and control functions of boards of directors in Hong Kong and Taiwanese firms. *Asia Pacific Journal of Management, 18*(2), 223–244.

CHAPTER 3

Theories of Governance
Structure, Culture, and Internal Dynamics

This is the second of two chapters that focus on theories that are relevant and applicable to higher education governance. Six theoretical frames are discussed: structural theory, human relations theory, cultural theory, cybernetics, social cognition theory, and open systems theory. These theories provide useful lenses through which to analyze and understand governance in the academy at the meso or organizational level. Some of these theories have already been applied extensively to higher education governance (e.g., structural), while others have played a far more modest role within the scholarly literature, or none at all.

While the structural focus has yielded powerful insights, the excessive conceptual emphasis on structural and rational models means that little attention has been paid to the role people play in the governing process. It has also limited the explanation of governance phenomena, constrained the discourse, and restricted the depth and accuracy of our understanding of governance in the academy. If we expand the focus of governance research to include human and interpersonal dynamics, considerations of alternative theoretical perspectives such as theories of human relations, social cognition, and organizational culture come to the fore. The human and interpersonal dynamics provide theoretical variety and additional analytical tools that allow us to explore how people's interactions in universities affect the functioning of governance, for example, how different groups come together, how inter- and intra-group/departmental relations are fostered in the governing process, and how these groupings shape the quality of governance practices. In this chapter, we will discuss these six theories in some detail and provide guidelines and considerations about possible ways in which they could be applied to explain and understand university governance.

STRUCTURAL APPROACH TO GOVERNANCE

The Structural Perspective

In this section, we briefly describe the structural perspective in order to lay a foundation for understanding how it has been used in higher education governance. Some writers prefer to use the term structural perspective rather than structural theory, but here we use both terms interchangeably. The structural perspective emphasizes the functional and/or mechanistic dimensions of an organization (Bolman & Deal, 2008; Morgan, 2006). The primary focus is on structural arrangements that are designed to facilitate the division of labor, establish lines of communication, create hierarchies of authority, and formalize rules and procedures. A fundamental assumption of this perspective is that the right formal structural arrangements of roles and relationships can minimize problems of communication, workflow, and the distribution of authority and increase an organization's overall performance capability (Bolman & Deal, 2008).

Bolman and Deal (2008) highlight six assumptions that undergird the structural perspective:

1. Organizations exist to achieve established goals and objectives.
2. Organizations work best when rationality prevails over personal preferences and external pressures.
3. Structures must be designed to fit an organization's circumstances—goals, technology, environment, etc.
4. Organizations increase efficiency and enhance performance through specialization and division of labor.
5. Appropriate forms of coordination and control are essential to ensuring that individuals and units work together in the service of organizational goals.
6. Problems and performance gaps arise from structural deficiencies and can be remedied through restructuring.

These assumptions are all embedded in one way or another in university governance and in related scholarship that utilizes the structural perspective. In the next section we examine this perspective and how it has been used to frame our thinking on higher education.

The Structural Perspective and Governance

Kerr (1963) was one of the early proponents of the structural approach as a means to analyze governance. Like Kerr, many of the early writers, especially in the 1960s and 1970s, viewed decision-making authority through this lens. It may be argued that since higher education was rapidly expanding during this era in some countries, these scholars were grappling with issues related to the increased size and complexity of universities and how to improve the decision-making process in order to make universities more efficient (Kezar & Eckel, 2004). Hence, it would have been appropriate to draw on the structural perspective to find answers to questions posed and challenges faced. Kezar and Eckel argue that since those early works of the 1960s and 1970s, governance scholarship has continued to rely almost exclusively on structural theories.

Structural theories as applied to governance in higher education highlight authority, rules, procedures, and decision-making bodies such as boards and committees (Kezar & Eckel, 2004). Some of the actual governance structures in universities include academic senates, faculty advisory councils, governing boards, and student councils or unions. These are all formal forums and decision-making bodies where stakeholders with the legitimate authority assemble to engage in collective action. Enshrined in these structures are decision-making rights and formal authority that specify who participates in the process and the types of decisions that can be made (Kaplan, 2004). That is, the structural parameters of these bodies determine who has the authority over certain decisions along with the associated rules and procedures; for example, who has the authority to decide? At what level is the final decision made? Or, is the decision-making process centralized or decentralized? These questions typify the focus of the structural perspective as it applies to governance. It is also about defining roles, functions, and levels of authority in campus governance. For instance, in most Canadian universities, as is the case in many jurisdictions, the academic senate has the legitimate authority to make decisions on academic matters while the governing board has legitimate decision-making authority over administrative matters (Jones, 2002).

Decision-making authority sometimes devolves to other governance bodies. Oftentimes, higher level governing structures delegate some of their authority to other governing entities such as a standing committee or a subcommittee. For instance, although formal authority resides with a board of governors or some other entity that appoints the president of an institution, the board delegates authority to the president and other top-level administrators, who, in turn, delegate authority to the faculty for certain academic matters. This highlights the structural duality of governance that is unique to the academy. Devolution is further exemplified at some universities in instances where the academic board functions as a standing committee of the academic senate or a university strategy committee may be a standing committee of a university council or board of trustees. A presidential search committee could be an ad hoc committee of a governing board that is vested with authority to conduct a search and recommend a candidate for the university presidency. The terminology and roles assigned to these bodies can vary tremendously by institution, so careful attention needs to be paid to the specific structural arrangements associated with institutional governance. Whether they are created as primary governing entities, ad hoc, or standing committees, these bodies all constitute governing structures of a university and they have defined roles, functions, and specified decision-making authority granted to them.

Two structural descriptors arising from governance studies are hierarchical and bureaucratic. Hierarchy refers to a formal chain of command. Structurally, this varies depending on whether functions are administrative (e.g., admissions and enrollment management, information technology, budget and finance) or academic (e.g., teaching and research within academic departments, including research centers and institutes of universities). Administrative structures tend to be taller, more vertical, and based on position. Administrators have what Weber describes as rational-legal authority that is defined along formal organizational lines and hierarchy of offices (as cited in Bess & Dee, 2008). The academic structures are flatter, positions are more lateral, and authority is based on professional expertise (Bush, 2011; Hardy, 1996; Rhoades, 1992). This structural configuration of authority is captured in Mintzberg's (1979) term "professional bureaucracy." Decision-making in this context follows a collegial process in which there is an assumption of equal rights in policy determination and decision inputs among colleagues. Academics in leadership roles function on the principle of *primus inter pares*, or first among equals. In other words, power and authority are disseminated directly to academic professionals whose involvement in the governance process is based on democratic principles (Kezar & Eckel, 2004). The important point here is the structural distinctions between administrative/managerial and academic governance and the hierarchical differences that exist between these different parts of the academy. A more detailed discussion of collegiality is found in chapter 6.

Bureaucracy is based on Weber's (1947) notion of how to organize structurally for efficiency in which decision-making and planning takes place in an authority, rules, and procedurally-driven environment. Herbert Stroup's *Bureaucracy in Higher Education* (1966) is perhaps the foundational work in the application of Weber's model to higher education. Bureaucratic features embedded in a university's governing structures include: state charters as an organizing authority; formal channels of communication; clearly defined authority relations, such as the type of authority assigned to a senate versus a governing board; coordinated division of labor; formal policies; standardization of rules and regulations; record keeping; and the specialization of roles for the decision-making process (Hardy, 1990; Jones, Shanahan, & Goyan, 2004). Some administrative offices of the university, such as the finance office or the registrar's office, usually possess many of the features of a bureaucracy. In fact, as massification in higher education took root and campuses became increasingly larger, alternative structures were sought and some universities adopted more bureaucratic approaches as a means to increase efficiency in the decision-making process, including increased formalization and standardization. Tierney (2004) argues that bureaucracy in universities functions in a different manner from traditional bureaucracies because universities have two different types of bureaucratic structures: administrative and academic. On the academic side, bureaucracy is based on decentralized power that resides at the unit or department level among the faculty. Essentially, bureaucracy on the academic side of universities has been largely legitimated in units and departments where decentralization is discipline-based (Tierney, 2004) and reflects what Mintzberg (1979) terms a professional bureaucracy. However, bureaucracy on the administrative side is stronger and reflects a more traditional type of bureaucracy. Hence, bureaucracy may be viewed as segmented in the academy—professional bureaucracy versus traditional administrative bureaucracy. From the structural perspective, universities are governed collectively by these two "branches" of the academy whose configurations are somewhat different—the notion of dual or shared governance (these concepts are discussed in greater detail in chapter 6).

Structural Perspective and the Governing Environment: The Internal Environment

The governing environment of universities has both internal and external structural elements. Higher education scholars examining internal governing structures have engaged themes such as centralization, decentralization, authority, hierarchy, size and composition of governing bodies, efficiency, and effectiveness. For example, they have investigated how the size of governing bodies such as senates, governing boards, and committees affects efficiency and effectiveness of university governance. Studies have found a relationship between the size of governing structures and decision-making efficiency; essentially, larger bodies are viewed as less efficient (e.g., Lee, 1991; Schuster, Smith, Corak, & Yamada, 1994).

At the organizational level, size and complexity (the number of loosely coupled academic units, a high level of variety in their functions and goals, and a dual administrative-academic design) shape the way in which structures are designed. Based on size and complexity, a university's governance arrangements may be located some-where on the centralized-decentralized continuum. The larger and more complex a university is, the more decentralized it tends to be because decentralized structures can better facilitate the distribution of decision-making authority. Because large institu-tions tend to have a high level of variety in their functions and goals (i.e., a high level of complexity), decision-making is often more effective when the process is decentral-ized, so that "local-level" expertise can inform the decision. Hence, in a large institu-tion with multiple specialized academic units, centralization can lead to decisions with very little perceived legitimacy.

Small institutions tend to have a lower level of complexity, and they can therefore make effective decisions through centralized processes that involve nearly all organi-zational members. Major academic decisions in a small university might therefore be made by a council involving all 50 of its professors, but at a large university with many hundreds of faculty, the council might be composed only of representatives from each academic unit. Hence, larger universities tend to be designed and governed as representative democracies in which there is representation from other units, divisions, or faculties in the decision-making process. Smaller universities and colleges have the potential for more direct participation.

Beyond size and complexity, governance structures are designed in accordance with established goals and objectives that are linked to a university's mission. The governing board is an example of a governance structure with an important role in ensuring that a university does not drift away from its mission and engage in *ultra vires* activities. In other words, it is a governance mechanism that holds universities accountable for their actions and provides safeguards against reckless or inappropriate decisions. For exam-ple, a university president wishing to purchase real estate for the institution must first seek the approval of the university governing board and would, in the process, have to convince the board that it is in the furtherance of the institution's mission.

In addition to highlighting goals and objectives, division of labor, specialization, and so on, the structural perspective emphasizes coordination and control. Coordina-tion and control are essential elements in an organizational structure in which there is specialization because specialization creates differentiated roles across units within an organization and, hence, the tendency for individual units to focus on their own priorities. As loosely coupled entities (Weick, 1979), academic specialization in univer-sities usually occurs at the departmental level. Loose coupling is a structural configura-tion in which departments and faculties come together in a loosely federated manner. It represents a form of coordination and control, which is different from traditional bureaucratic coordination/control, and which is more consistent with professional bureaucracy, more aligned with the professionalized expertise and status of faculty, and more appropriate for the specialized work of academic departments.

Furthermore, with loose coupling, professional authority is devolved to units and departments within their disciplinary specialties in a manner that facilitates innovation, flexibility, and responsiveness but simultaneously limits the degree to which the actions and decisions of one unit impact others in a university. Such a decentralized environment requires coordination and control to ensure that a university remains a single organization, especially for large universities with multiple departments, institutes, and colleges, the orga-nizational form that Clark Kerr (2001) described as the "multiversity." Tierney (2004) argues that loose coupling is an institutional framework best suited for academics to be aligned with their discipline while simultaneously providing them with standardized and predetermined processes for organizational decision-making such as recruitment, tenure, and curricular issues.

Universities tend to have loosely coupled academic structures, but more tightly coupled administrative structures. The question therefore becomes: how does university governance coordinate between loosely coupled and tightly coupled structures? From a structural perspective, it is achieved in two ways: through vertical coordination and lateral coordination. Vertical coordination uses top-down devices in which the work and action of university agents are controlled and coordinated through devices like authority, rules and policies, planning, and budgetary control mechanisms (Bess & Dee, 2008; Bolman & Deal, 2008). Governing structures are organized as a chain of command and there are rules governing how a university carries out its daily functions, how it deals with issues that arise, and how it maintains some level of organizational uniformity. In essence, the chain of command in governance structures is a hierarchical system of authority through which decisions are legitimated. For example, a committee that has been assigned responsibility to investigate campus hazing but does not have the authority to make a final decision can only recommend a course of action to the higher level council that has the authority to make a decision. Similarly, an academic department can propose a new program, but this proposal usually is approved by higher-level bodies before the new program can actually be offered. Coordination is achieved because the rules regarding who has the authority to decide on which issue are clear, and, generally speaking, the more important the decision, the higher the level of authority assigned to make the final approval.

Lateral (or horizontal) coordination is achieved through structural mechanisms that link units and departments that function at the same level. This facilitates interdepartmental and interfaculty governance. These governing structures provide university-wide interactions and exchanges that facilitate lateral coordination. An example of a lateral governing structure would be a committee of deans. In some universities, such a structure serves as a mechanism to coordinate faculties and departments and to provide some measure of institutional coherence. For example, at the University of the West Indies (UWI), the Committee of Deans serves as "a forum for the coordination of inter-campus discussions among Deans [and to] hold consultative and advisory meetings with the Vice-Chancellor on major and important matters in the University" (University of the West Indies, 2008, p. 67).

Structural Perspective and the Governing Environment: The External Environment

Governing structures connect the microworld of higher education organizations to the desires of the external macroworld of state and global policymakers. Through the authority granted to governing instruments, states/governments shape universities academically and organizationally (Ferlie, Musselin, & Andresani, 2008) and influence universities' actions. Among the external environmental influences on campus governance are the state and its legislature, external bodies such as accreditation and bond-rating agencies, and international entities with global governing authority such as the World Trade Organization (WTO). The nexus between governing structures and external environmental influences on universities has been studied extensively;

for example, the mechanisms through which the state influences the policy direction of universities. Included among these governing mechanisms is the matrix model of governance which facilitates dual accountabilities and has been advanced by Mortimer and McConnell (1979) as a structural mechanism to address issues of internal and external environmental governing relations.

Finally, there has been much criticism about the functional capability of governance to handle contemporary demands being made on higher education. The focus of most of this criticism has been on governance structures and on how they constrain efficiency, effectiveness, and speed of response. In particular, the slow speed of response is arguably due to the dual authority system (administrative and academic structures) and the need to coordinate between loosely coupled and tightly coupled structures. This may partly explain why university administrators almost instinctively resort to structural changes in an effort to improve campus governance. However, there is no guarantee that making structural changes alone will improve governance (Schuster et al., 1994), and Kezar and Eckel (2004) argue that people within universities and the culture of these organizations are equally important considerations.

Although there has been an extensive corpus of research using the structural perspective, many of the findings point to the effect that people, interpersonal dynamics, and culture have on governance efficiency, responsiveness, and participation. This is consistent with a line of thinking that proffers structure, culture, and human agency as separable but not separate (Willmott, 2000). In other words, to improve governance, human agency and culture must be factored into structural considerations. In fact, Greenwood and Hinings (1988) conceptualized structures as "embodiments of ideas, beliefs and values" and argued that "structures are the reflexive expressions of intentions, aspirations, and meanings" (p. 295). Put another way, decision-making systems and governance structures are shaped by deeper underlying ideas, values, beliefs, intentions, and aspirations or "interpretive schemes" (Greenwood & Hinings, 1993).

While governance structures matter, the governance practices that are sometimes observed in universities are related more to the relationships that university members establish with colleagues in the governing process than with structural configurations. Governing structures should therefore not be viewed as somehow separated from the human agents who participate in and use them, but rather as complex networks of interdependence between structure and human agency. In the following section, we will examine the complex nexus between structure and agency in governance by viewing it through the human relations lens.

GOVERNANCE AND THE HUMAN RELATIONS PERSPECTIVE

The human relations perspective presents an alternative way of coming to grips with and conceptualizing governance. It encompasses the emotional, behavioral, and relational aspects of an organization. At its core are people, their interaction with each other, and how these interpersonal relations shape the governance process. Issues such as motivation, leadership, personality, employee engagement, and workplace climate are central to this perspective (Bolman & Deal, 2008; Kezar & Eckel, 2004). Despite the importance of people to the governance process, there is still a noticeable absence of governance research utilizing this perspective (Kezar & Eckel, 2004). In commenting on shared university governance in the United States, Tierney (2004) laments the lack of governance research utilizing the human relations perspective to address issues associated with the participation of faculty and students in institutional governance, issues related to community members on state boards, and the actions and behaviors of governing boards.

There is a clear relationship between structures and human agency. Generally, structures define who may interact and engage with whom and how often (Lawler, Thye, & Yoon, 2008) in that they define formal group membership. For instance, membership of a governing board or senate is constituted according to the functional parameters of these structures. While governance structures provide a mechanism for assembling groups of people to channel decision-making authority and govern universities, it does not address the human dynamics and interactions that occur in these groups. Nor does it address an individual's willingness (or unwillingness) to participate in the governance process. Issues such as these are better understood by seeing governing instruments/mechanisms, such as the senate, as subdivisions of a larger social order of human interactions—the university. In other words, since people interact in the governance process, there is a human-social element that is at the heart of governance and the way governing instruments function.

The type of human interactions that exist generally in a university could affect how well governing instruments function. For example, does the workplace climate foster faculty engagement in the governance process? Are there clear role definitions that promote consensual decision-making versus tension and conflict among members of a governing body? These questions are best answered by examining the human dynamics in governance including the relational and behavioral dynamics that occur within governing mechanisms. This goes beyond the demographics and characteristics of individuals in the governance process (Kezar & Eckel, 2004) and includes the manner in which human interactions manifest themselves in a university's governance process.

In the study of governance, it is important to understand how individuals engage with each other within social exchange structures, and the extent to which these individuals define themselves by referencing the group and are prepared to act on its behalf. For example, "I am a member of the governing council" would constitute a self-definition by reference to this group, while "I am a faculty representative on the governing council" suggests a subtle yet different self-definition and reference group. The ways in which individuals define themselves are expressions of how social actors within a governance structure interact and signal their emotional experiences with and ties to a social unit (Lawler & Yoon, 1996; Lawler et al., 2008). Hence, the practice of governance cannot ignore the social space and social order that actors in a university share with one another. By understanding this, we develop a clearer picture of how governance works and what is required to improve its functioning. Thus, pertinent to the functioning of governance from the human resource perspective are considerations such as leadership development, training, and relationship building. These considerations are germane to understanding governance and how universities may improve the efficiency and effectiveness of their governance arrangements (Kezar & Eckel, 2004). For example, Pope and Miller (2000) advocate for leadership training and development as important links in the functioning of governance processes. This is premised on the notion that although structures exist, individuals who chair and lead these structures need human relations skills and should have a keen sense of how to negotiate and direct agendas in a manner that achieves the greatest outcomes. For example, the manner in which a university's president relates to the senate can impact how well a university functions and the kinds of outcomes that are accomplished. Thus, an adversarial relationship could result in contestation and limit the achievements of a president's agenda despite having the legitimate authority by virtue of office.

Focusing on the human relations side of governance can raise very interesting questions on how members of governing bodies are oriented to their roles, whether there are opportunities and support for continuing growth within the roles, and issues of performance. Human relations management practices can be used to strengthen certain board management practices (Gannon, 2013), including the selection of individuals to lead governance bodies and the types of leadership training and development they may require (Pope & Miller, 2000). Pope and Miller argue that there are important characteristics that should be considered in selecting faculty members for leadership positions in governance, including moderate to low levels of oral and written communication apprehension, the capacity to direct an agenda, good judgment, and the ability to navigate the political terrain of a university. These characteristics all speak to building mastery of human relations in the governance process.

It is well known that power and politics play a major role in universities. This view is predicated on the notion of universities as miniature political environments and sites of interest group competition over a range of issues (Ordorika, 2003; Pusser, 2003). The political dynamics of universities involve interest group coalitions, conflict, values, power and influence, negotiation, and bargaining, and these are all actions and reactions of human beings involved in the governance process, not just structures to channel authority (Kezar & Eckel, 2004). Governance in the academy may therefore be viewed as being at the intersection of human relations and politics. Baldridge (1971) was one of the early scholars to connect the human side of university governance to its internal political environment. Some scholars suggest that power/politics constitutes a theory of governance that is different and separate from the human resources theory/perspective. While this is true, the politics of governing is closely connected to people's actions, interactions, and relationships. Kezar and Eckel (2004) point out that political elements are important for understanding the conditions and factors that affect governance and the way in which interpersonal relations within this context shape governance—the informal deal making and negotiations that occur in the academy. Hence, navigating the governance process of a university requires a solid understanding of organizational politics and people's actions and reactions both formally and informally within a politically driven social space.

THE CULTURAL LENS OF GOVERNANCE

In this section, we examine governance in the academy through the cultural lens. This conceptualization invokes an interpretive approach and symbolism to understand and analyze governance. At the center of the interpretive view are university actors' perspectives on what governance means and the manner in which these actors construct the social reality of their daily organizational existence. Institutionalists view this as the way in which actors construct and interpret their environment. Seeing a university as a cultural entity within some environmental context and its governance as socially constructed diverges from the traditional rational and linear conception of the structural perspective. Such a conceptualization provides a springboard for understanding the interplay between governance structure, culture, and human agency, and the way in which culture shapes the governance process. For instance, Birnbaum (1988) found that efficiency and effectiveness of universities' governance varied depending on the institutional culture. That is, institutional culture can limit or advance a university's governance process (Lee, 1991).

Culture can be defined as a shared set of meanings and symbols around which groups of individuals within the organization coalesce (Alvesson, 2002). Kuh and Whitt (1988) define it as "the collective, mutually shaping patterns of norms, values, practices, beliefs, and assumptions that guide the behavior of individuals and groups" (pp. 12–13). The concept of culture in a university context relies on shared ideas and cognition and is manifested through symbols and meanings, values and ideologies, rules and norms, collective consciousness, structures and practices, and behavior patterns (Alvesson, 2002). In other words, the cultural perspective portrays universities as systems of meanings that are shared among individuals and groups in different ways (Smircich, 1985).

These definitions highlight the idea that a university is a social unit where people interact, construct their reality, and establish shared meanings of their environment among themselves. In other words, people are at the heart of an organization's culture, and university governance is shaped or influenced by how people interact; how people in a university feel, think, and act; and how their values are shaped by shared ideas, meanings, ideologies, symbols, and beliefs (Alvesson, 2002; Schein, 2010).

University Governance and the Cultural Perspective

Tierney (2004) argues that governance is a symbolic process that underscores the fundamental values of universities. In this sense, governance is a cultural phenomenon and should be viewed as the symbols, stories, myths, sagas, ceremonies, and rituals (Bolman & Deal, 2008) through which individuals draw meaning. Thus, the cultural prism allows us to see how these cultural elements are embedded in the governance structures and practices of universities and how values in a particular institution shape ideas about governance. For instance, the structure and process of a graduation ceremony is symbolic of a rite of passage that conveys the meaning that a student has satisfied the university's academic requirements. At a religious-based university, it may be mandatory for students and faculty to attend prayer services together. This may be symbolic of some deeper religious belief that is an integral part of the institution's fabric. Additionally, the cultural frame helps us to understand how the interpretation and conveyance of meaning in governance structures and practices creates institutional order so that a university can function day-to-day.

To advance this line of thinking further, culture in a university has to be understood as embedded in a loosely coupled (Weick, 1979), highly differentiated, and complex organization. This is especially true of large research universities. How the culture is formed and shaped is related to the internal complexities of a university and also the external dynamic environment in which it functions (Smerek, 2010). That is, the culture of a university is shaped by a confluence of internal and external forces that are interpreted to and by both internal and external actors.

The internal forces include leadership style (Schein, 2010), a university's history (Clark, 1970), and the presence of subcultures (Van Maanen & Barley, 1985). Kunda (1992) defines a typical university culture as one that provides "shared rules governing cognitive and affective aspects of membership. . . . and the means whereby they are shaped and expressed" (p. 8). Austin (1994) describes universities as normative institutions in which collegiality and autonomy are central cultural norms among faculty, but there is also a parallel managerial and bureaucratic culture. How well internal governance in a university is practiced and its effectiveness depend on the collective consciousness of these various individuals at the group, unit, faculty, or administrative levels and the meanings and interpretations they ascribe to governing rules, regulations, and practices.

The cultural perspective helps us understand governance as a means to an end and not an end in itself (Tierney, 2004). In this regard, governance is viewed as both process- and procedure-oriented. For most universities, especially those rooted in European and Anglo-Saxon institutional models, these processes and procedures are symbolic of the collegial tradition which has been part of universities for centuries. At the same time, it also explains why the adoption of new processes and procedures that are derived from other institutional forms, such as business, can be perceived as far more than simply modifications to governance but rather an affront to established cultural norms.

External cultural forces that shape governance include the society in which a university is located and the broader institutional field of higher education. For instance, a norm of the academic profession is the expectation of professional autonomy in faculty members' work, coupled with high levels of specialization in the academy. This is an external cultural field level practice that is reflected in academic governance. According to institutional theory (DiMaggio & Powell, 1983), there are local and field level processes that shape a university's governance. That is, local societal forces and institutional forces combine to shape structures and practices. Meanings from these levels are encoded in structures and practices of governance. They reflect and are shaped by societal values and the maintenance and transmission of institutional values and traditions associated with the field of higher education (Scott, 2007; Zilber, 2008). Through these meanings embedded in governance, individuals develop shared cognition, rules, roles, cultural expectations, and beliefs, which in turn shape collective actions (Smircich, 1983; Zilber, 2008). This collective action, framed by meaning and symbolic prescriptions conveyed in governance structures and practices, is the scaffolding of institutional order. Thus, using Scott's (2007) conceptualization of "institutional carrier," governance may be conceptualized from a cultural perspective as a carrier of institutional order. And as a carrier of institutional order, there are artifacts (material culture), routines (habitualized behavior), relational systems (personal and organizational networks), and symbolic systems (Scott, 2007; Zilber, 2008) that all come together to define governance in the academy.

The cultural perspective helps us to view governance as functioning within an environmental context. According to Tierney (2004), "the underlying tenet of the cultural perspective is that one needs to constantly interpret the environment and the organization to internal and external constituencies" (p. 115). Such interpretation is necessary for both internal and external stakeholders to develop a shared meaning and the collective consciousness about governance: what it is, why universities have it, and how it should be practiced. University professors or senior administrators who accept a position at a new university need time to acclimatize, even though they may have had a long career in higher education. They will note subtle differences in institutional routines and practices. They will gradually learn the institutional legends and stories that help them understand certain rituals and symbols, just as they will see the important differences in university emblems, colors, and icons. If they look carefully they may see how differences in both local and institutional culture have influenced university governance. Thus, a university's systems of decision-making and resource allocation, mission and purposes, patterns of authority and hierarchy, relationship with other universities, and relationships with government, business, and community as external stakeholders (Marginson & Considine, 2000) must all be interpreted within a wider cultural context.

Kezar and Eckel (2004) point out that the cultural perspective is seldom used in research on university governance and they call for more studies in this area. They argue that an emphasis on scholarship utilizing the cultural perspective would answer questions about whether there is a core set of cultural issues that shape governance; whether or not there are values that are germane to successful governance, and what they are; and the cultural interaction that occurs when diverse groups' values come together in the governance process. An example of this would be the distinct subcultures of faculty and administrators interacting to govern the academy.

The cultural perspective may be particularly helpful in international and comparative studies of university governance. Universities in different jurisdictions have different histories and are embedded in different sociopolitical systems, and a cultural perspective can assist in illuminating the complex web of understandings that underscore these differences. We will discuss some of these differences in the next chapter.

GOVERNANCE AND OPEN SYSTEMS THEORY

The term "system" in system theory implies that there is a set of interrelated and interdependent parts that make up the whole. In this sense, a university may be conceptualized as system in which the units, departments, and faculties come together to form the whole—the university. The system can also be a collection of universities within a particular jurisdiction. Because the parts are interrelated and interdependent, changes in one part of the system could affect other parts. As we have already noted, the extent of the effect depends on the looseness or tightness of the coupling among the parts. Weick (1979) refers to academic departments in universities as loosely coupled entities which seldom interact, for example, the departments of philosophy and chemistry. Actions with negative consequences that are taken by one department may be insulated from the rest of the university because of the looseness of the coupling.

Universities are shaped by the social, economic, political, and cultural constructions and reconstructions that occur in the societies in which they exist. The complexities, tensions, and ambiguities that are within the larger society project onto higher education institutions (Rosow & Kriger, 2010). As countries shift their policy priorities, universities and their governance mechanisms are expected to adjust to new environmental demands. For example, shifts in funding priorities at the state level may impact funding to universities; universities are expected to make adjustments that are aligned to the funding priorities of the state. Universities are therefore susceptible to, dependent on, and are expected to respond to their external environment. This is reshaping governance in the new environment.

However, it is quite important to recognize that this connection between the university and society is far more complex than a simple hierarchy; this is not an hourglass with funding and regulation dripping down from above through the primary relationship between the state and the university leadership. Universities are shaped by a broad range of interactions and interrelationships with society far beyond the direct relationships they have with formal government authorities. For example, increasingly universities are interacting with industry partners and seeking private external funding sources. Market forces too also shaping decision making, policy and governance in universities.

At the same time, the fact that universities are embedded in their local context also means that they play a role in shaping the world around them. University leaders are more than simply responsive actors. They advocate on behalf of their institution in its relationships with the broader society. More importantly, a complex arrangement of relationships with society can be found at every level of the institution (Jones, 1991). Given its mission and expertise, a faculty of agriculture will have a wide range of relationships with the government department responsible for policy in this area, as well as with sector organizations, businesses, and even individual farmers requesting advice on how to deal with a particular problem. A faculty of medicine, through its complex connections with health departments, professional organizations, and individual practitioners, may influence national policies, standards of health care, the introduction of new procedures based on recent research, and professional ethics. Individual faculty members may influence policy by providing expert advice to government and advocacy groups (Jones, 1993) or taking on research contracts with private industry. These relationships are in no way limited to professional faculties. Scholars of religion may play an important role in the interpretation of religious scriptures. Sociologists may illuminate social inequities. Historians may challenge existing understandings of key events. From this perspective, the university is not simply a subject of societal pressures and elements, but rather deeply embedded in a complex web of interactions with the society in which it functions.

Given this context, open systems theory provides a useful theoretical framework from which to understand higher education governance. The open systems concept implies that an organization interacts with its environment, but organizational boundaries determine the extent of such interactions. However, the extent to which an organization or system is open depends on how the boundaries are defined (Scott, 2003). The loosely coupled nature of the university and the decentralization of authority may allow local units to respond directly to the needs of the external environment through their relationships with government, organizations, agencies, and commercial entities. However universities might also establish boundaries for this interaction that limit the open nature of the system. The senior leadership may limit the interaction between faculties and local units with government in order to ensure that university-wide interests are articulated. There may be stringent criteria governing contracts with industry or agreements with private donors that limit the nature of these relationships. These are all examples of how university governance is shaped by and shapes the external environment.

CYBERNETICS AND GOVERNANCE

Birnbaum (1989) describes universities as having large, dynamic, and complex social systems in which there is contention, biases, goal ambiguity, and the appearance of chaos. Compounding this complexity is the dynamic and uncertain environment that defines the current context of higher education globally. Universities now have to contend with environmental uncertainty, the rapid speed of events such as media invasions, and the general uncertainty that has become pervasive in higher education about issues like funding. In the midst of all this, universities carry out their mission, grapple with the many challenges that characterize day-to-day activities, and continue to survive. Birnbaum argues that the principles of cybernetics and cybernetic control are the means by which such a complex and unpredictable system functions. In this section, we examine governance through the cybernetic lens.

Cybernetics emerged largely from the early work of Weiner (1948) and the design challenges of World War II. The basis of this design challenge was resolving the complexity of striking a moving target such as an airplane. This led to sophisticated models of communication, control, and information exchange that simulated the adaptive capacities of the human brain to process information and take corrective action when needed (Morgan, 2006). This thinking was later adapted to organizations. Much of the theoretical and methodological development of organizational cybernetics that followed is largely the work of Stafford Beer (e.g., Beer, 1979; 1981; 1985). It was later applied to social institutions such as universities. Birnbaum (1989), for example, was an early proponent of its application for understanding the functioning and design of universities.

From an organizational perspective, cybernetics is about creating the capabilities within an organization to learn in a "brain-like way." Central to this are purposeful information processing, communication, and control systems of which a key element is information variety. Information variety comes from Ashby's (1956; 1968) concept of requisite variety. For an organization to attend properly to the complexities and diversity of its environment, it must have the requisite variety in its information and control system (Turnbull, 1997). Information is needed to determine: what goals and performance standards are to be set; the environmental parameters in which they will be attained; the means for measuring performance; when there are deviations from the normative or desired level of performance; and what corrective actions are needed. Because governance is so central to the functional capability of a university, internal systems of control such as governing mechanisms (which might, for example, closely monitor financial data and enrollment rates) are designed to capture the requisite information needed in a cybernetic system. Feedback mechanisms, the processing of information attained, and the decision authority to make changes based on feedback would constitute a communication, information gathering, and learning cybernetic approach to governance.

Morgan (1997, p. 86) outlines four key principles of communication and learning associated with cybernetics as:

1. Systems must have the capacity to sense, monitor, and scan significant aspects of the environment.
2. They must be able to relate this information to the operating norms that guide system behavior.
3. They must be able to detect significant deviations from these norms.
4. They must be able to initiate corrective action when discrepancies are detected.

Morgan argues that if these four conditions are satisfied, an organization can function in an intelligent and self-regulating manner by engaging in the continuous processing of information exchange with its environment, which in turn allows for the monitoring of performance changes and the taking of corrective actions.

In its simplest form, the cybernetic organization is able to detect and correct deviations from predetermined norms and standards but does not have the capability to question or challenge these predetermined norms and standards. Taking corrective action requires organizations to articulate the goals and objectives towards which they are striving and to create feedback loops. The feedback loops alert the organization that it is off course and that corrective adjustments are needed to bring the organization back on course towards its established goals and objectives. Because the system is designed to detect deviations, the feedback is always negative. This system of learning, referred to as "single-loop" learning, "permits the organization to carry on its present policies or to achieve its present objectives" (Argyris & Schon, 1978, p. 2). This is essentially a consolidation process in which there are no changes to present policies, objectives, or mental maps in an organization but simply an improvement in knowledge and competency (Romme & van Wittleoostuijn, 1999; Snell & Man-Kuen Chak, 1998).

In a more complex cybernetic system, the organization is not only able to detect and correct deviations from operating norms and standards but also has the capability to question those operating norms and standards. The more complex system relies on double-loop learning. Double-loop learning "manifests itself as a transformation process, that is, changes in the organization's knowledge and competency by collectively reframing problems and developing new policies, objectives and mental maps" (Romme & van Wittleoostuijn, 1999, p. 440). Thus, double-loop learning not only causes corrective action to be taken, but also establishes new visions, norms, and reference points (Morgan, 2006). This constitutes the essence of governance in a cybernetic governing system. Governance does not create "a straitjacket" but allows space for learning and innovation in a dynamic and complex higher education environment. The governing board of a university is an example of a governing entity with the authority to challenge and where appropriate, change existing goals and standards—the double-loop learning of a cybernetic university.

Romme and van Wittleoostuijn (1999) posit that double-loop learning requires open dialogue with free and unrestricted conversations among key actors. One can argue that this is typical of the collegial model of governance. However, there has to be a willingness to subject individuals' views and positions to the scrutiny of others in an environment free of defensive posturing and behaviors and in ways that would not impede the learning process. Bess and Dee (2008) posit that double-loop learning has the greatest chance of success in environments where there is open communication, decentralized authority structures, and a culture of inquiry and experimentation. They argue that in a university, it may lead to higher levels of faculty and staff participation in the governance and decision-making process.

Information garnered through a diversity of participants and control systems is pertinent to governance. For example, forums like senates or governing boards can be venues of rich discussion and debate on issues of major significance and serve as an information exchange that could enhance decision-making effectiveness. Requisite variety would suggest that attention should be paid to the membership composition of these bodies to ensure that the right mix of information emerges. For instance, some governing boards or councils have a mix of internal and external stakeholders whose participation brings variety to debates and discussions associated with planning. This cross-fertilization of ideas could provide the variety needed for a university to cope with or reduce uncertainty about its environment and ensure that the university does not drift away from its standards, goals, or mission. In other words, embedded in the governance are methods of diagnosis and correction. Simultaneously, these activities serve as a control function through feedback mechanisms such as reports and data presented at these governing forums. In essence, the requisite variety of information along with a feedback mechanism allows a university to engage in monitoring, self-correction, error elimination, and self-regulation activities (Birnbaum, 1989; Morgan, 2006). Kezar (2001) explains that the cybernetic model in a university setting "is a loosely coupled, open system in which multiple organizational realities such as the collegium, bureaucratic organization, organized anarchy, and political system exist simultaneously to greater and lesser degrees, depending on the institution" (p. 110). We argue that the complexity of the internal environment and the way in which these multiple forces come together could provide a governing forum for organizational learning and innovation to occur.

SOCIAL COGNITION AND GOVERNANCE

Social cognition theory (SCT) is a product of the work of prominent psychologist Albert Bandura. Social cognition theory is about human behavior, how individuals and organizations learn, and how people make sense of their environments (Argyris, 1994; Kezar & Eckel, 2004). Stajkovic and Luthans (1998) point out that the social part of the theory is related to the social origins of how people think and act, and this is driven by what people learn by being members of society. Hence, in an organization, a lot of what individuals know and how they behave is related to the organizational environment in which they function. On the other hand, the cognitive elements of the theory are about how thought processes influence human motivation, attitudes, and action. It also highlights that, depending on unique characteristics, each individual within an organization processes and acts differently on the same information (Stajkovic & Luthans, 1998). Thus, there is no single organizational reality shared by all employees which is typical of the functionalist perspective. Rather, organizations such as universities have multiple socially constructed views of organizational reality: a social-constructivist perspective. Hence, social cognition theorists are concerned with how individuals within an organization frame their reality, how the social context influences the framing, how people reconstruct their reality on an ongoing basis, and the ways in which learning can shape and reshape existing views (Kezar, 2001). Bandura conceptualizes these multiple influences and interactions as a triadic reciprocality of the environment, the individual, and behavior—these three elements exerting influence on each other. Thus, the actions taken by individuals in the governance process and how these individuals initiate, execute, and maintain behaviors and practices are explained by reciprocal causation among cognitive, behavioral, and environmental activities (Bandura, 1986; Stajkovic & Luthans, 1998).

How is this theory relevant to university governance? Social cognition theory offers a theoretical foundation that allows behavior, cognition, and learning to be applied to institutional governance. This is in consonance with the notion that the practices and performance capability of institutional governance cannot ignore the human element. In fact, we argue that a significant aspect of the performance of governing instruments is directly linked to the actions and practices of the individuals involved. It relates to the way people learn the routines of the governance process; how they perceive and define the consequences of their behaviors—rewards versus punishment; how individuals encode information from the environment to construct their reality about the governance process and then act accordingly; and the manner in which the organization's environment shapes an individual's cognition, competencies, expectations, and beliefs about the governance processes and practices. Hence, it is wise not to overlook the behavior element when examining the complexities of university governance. Additionally, because governance capitalizes on the intelligence of an organization (Kezar & Eckel, 2004), organizational learning also has to be factored into analyzing it. This is also consistent with the cybernetic perspective. Stated another way, how individuals think about and interpret a university's environment, including the governance practices they observe daily, are germane to institutional governance through a social cognition lens.

SCT provides five human capabilities that allow us to understand how this process works: symbolizing capabilities, forethought capability, vicarious learning capabilities, self-regulatory capability, and self-reflective capability. *Symbolizing capability* refers to the extent to which individuals have the capability to rely on symbols to interpret and adjust to their environment (Stajkovic & Luthans, 1998). It is the way in which people see and process symbols and ascribe meaning, which is then used as a guide for their action. A junior faculty member may interpret the subtle symbols within a department in order to learn important differences in status associated with participating in different committees.

Forethought capability highlights how people can self-regulate future behavior (Stajkovic & Luthans, 1998). Employees think about their future, determine the consequences of their actions, and set goals. For example, an individual may set his or her sights on becoming a dean in the future and observe how the governance process works, note the profile of accomplishments expected of successful candidates, set the appropriate goal (becoming a dean), and take the appropriate actions to achieve it.

Vicarious learning capability is the notion of learning by observing the behavior of others and the consequences of their behaviors (Stajkovic & Luthans, 1998). Thus, individuals do not have to learn the way in which governance functions from trial and error and thereby risk consequences. Rather, they learn by observing the practices of competent others. For example, junior faculty may learn how to influence decision-making in department meetings by observing the behaviors of influential senior colleagues.

Self-regulatory capability suggests that people have self-set standards and methods of self-evaluations of their behaviors. Through self-evaluations, they are able to ascertain if there is congruence between their self-set standards and performance or if they simply need to set higher standards. In other words, the self-regulatory mechanisms of individuals function in three ways: through self-monitoring of one's behavior, its determinants, and its effects; the way in which behavior is judged by the individual in relation to personal standards and environmental circumstances; and effective self-reaction (Stajkovic & Luthans, 1998). For example, a senior academic leader may have high standards related to the quality of public presentations and devote considerable time and energy to crafting the text and practicing the speech. The process involves multiple revisions and iterations based largely on a self-standard for excellence, a standard that may be well above the normal expectations of someone in this situation.

Self-reflective capability allows employees to reflect on their personal experiences and thought processes. Through this, they are able to generate specific knowledge about their environmental reality and how to deal effectively with their environment (Stajkovic & Luthans, 1998). For instance, a good committee chair may reflect on the events of each meeting in order to learn lessons for the next. Was enough space provided for thoughtful discussion? Did the meeting proceed efficiently? What can the chair do to increase the effectiveness of the decision-making process?

Given the influence that social cognition theory has had on understanding people's actions, motivations, and learning in organizations, Kezar and Eckel (2004, pp. 392–393) posit that it should be applied to the study of institutional governance. They believe it may provide answers to questions like:

- "What level of redundancy within the decision-making processes is needed to create learning?
- What process and expertise are more effective for addressing complex decisions . . . in the new governance environment?
- How do group dynamics facilitate or hinder learning about governance?"

SUMMARY

In this chapter, we have reviewed six quite different theoretical frames that may be useful in understanding and exploring university governance. Structural theory has provided the foundation for the vast majority of studies of university governance to date and has contributed a great deal to our understanding of higher education governance structures and arrangements. Though used far less frequently, human relations theory, cultural theory, cybernetics, social cognition theory, and open systems theory offer very different perspectives on governance and hold tremendous potential as tools for research in this important area.

DISCUSSION QUESTIONS

1. Based on the discussion of the six theoretical frames, what do you think would be a good research question for each of the frames?
2. What do you see as the key strengths and limitations associated with structural theory in the study of university governance?
3. Which framework do you believe offers the greatest potential in terms of contributing to our knowledge of governance practices that will lead to effective decision-making? Why?

REFERENCES

Alvesson, M. (2002). *Understanding organizational culture*. Thousand Oaks, CA: Sage.
Argyris, C., & Schon, D.A. (1978). *Organisational learning: A theory of action perspective*. Reading, MA: Addison-Wesley.

Argyris, C. (1994). *On organizational learning* (2nd ed.). Cambridge, MA: Blackwell.

Ashby, W. R. (1956). *An introduction to cybernetics.* New York, NY: John Wiley.

Ashby, W. R. (1968). *An introduction to cybernetics.* London, England: University Paperbacks.

Austin, A. E. (1994). Understanding and assessing faculty cultures and climates. *New Directions for Institutional Research, 84,* 47–63. doi.10.1002/ir.37019948406

Baldridge, J. (1971). *Power and conflict in the university.* New York, NY: John Wiley.

Bandura, A. (1986). *Social foundations of thought and action: A social cognitive theory.* Englewood Cliffs, NJ: Prentice-Hall.

Beer, S. (1979). *The heart of enterprise.* Chichester, England: John Wiley.

Beer, S. (1981). *Brain of the firm* (2nd ed.). Chichester, England: John Wiley.

Beer, S. (1985). *Diagnosing the system for organizations.* Chichester, England: John Wiley.

Bess, J., & Dee, J. (2008). *Understanding college and university organization: Theories for effective policy and practice.* Sterling, VA: Stylus Publishing.

Birnbaum, R. (1988). *How colleges work: The cybernetics of academic organization and leadership.* San Francisco, CA: Jossey-Bass.

Birnbaum, R. (1989). The cybernetic institution: Toward an integration of governance theories. *Higher Education, 18,* 239–253.

Bolman, L. G., & Deal, T. E. (2008). *Rearming organizations: Artistry, choice, and leadership.* San Francisco, CA: Jossey-Bass.

Bush, T. (2011). *Theories of educational leadership and management.* Los Angeles, CA: Sage.

Clark, B. R. (1970). *The distinctive college: Antioch, Reed & Swarthmore.* Chicago, IL: Aldine.

DiMaggio, P. J., & Powell, W. W. (1983). The iron cage revisited: Institutional isomorphism and collective rationality in organizational fields. *American Sociological Review, 48,* 147–160.

Ferlie, E., Musselin, C., & Andresani, G. (2008). "The steering" of higher education system: A public management perspective. *Higher Education, 56,* 325–348.

Gannon, G. (2013). *Human resources programming and its impact on leadership within governing boards of Ontario community colleges.* (Unpublished Ph.D. thesis). University of Toronto, Toronto, Ontario.

Greenwood, R., & Hinings, C. R. (1988). Design archetypes, tracks and the dynamics of strategic change. *Organization Studies, 9,* 293–316.

Greenwood, R., & Hinings, C. R. (1993). Understanding strategic change: The contribution of archetypes. *Academy of Management Journal, 36,* 1052–1081.

Hardy, C. (1990). Putting power into university academic governance. In J. Smart (Ed.), *Higher education: Handbook of theory and research* (Vol. 4, pp. 393–426). New York, NY: Agathon.

Hardy, C. (1996). *The politics of collegiality: Retrenchment strategies in Canadian universities.* Montreal, Quebec: McGill-Queen's University Press.

Jones, G. A. (1991). *Pressure groups and secondary relations: A pluralist analysis of the interface between the University of Toronto and the government of Ontario.* (Unpublished Ph.D. thesis). University of Toronto, Toronto, Ontario.

Jones, G. A. (1993). Professorial pressure on government policy: University of Toronto Faculty. *Review of Higher Education, 16*(4), 461–482.

Jones, G. A. (2002). The structure of university governance in Canada: A policy network approach. In A. Amaral, G. A. Jones, & B. Karseth (Eds.), *Governing higher education: National perspectives on institutional governance* (pp. 213–234). Dordrecht, The Netherlands: Kluwer.

Jones, G. A., Shanahan, T., & Goyan, P. (2004). The academic senate and university governance in Canada. *The Canadian Journal of Higher Education, 34*(2), 35–68.

Kaplan, G. E. (2004). Do governance structures matter? *New Directions for Higher Education, 127,* 23–33.

Kerr, C. (1963). *The uses of the university.* Cambridge, MA: Harvard University Press.

Kerr, C. (2001). *The uses of the university* (5th ed.). Cambridge, MA: Harvard University Press.

Kezar, A. (2001). *Understanding and facilitating change in higher education in the 21st century.* (ASHE-ERIC Higher Education Report). Washington, DC: Association for the Study of Higher Education.

Kezar, A., & Eckel, P. (2004). Meeting today's governance challenges. *Journal of Higher Education, 75*(4), 371–399.

Kuh, G. D., & Whitt, E. J. (1988). *The invisible tapestry: Culture in American colleges and universities* (ASHE-ERIC Higher Education Report no. 1). Washington, DC: Association for the Study of Higher Education.

Kunda, G. (1992). *Engineering culture: Control and commitment in a high-tech corporation.* Philadelphia, PA: Temple University Press.

Lawler, E. J., Thye, S. R., & Yoon, J. (2008). Social exchange and micro-social order. *American Sociological Review, 73*(4), 519–542.

Lawler, E. J., & Yoon, J. (1996). Commitment in exchange relations: Test of theory of relational cohesion. *American Sociological Review, 61*(1), 89–108.

Lee, B. (1991). Campus leaders and campus senates. In R. Birnbaum (Ed.), *Faculty in governance: The role of senates and joint committees in academic decision making* (pp. 41–62). (*New Directions for Higher Education, No. 75*). San Francisco, CA: Jossey Bass.

Marginson, S., & Considine, M. (2000). *The enterprise university.* Melbourne, Australia: Cambridge University Press.

Mintzberg, H. (1979). *The professional bureaucracy.* Englewood, NJ: Prentice-Hall.

Morgan, G. (1997). *Images of organization* (2nd ed.). Newbury Park, CA: Sage.

Morgan, G. (2006). *Images of organization* (Updated ed.). Newbury Park, CA: Sage.

Mortimer, K., & McConnell, T. (1979). *Sharing authority effectively.* San Francisco, CA: Jossey-Bass.

Ordorika, I. (2003). *Power and politics in university governance: Organization and change at the Universidad Nacional Autónoma de México.* New York, NY: RoutledgeFalmer,

Pope, M. L., & Miller, M. T. (2000). Community college faculty governance. Leaders: Results in a national survey. *Community College Research and Practice, 24*, 627–638.

Pusser, B. (2003). Beyond Baldridge: Extending the political model of higher education governance. *Educational Policy, 17*(1), 121–140.

Rhoades, G. (1992). Governance models. In B. Clark and G. Neaves (Eds.), *The encyclopedia of higher education* (Vol. 2, pp. 1376–1384). Oxford, England: Pergamon Press.

Romme, A.G.L., & van Wittleoostuijn, A. (1999). Circular organizing and triple loop learning. *Journal of Organizational Change Management, 12*(5), 439–453.

Rosow, S. J., & Kriger, T. (2010). Introduction. In S. J. Rosow, & T. Kriger (Eds.), *Transforming higher education: Economy, democracy, and the university* (pp. ix–xvi). Lanham, MD: Rowman & Littlefield.

Schein, E. H. (2010). *Organizational culture and leadership.* San Francisco, CA: Jossey-Bass.

Schuster, J., Smith, D., Corak, K., & Yamada, M. (1994). *Strategic academic governance: How to make big decisions better.* Phoenix, AZ: Oryx.

Scott, W. R. (2003). *Organizations: Rational, natural and open systems.* Upper Saddle River, NJ: Prentice-Hall.

Scott, W. R. (2007). *Institutions and organizations.* Thousand Oaks, CA: Sage.

Smerek, R. E. (2010). Cultural perspectives of academia: Toward a model of cultural complexity. In J. C. Smart (Ed.), *Higher education: Handbook of theory and research* (Vol. 25, pp. 381–423). Dordrecht, The Netherlands: Springer.

Smircich, L. (1983). Organizations as shared meanings. In L. R. Ponty et al. (Eds.), *Organizational symbolism.* Greenwich, England: JAI Press.

Smircich, L. (1985). Is organizational culture a paradigm for understanding organizations and ourselves? In P. J. Frost et al. (Eds.), *Organization culture.* Beverly Hills, CA: Sage.

Snell, R., & Man-Kuen Chak, A. (1998). The learning organization: Learning and empowerment for whom? *Management Learning, 29,* 337–364.

Stajkovic, A. D., & Luthans, F. (1998). Social cognitive theory and self-efficacy: Going beyond traditional motivational and behavioral approaches. *Organizational Dynamics, 26*(4), 62–74.

Stroup, H. (1966). *Bureaucracy and higher education.* New York, NY: Free Press.

Tierney, W. G. (2004). A cultural analysis of shared governance: The challenge ahead. In J. C. Smart (Ed.), *Higher education: Handbook of theory and research* (Vol. 19, pp. 85–132). Dordrecht, The Netherlands: Kluwer.

Turnbull, S. (1997). Stakeholder governance: A cybernetic and property rights analysis. *Corporate Governance: An International Review, 5*(1), 11–23.

University of the West Indies. (2008). *Statutes and ordinances.* Kingston, Jamaica: University of the West Indies.

Van Maanen, J., & Barley, S. (1985). Cultural organization: Fragments of a theory. In P. Frost, L. Moore, M. R. Lewis, C. Lundberg, & J. Martin (Eds.), *Organizational culture* (pp. 31–53). Beverly Hills, CA: Sage.

Weber, M. (1947). *The theory of social and economic organization.* New York, NY: Free Press.

Weick, K. (1979). Educational organizations as loosely coupled systems. *Administrative Science Quarterly, 21*(1), 1–19.

Weiner, N. (1948). *Cybernetics.* New York, NY: Wiley.

Willmott, R. (2000). The place of culture in organization theory: Introducing the morphogenetic approach. *Organization, 7*(1), 95–128.

Zilber, T. B. (2008). The work of meanings in institutional processes and thinking. In R. Greenwood, C. Oliver, K. Sahlin, & R. Suddaby. *The Sage handbook of organizational institutionalism* (pp. 151–169). Los Angeles, CA: Sage.

CHAPTER 4

State-University Governance
Concepts, Perspectives, and Shifting Tides

Many universities are public institutions and therefore have direct interactions with the state, but even private institutions frequently interact with and are in some ways regulated by government. The mechanisms that facilitate this interaction and help to define levels of authority constitute important elements of state-university governance. These mechanisms include funding, policy promulgation on higher education, legal requirements, rules and regulations about the general administration of public entities and quasi-public institutions, and the oversight function exhibited through membership of boards of governors and other governing bodies. Different countries use these mechanisms in different ways. Some use them to be more interventionist while others, although discharging their oversight responsibility, are less intrusive and allow institutions to have autonomy and latitude.

This chapter focuses on public universities. By drawing on examples of policies, practices, and governance reforms from around the world, we discuss in this chapter the theoretical and conceptual underpinnings of state-university governance. Specifically, the chapter examines the "system" concept of higher education governance and focuses on the conceptual underpinnings and policy issues that shape the balance between state responsibility and university autonomy; the philosophical basis for some types of system governance; the type and degree of government control versus university autonomy; how alteration of the balance between these two has implications for higher education governance; the changing role of the state and its impact on higher education governance; and the way in which public policy promulgation is reforming higher education governance.

The chapter is divided into two broad sections. In the first section, we discuss conceptualizations of state-university-market and state-university-industry relationships. In section two, we discuss the "system" concept of higher education, policy issues and recent promulgations, the changing nature of the state, and how all these factors are impacting state-university relationships.

CLARK'S TRIANGLE OF COORDINATION

Burton Clark's (1983) pioneering work on the "triangle of coordination" has become one of the most influential conceptualizations used in higher education to understand state-university relations and authority lines (Burke, 2005; Pusser, 2008). The key elements (or vertices) of the triangle are state authority, the market, and the academic oligarchy (see Figure 4.1). The model is a useful tool for analyzing shifts between these elements in a higher education system (McNay, 1999). It also provides a useful way of comparing national systems and inter-country variations of higher education governance (Braun & Merrien, 1999). For instance, coordination could be achieved through state-driven coordination, with Sweden as a good example of this, or through market-like mechanisms as is the case in the USA, or through the rule of the academic oligarchy which, at the time of Clark's writing, was typical of Italy and the United Kingdom (Braun & Merrien, 1999).

Clark initially conceptualized lines of authority moving along a continuum from state-controlled to market-controlled. The state and the market were perceived as having significant influence on higher education coordination and issues of how authority was exercised (Salazar & Leihy, 2013). Clark recognized that in some instances the state is weak and the market underdeveloped. Thus, he added the academic oligarchy dimension to the model in order to capture the structure of systems and lines of authority in situations where powerful academics exercise significant authority (Pusser, 2008).

Central to the market dimension of the model are notions of consumers and competition. Students are considered consumers and there is competition for tuition fees; institutions also compete for research grants, faculty, and staff and for donations from private foundations and benefactors. In countries like the UK and USA that are more aligned with this type of coordination, the government plays a facilitative role and creates conditions that foster the growth and development of the market. One current manifestation of the market influence in higher education is the increased number of publicly traded, degree-granting, for-profit universities (Breneman, Pusser, & Turner, 2006; Pusser, 2008).

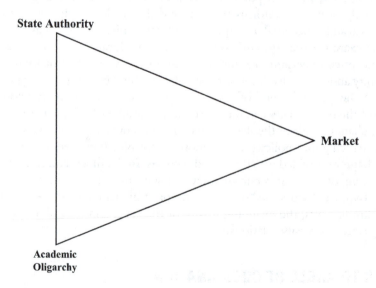

Figure 4.1 Clark's Triangle of Coordination

Another element of the triangle of coordination is the state, which is articulated as a broader and more nuanced concept than that of government (Pusser, 2008). According to Skocpol (1985, p. 7),

> the state must be considered as more than the "government." It is the continuous administrative, legal, bureaucratic and coercive systems that attempt not only to structure relationships between civil society and public authority in a polity but also to structure many crucial relationships within civil society as well.
>
> (quoted in Pusser, 2008, p. 110)

In Clark's conceptualization, the state is split into bureaucratic and political components (McNay, 1999). Hence, colleges and universities as institutions of the state are subject to political action and bureaucratic administrative influences (Ordorika, 2003). In highly bureaucratic environments, one can observe multiple formal levels of coordination, complex rule-based administrative structures, and administrative agencies with defined jurisdictional scope (Salazar & Leihy, 2013). The degree to which this occurs depends on how much the state is directly involved in the administration of university governance. In some countries the system is centralized and universities are homogeneous bodies with very limited autonomy (Reale & Poti, 2009). In other situations, the state plays a supervisory role and allows institutions the freedom to regulate themselves (van Vught, 1993).

Under the third dimension of Clark's model, the university is viewed as a state agency but at the same time it is an autonomous corporation governed by an academic oligarchy. Senior academics and professors are powerful individuals who occupy important positions in the governing bodies of the university. This academic oligarchy can also operate at the system level, with councils composed of academics assigned responsibility for decisions related to system finance, funding, and quality assurance.

The three dimensions of Clark's model encompass a space that is delimited by tensions among the state, the market, and academic leaders. It also captures shifting power and authority relationships among these three dimensions over time and in different nation-states. In some countries, one dimension may assume more prominence than the others at a point in time or in a specific context. Although this model continues to be used as a heuristic guide by scholars analyzing governing coordination within higher education systems, it must be acknowledged that the contextual reference point on which it was based has changed.

THE TRIPLE HELIX OF GOVERNMENT-UNIVERSITY-INDUSTRY RELATIONSHIP

The Triple Helix thesis advances the idea that the university can be a critical player in contributing to innovation in knowledge-based societies (Etzkowitz & Leydesdorff, 2000). It is built on the reflexive network linkage of universities-industry-government and places the universities at the center of technology advancement and knowledge transfer. This model expands the purpose of universities beyond teaching and research to include a third mission of economic development. In this case, the relationship between universities and industries in knowledge transfer extends beyond the traditional means of journal publications and the hiring of graduate students and includes negotiated agreements between the parties (Etzkowitz, 1999).

Etzkowitz and Leydesdorff (2000) suggested three categorizations of the Triple Helix model. In the first model, industry and academia are subsumed under the nation-state and the relations between them are directed by the state. They point out that strong versions of this model are found in the former Soviet Union and in Eastern Europe and the weaker versions in some Latin American countries, although in some countries previously influenced by communist ideology such as Poland and Romania, the level of state influence has diminished from the late 1990s onwards and the market model is now a more prominent practice. These changes were driven largely by the liberalization of higher education and the influence of transnational networking (Dobbins & Knill, 2009). Etzkowitz and Leydesdorff refer to countries with strong state-driven and centrally planned models as having an etatistic model of university-industry-government relations, and it is viewed as a failed developmental model (Figure 4.2). It is considered as too top-down, involving little or no provision for bottom-up initiatives, and as a result it has hampered innovation (Etzkowitz & Leydesdorff, 2000).

With the second Triple Helix policy model, each of the three elements of the model has highly circumscribed borders and defined relational linkages with the other elements. Etzkowitz and Leydesdorff termed this the laissez-faire model of university-

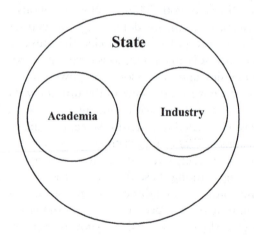

Figure 4.2 Model 1: Etatistic Model of University-Industry-Government Relations

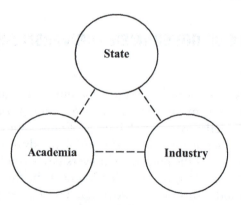

Figure 4.3 Model 2: Laissez-faire Model of University-Industry-Government Relations

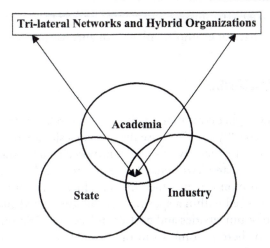

Figure 4.4 Model 3: The Triple Helix of University-Industry-Government Relations

industry-government relations (Figure 4.3). Sweden would be a typical example of this kind of arrangement.

The third category of the Triple Helix model has overlapping elements among academia, the state, and industry. Hybrid organizations are created as a result of this trilateral network (Figure 4.4). This model has gained popularity in most countries now with the USA as a leading example. Although this relationship is encouraged by government, and, as is in the case of the USA, fostered through legislation such as the Bayh-Dole Act, the government plays less of a controlling role. The state/government essentially seeks to foster an innovative environment in which universities spin-off firms and engage in trilateral innovations geared towards knowledge-based economic development. Again the state plays less of a direct controlling role in governing universities but at the same time creates conditions that would encourage the overall attainment of a national policy goal such as economic development. Hence, in places where this category of the Triple Helix is more prevalent, there is an expansion of or shift in missions and paradigms towards what Mok (2005) termed academic entrepreneurialism. Universities in this context have become more entrepreneurial by strengthening their relationship with the business and industrial sectors and other non-state actors (Mok).

Mok (2005) contends that in jurisdictions like Hong Kong, Singapore, and Taiwan the state has retreated from its previous direct controlling role to being a "market-facilitating state." He points out that the post-war state in East Asia played a direct and interventionist role in coordinating research and development, guiding entrepreneurial activities, and governing market processes of resource allocation. However, in more recent times the state has changed its role from that of a "market constructing state" to a "market facilitating state." Emerging in this process are technology parks where Triple Helix interactions occur and create the conditions to transfer technology and innovation into commercial activities. It is in this context that the Triple Helix government-university-industry/business network system functions in these countries. Although this represents a transformation in the mode of governance and it may appear as if the state is weakened in this process, Mok argues that the state not only plays a coordinating and facilitating role to drive entrepreneurial activities, but also may be playing an enhanced role in governing universities. This may be achieved through policy formulations that, for example, enhance quality assurance requirements.

SYSTEMS GOVERNANCE

While the sum of the higher education institutions and related structures in a jurisdiction is frequently called a "system," we use the term in a slightly narrower sense to refer to a set of interrelated parts that have a set of common characteristics, cohere towards a set of common objectives, and have some defined boundary. A higher education system broadly refers to a common way in which higher education institutions are organized, coordinated, and governed within a specific jurisdiction. Stated another way, a system refers to a collection of universities and postsecondary organizations within a specified jurisdiction in which there is some form of national, state, or provincial reporting, monitoring, and oversight, and institutions are guided by the rules and regulations of the jurisdiction. For example, the British higher education system was created by bringing together a collection of uncoordinated universities into a highly structured state-run higher education enterprise (Shattock, 1996).

It is also important to note that different jurisdictions have quite different traditions and policy arrangements defining the boundaries of what is called the higher education system. The British higher education system (primarily England and Wales) is dominated by universities, and operates in parallel with a relatively distinct further education sector that offers vocational and a wide range of adult education programming. The Canadian provinces use a much more inclusive definition of higher education, and these provincial systems include universities, community colleges, technical institutes, and other institutions. In other words, some countries define higher education as synonymous with postsecondary or tertiary education, while others have a much narrower, elite definition. One cannot assume that the term higher education is being used in the same way in different countries.

Generally, the underlying modus operandi for a system and its system-defining distinctive characteristics reside in state or governmental policy about the administration, funding, and societal conceptions of higher education. In some jurisdictions, national/federal legislation forms the basis of governance practices, in others, boards of governors are granted wide governing authority over the system, and in other countries financial instruments and other planning tools are used as the basis for governing institutions (McDaniel, 1996). Such distinctiveness arises also because within a system there are usually defined notions of the purposes of higher education and the manner in which universities achieve those purposes (Filippakou, Salter, & Tapper, 2012a). Thus, universities in a system operate within an institutional context that is related to a particular jurisdiction. This institutional context has embedded rules, regulations, ideologies, values, and practices that are system-defining and jurisdictionally located. In this sense, there is a sharing of common values and practices among higher education institutions within a jurisdiction, and the state's regulatory apparatus holds the interconnecting parts of these institutions together, thereby creating a system (Filippakou et al., 2012a).

A country could have a unitary higher education system where there is one set of structures and practices, or it could be divided into two groups with different institutional identities, structures, and practices to form a binary system. English higher education is a case in point in which there was a binary system prior to the 1992 Further and Higher Education Act (Filippakou, Salter, & Tapper, 2012b). The binary system in the UK consisted of two parallel systems of higher education with one part of the system governing the polytechnics and the other part catering to the older and more traditional universities. It was seen as a means of encouraging diversity among higher education institutions within the same jurisdiction. According to Taylor (2003), the binary system reflected differences in the profiles of the two groups of institutions. For example, differences in the balance between teaching and research and how institutions were funded created defining parameters between the groups in the system. But even more significantly, the binary system reinforced fundamental differences in approaches, philosophy, practices, and priorities between traditional universities and the polytechnics (Taylor, 2003). After 1992, the binary system was abolished and a unitary system was adopted in which diversity is pursued "based on institutional self-determination with a common overall framework" (Taylor, 2003, p. 266). From this example, it can be seen how within a single jurisdiction there could be different sets of rules, regulations, and practices, but they are all defined according to the country's notions of higher education and how it should be structured to achieve its purpose.

The important thing about a system is that it delineates common distinctive characteristics about the structure and practice of interconnected higher education institutions within a defined territorial boundary. The boundary could be the nation-state or a province, as is the case in some federal systems such as Canada or the United State. It could also be a region where multiple countries are signatories to a common agreement, such the European Higher Education Area, although this is not a system in the strictest sense of the word since the EU does not have jurisdiction over higher education. The bottom line is that a system is a macro way of organizing and governing higher education institutions.

State-University Relations

Making specific reference to the United States, Lane (2007) captures the state-university relationship in this way:

> the relationship between state governments and public institutions of higher education resembles an intricate and clumsy dance with both partners often trying to play the role of the lead dancer.
>
> (p. 615)

Such a depiction is equally applicable to several other countries. It highlights the constant struggle faced by universities that are funded from the public's purse and the delicate balance between state responsibilities and university autonomy. In addition to institutional autonomy, academic freedom and open and responsive governance arrangements are also important guiding principles of governance that have significant bearings on the state-university relations balance (Trakman, 2008; Sirat & Kaur, 2010). The relationship between the states and higher education institutions is further complicated by the role universities have played as instruments of state development and states' political legitimacy. Pusser (2008) reminds us that in the United States as well as in several other countries, many higher education institutions were established before the formation of the states themselves but became instrumental to their advancement and continue to be so.

An examination of state-university relations across different countries reveals variations in this balance. Sirat and Kaur (2010) suggest that the level of autonomy and control experienced by universities is a reflection of the maturity of a society and its higher education system. Sawyerr (1994) points out that the historical, political, and cultural landscape of a nation shapes the balance in state-university relationships. Hence, depending largely on how these societal factors impact the nation-state, state-university models of higher education governance at the national or "system" level show variations and could be viewed along a continuum.

At one extreme are those countries that allow universities to have significant autonomy, both procedural and substantive autonomy (Berdahl, 1999). At the other extreme are those countries that have a tightly controlled state-centric approach to governing universities. Along this continuum are various configurations of state-level control and institutional autonomy. For example, the traditional British model of governance such as is found at Oxford and Cambridge Universities allowed significant procedural and substantive autonomy from the state, although the Oxbridge model was not typical of all British universities. Nevertheless, the older British universities were granted significant autonomy from the state. Other countries have some blend of procedural and substantive autonomy that allows varying levels of partnerships and power-sharing between the state and universities. On the other hand, the former Soviet Union and the pre-1970s model of Chinese higher education were tightly state-centric and universities had very limited autonomy (Zha, 2009).

Variants between these two extremes of state-university governance also have existed in the continental model of Europe and in the USA. For example, in Germany prior to the 1990s, the state controlled universities were administered in a manner similar to a state agency but the academic arm of universities was controlled by the academic oligarchy. Governance in this context was a combination of state regulation and direct government interference but with a strong academic oligarchy (Orr & Jaeger, 2009). Similarly, Italy, prior to 1989, had a highly centralized higher education system in which the Minister of Education had very strong formal powers and universities adhered to strict governmental rules and regulations, while small circles of influential academics comprised of professors, deans, and rectors negotiated and made decisions for universities (Rebora & Turri, 2009).

Three important conceptual underpinnings are embedded in state-university relations: monitoring, control, and partnership. Lane (2007) and Lane and Kivisto (2008) apply the principal-agent theory to state-university relations to show how the state, as principal, funds its public universities (the agents) and monitors them to ensure that they are acting in the best interest of the state and the public at large. Monitoring is captured within the notion of governmental oversight which, according to Ogul (1976), may be differentiated into manifest and latent oversight mechanisms. Manifest oversight refers to formal monitoring mechanisms such as appropriations hearings, while latent oversight mechanisms are informal activities (Lane, 2007). Lane argues that governing mechanisms such as those that allow a government to appoint members to a university governing board are one of the direct means used by governments to have oversight. Individuals appointed by, and who have the confidence of, government will play a role in monitoring universities and/influencing decisions. In some instances, the state goes beyond monitoring institutional behavior and attempts to control universities by influencing or regulating what they do and how they do it (Sirat & Kaur, 2010). This would be typical of state-centric higher education environments in which limits on academic freedom and institutional autonomy are typically imposed.

Partnership is another conceptual approach to state-university relations. This approach, as espoused by Levy (1980), emphasizes reconciliation instead of control but also accepts universities' surrender of the notion of full autonomy and independence from the state to undertake their own activities. This partnership concept is rooted in the idea of mutual dependence and mutual acceptance. The idea, according to Levy, is that universities rely on the state for official legitimacy and the state depends on universities to fulfill its national developmental goals, and this dynamic creates mutual dependence and mutual acceptance.

Sirat and Kaur (2010) express concerns about the viability of the partnership approach, given the resource-dependent nature of higher education institutions and the state as a resource provider with powers over decision-making. It must be pointed out though that resource provision to higher education institutions is becoming more diverse and diffused through endowments, tuition fees, and research funding. The question would be how much self-governing power the state or government would be willing to surrender to its public universities, particularly in tight fiscal times.

THE PUBLIC POLICY PERSPECTIVE, THE STATE, AND HIGHER EDUCATION SYSTEMS

Higher education institutions have been described as "a curious mix of public and private entities" (Fowles, 2014, p. 272) and have been viewed historically as constituting a distinctive sector, particularly compared with other public entities. In other words, public higher education institutions are frequently seen as "creatures of the state" just as other public agencies are seen, with their legal structures and modes of governance enshrined in the state's legal framework. However, higher education institutions have had much greater autonomy than the typical public sector bureaucracy (Berdahl, 1999; Fowles, 2014; McLendon, 2003) and have even been referred to as a "standalone" sector (Ferlie, Musselin, & Andresani 2009). In this latter sense, they appear, and in many regards traditionally functioned, as private entities even though they are public or publicly funded institutions. This sectoralist view is in consonance with the traditional Mertonian ideology of academic and institutional autonomy of universities (Ferlie, Musselin, & Andresani, 2008). This perspective on higher education has traditionally guided how governments or states have related to universities versus how they have related to other public entities; how involved states are in directing higher education; and how much direct interference there is from governments. Much of what is observed among universities and their respective governments is the outcome of governmental policy-making and its associated economic-political ideology. Thus, the nature of the relational interaction is closely tied to the nexus between states' policy perspectives on higher education and the structural tradition of higher education in respective countries. For instance, the UK tradition and practice prior to 1992 was to permit extensive institutional autonomy through the University Grants

Committee (UGC) structure. This governance mechanism ensured the maintenance of the idea of a liberal university (Tapper, 2007). On the other hand, China adopted a state-centric policy-making approach, and as a result higher education institutions did not have the level of autonomy as experienced in the UK. An important point to grasp here is that governments rely on policy instruments as one way of governing systems of higher education. These policy instruments vary considerably in their application across jurisdictions (McDaniel, 1996).

Policy shifts that are arguably influenced by a neoliberal world view are now supplanting the traditionalist policy view of higher education in many systems, an issue that we will return to in chapter 9. As policy positions change, concomitant shifts are being observed in higher education, specifically in the type of governance arrangements. Ferlie et al. (2008) argue that state-university governance is understood better by examining public policy shifts and developments along with the policy regimes from which these policies originate. For example, Bleiklie (1998) notes that public involvement in higher education may be viewed from two different policy perspectives: (1) the cultural view, and (2) the utilitarian view. The cultural view emphasizes the teaching of science and scientific pursuits of knowledge as an emancipator for societies and as important in the transfer of cultural values. The utilitarian view advances the idea of universities contributing to the economic growth of societies, developing a trained workforce, and conducting applied research. Traditionally, the cultural argument was more dominant, but more recently a greater emphasis has been placed on the utilitarian argument in most countries (Bleiklie, 1998; Slaughter & Leslie, 1997). Much of the current policy promulgations have their origins in the utilitarian argument and have reshaped the way in which states relate to universities.

To illustrate the importance of the policy perspective and policy priorities to higher education governance, we draw on a 1999 study conducted in the USA by Richardson and his colleagues. Richardson, Reeves-Bracco, Callan, and Finney (1999) conducted a study of seven higher education state systems to ascertain the relation between states' policy priorities and the structural mechanisms used to achieve them. From this study, they derived a policy model with three levels: the policy environment, the system design, and work processes. The policy environment constitutes the first level. Here, the structure, history, and traditions of the state and its governmental processes are key elements. This policy environment is shaped by the approach adopted by the state to achieve its higher education policy priorities (Martinez, 2002). In this regard, states vary based on their different political and philosophical policy approaches, which reflect the type of policy environment in which higher education functions. For example, some states view themselves philosophically as providers of resources to higher education and view universities as purveyors of knowledge, research, teaching, and societal development. These states usually adopt a hands-off approach, are less definitive in their policy prescriptions, and give great deference to universities (Martinez, 2002). On the other hand, some states are more actively involved in steering higher education. These states are more concerned about policy outcomes and design structural mechanisms to achieve them.

The system design is the second level in the Richardson et al. (1999) framework. The system design that is adopted dictates the type of governance and institutional structure found in a particular jurisdiction. Segmented systems, unified systems, and federalist systems are designs commonly found within American states. Again, different states have adopted different systems, but they all operate within some larger policy context.

Segmented systems have multiple governing boards within the state; unified systems have a single governing board; and federal systems have multiple governing boards but also a state-wide board (Martinez, 2002).

The third level in the model is work processes. Work processes are concerned more with the day-to-day practices and activities associated with managing an institution. Policy-makers use tools such as state budgeting, program planning, and articulation arrangements to guide the administration of universities. Although the three elements of the Richardson et al. (1999) framework were presented as discrete, they pointed out that each level within the model is affected by the other levels. Hence, for a governing relationship to work well, the system design and the work processes should be compatible with their policy environment. This means that as the policy environment and priorities change, so too does the governance relationship, a phenomenon that has been observed in many countries over the last few decades.

Policy Change Reshaping State-University Governance

Structuring policy to effect change in behavior and practices in higher education, particularly in public universities, has occupied state policy-making agendas more and more in recent times. As this policy approach takes root, one common observation is a movement away from the traditional cultural and Mertonian view of higher education and the governance arrangements associated with it. Ferlie et al. (2008; 2009) advanced three reasons for higher education's divergence away from the traditional Mertonian concept:

1. The growth in the higher education subsector, largely as a result of mass higher education, has made it more expensive, politically more visible, and economically more strategic. Pertinent to this is the nexus between policy goals of economic growth and higher education as a critical driver. Countries have repositioned higher education institutions as vehicles of nation-building and nations' global competitiveness. There is now significantly less emphasis on the traditional ideal of the university as a liberal institution of enlightenment and an embodiment of the public interest (Schuetze, 2012; Wolf, 2002).
2. The public, politicians, and policy-makers are less trusting of publicly funded services such as higher education. Governments are therefore now more involved in trying to ensure that the public gets "value for money."
3. The market is now perceived as a more efficient mechanism for resource allocation and hence plays a more integral role in public sector administration and higher education governance. As a result, universities are expected to be more market-driven, to be more entrepreneurial, and to seek alternative streams of revenue.

The combination of these three factors is a driving force behind public policy changes that are reshaping and rebalancing state-university governance. While higher education continues to be a distinctive sector, recent trends suggest that public policy shifts are creating similarities between universities and other public sector organizations such as the healthcare sector (Paradeise, Reale, Goastellec, & Bleiklie, 2009). Although to varying levels across different countries, governments are developing policy prescriptions that are intended to "steer" higher education and universities in a manner that is closer to what obtains in other public sector entities. For example, in an examination of the higher education systems of seven European countries, Paradeise et al. argue that in all of these jurisdictions the state, although to varying degrees, increasingly sought to steer and govern higher education systems and that this policy approach was the result of the adoption of new public management—a shift in ideology about the public sector—as a way to manage public sector entities in order to achieve desired outcomes in the new policy environment. These changes in approach to state-university relations clearly are linked to a general reorganizing of the state and the way it interacts with the public sector, with higher education being one of the sectors. Additionally, across many jurisdictions and countries, these policy changes are in line with broader changes in the global higher education political economy (Pusser, 2008).

Thus, in the current environment, changes are occurring in places where the traditional Mertonian concepts of academic and institutional autonomy were fundamental values and the basis on which universities functioned, and the state is now a more active player in shaping higher education systems (Paradeise et al., 2009). Higher education is no longer as insulated as previously from governmental steering (Ferlie et al., 2008). In fact, Maassen, Moen, and Stensaker (2011) argue that in a number of European countries, the traditional state-university model was characterized by close informal linkages. However, since the mid-1980s, questions have been raised about maintaining these close relationships given the potential adverse impact that they could have on institutional efficiency and effectiveness. This has been a key driving force in the emergence of alternative models of state-university relations (Gornitzka, 1999; Maassen et al., 2011). Hence, the traditional "guardian angel" role towards universities practiced by these European states has virtually disappeared (Nybom, 2007).

In the UK, changes in governance practices between the state and universities have been in part driven by the state's shifting interpretation of higher education as a public good (Fulton, 2002), the economic role higher education plays in the nation-state's global competitiveness, and broader ideological views associated with new managerialism as a way of managing public services and state entities (Deem, 1998). More recently, China has reformed the higher education sector and its governance in order to advance its policy pursuit of being a global economic and competitive player in the knowledge economy (Zha, 2009). The structure of governance in China is now shaped by the policy shift from elite to mass higher education, which is directly related to the country's global economic competitive agenda (Gu, Li, & Wang, 2010). Not only have there been changes to state-university governance, but there have been changes to the internal governance structures and authority relationships in universities (de Boer & File, 2009). These internal changes are in many regards the result of broad macro policy developments that are impacting the microworld of higher education institutions. Higher education state-university governance must therefore be examined and understood within the context of changes in normative conceptions of public policies and the broader ideological frameworks within which policies are constructed and universities are embedded (Bleikie, 1999).

State Funding and Governance

First and foremost, an important factor to grasp in state-university governance is that the state provides universities with funding in exchange for the education of its citizenry, the advancement of knowledge, and the maintenance of society. This constitutes an exchange relationship (Emerson, 1962) between universities and their respective states. In most countries, this was traditionally based on the principle of mutual dependency. In such cases, universities were given significant autonomy over academic programming, research, and resource utilization. In other words, universities as resource dependent entities in the exchange relationship were given the right to control the resources appropriated to them by the state in the exchange. This practice accords with Pfeffer and Salancik's (2003) notion of constraint absorption.

According to the theory of constraint absorption, the resource-holding entity relinquishes power in an exchange relationship to the less powerful party by granting it the right to control the resource. This was typical of traditional practice of public higher education in many of the Anglo-Saxon countries. It was based on the notion of institutional reliance on the public purse while maintaining autonomy and insulation from governmental interference—what Paradeise (1998) calls "regulation by the community" (cf. Ferlie et al., 2008).

Having responsibility for funding higher education created a pathway for states to assume greater involvement in directing and regulating the sector. By linking policies to funding, governments have gained more control over higher education. This is indicative of shifting modes of governance driven by specific policy orientations. For instance, Shattock (2008) notes that in the UK, the government has asserted greater control of higher education by making changes to public policy and in so doing moving higher education from being privately governed to being publicly governed. Higher education systems of governance can therefore be viewed as an instrument of public policy (Olsen, 1988). This suggests that the type of state-university governance practiced depends significantly on the public policy pursued and operationalized through funding, budgetary, and legislative mechanisms.

Redefinition of the State and Public Sector Management

As state entities, public universities are impacted and shaped in part by the defining characteristics of the state itself and the manner in which the state defines and relates to public entities. The state, as it was traditionally conceptualized, has undergone a redefinition and transformation driven primarily by globalization and its associated neoliberal narrative. Mok (2009) argues that the pressures of globalization have weakened the nation-state and limited its role in the management of the public sector. The diminished capacity of the state is captured in conceptualizations such as "wither the state" (Waters, 2001), "hollowing-out of the state" (Cerny, 1996), "dissolving the nation-state" (McGrew, 1992), and "governance without government" (Rhodes, 1997). The neoliberal narrative is captured by Harvey (2005) in this way:

> Neoliberalism is in the first instance a theory of political-economic practice that proposes that human well-being can best be advanced by liberating entrepreneurial freedoms and skills within an institutional framework characterized by strong private property rights, free markets and free trade. The role of the state is to create and preserve an institutional framework appropriate to such practices.
>
> (p. 2; cf. Pusser, 2008, p. 111)

It is within this conceptualization that in some countries government funding to universities has decreased, privatization and competition have taken root as guiding principles, and the states' roles in public sector projects have shifted (Castells, 1996; Pusser, 2008). Vidovich and Currie (2011) report that in Australia there is evidence that under conservative political leadership (1996–2007) a neoliberal policy agenda dominated, and during this period university funding from the state was significantly reduced while student fees increased. Vidovich and Currie called it the "hidden privatization from within" (p. 46). This has had a profound impact on public policy approaches generally, and for public universities it has refashioned state-university relations.

It is argued that the changes to the governance of higher education are the result of this broader philosophical thinking about the role, legitimacy, and authority of the traditional state model. Ferlie at al. (2008) argues that the "hollowing out" of the nation-state and the emergence of network governance modes of public management are among the forces driving the redefinition of the state and impacting higher education. Multinational corporations, nongovernmental organizations, social movement organizations, and supranational institutions such as the EU are now actors in network governance processes (Ferlie et al.) and this has resulted in a decline in the influence of the nation-state. In Europe, intergovernmental initiatives like the Bologna process now play a role in the governance of member countries.

The main criticism raised about the traditional conceptualization of the nation-state is that the centralized command and control model is an inefficient and ineffective means of planning, controlling, and regulating societal institutions, such as higher education. Hence, the network model has superseded the traditional nation-state model as a result of more actors now being involved in the process. Higher education institutions are networked regionally, nationally, and internationally with an expanded compliment of stakeholder groups (Ferlie et al., 2008). Ferlie et al. argue that such expansion in actors and stakeholder groups leads to a diffused and pluralist power base.

The second force driving the redefinition of the state is what Ferlie et al. (2008) call the democratic revitalization of the traditional bureaucratic public sector. Democratizing and thereby increasing stakeholders' participation in decision-making in the public management process is viewed as a strategic response to a decline in trust of government (DeLeon, 2005; Ferlie et al., 2008). As public institutions, democratization has expanded to higher education. For instance, university board membership in many jurisdictions now includes more individuals from outside the university. There is also a much closer link between civil society and the universities in some systems, including an increased emphasis on applied and funded research (Gibbons et al., 1994). Hence, universities are influenced much more by their local external communities and organizations that fund research. Because there is much more involvement from civil society in universities' decision-making and strategic direction, the state's role has changed and the governing dynamic is more participative.

The third force driving the redefinition of the state is a stronger emphasis on the management of the public sector. This is a major shift from the bureaucratic administrative approach which was accompanied by a large public sector and a welfare state ideology in many countries. A greater emphasis is now placed on marketization, on the belief that the market is an efficient means of resource allocation. This became a worldwide trend more deeply entrenched in countries like the UK, the Netherlands, and Australia.

With the diminution of the state has come reductions in public sector budget allocations and funding cuts to higher education in many countries. Universities are now expected to reduce operating costs, develop alternative sources of private funding, be more entrepreneurial, and attend more closely to the job market and societal needs (Dill & Sporn, 1995). Filippakou et al. (2012a; 2012b) describe it as an evolving relationship between the state and the market that is shaping and reshaping higher education institutions. On one hand, universities have been granted more procedural autonomy (Berdahl, 1999) in order to satisfy governmental expectations, and executive leadership has been strengthened while collegiality and the power of deliberative bodies have been weakened (Braun & Merrien, 1999). On the other hand, the role of government and the nation-state in countries like China and Japan shifted from welfare provider to market builder, facilitator, and regulator (Mok, 2009). This is seen throughout the public sector in various countries and is reflected in policy prescriptions. State governing relies on ex post evaluations rather than ex ante controls, and the use of intermediary bodies such as those responsible for quality assurance (Bleiklie, 2000; Braun & Merrien, 1999).

Despite having a diminished role, the state in many jurisdictions still seeks to have control over higher education. Governments are developing policy prescriptions that are intended to "steer" higher education and universities in a manner that is closer to what obtains in other public sector entities. In the UK for example, the government has asserted greater control of higher education by making changes to public policy and in so doing moving higher education from being privately governed to being publicly governed (Shattock, 2008). Like the UK, many modern states are steering higher education institutions by relying on regulations, incentives, accountability mechanisms such as quality assurance requirements, and sanctions to force universities to comply with government policy (Marginson, 1999). This is to ensure that universities are in compliance with the state's policy priorities, for example, graduating the caliber of citizen needed for the nation-state's global competitiveness. Another case in point is Australia. Vidovich and Currie (2011) report that government funding of higher education in Australia declined to one of the lowest levels in the OECD, yet the government seeks to have greater regulatory control over the sector. In such cases, while the nation-state has been weakened in this globalized era and universities have generally experienced reductions in appropriations from the state, the nation-state still seeks to assert more control over the strategic direction of universities. Essentially, the state seeks to have greater power and control over "what" universities do while granting greater responsibility to universities over determining "how" they do it. In other words, the state has restricted substantive autonomy but allowed more procedural autonomy (Berdahl, 1999).

These occurrences have created a shift in the level of institutional autonomy and control traditionally associated with universities. Although Maassen, Moen and Stensaker (2011) point out that university autonomy differs depending on the national setting in which autonomy is understood, translated, and implemented, current ongoing changes to autonomy represent a shift in power and authority. Tandberg (2013) notes that in the USA, several states have tinkered with public college and university governance by restructuring governing bodies and adjusting their power and scope of authority over universities. This power dynamic usually manifests itself in the levels of autonomy universities are allowed.

TYPOLOGIES OF STATE-UNIVERSITY GOVERNANCE

Evaluative State

Neave (1988; 1998; 2012) uses the term "evaluative state" to capture the shifting power dynamics between universities and the state and as a mode of system control for higher education. Its origin dates back to the mid- to late 1980s and it was first observed in France, the Netherlands, and the UK (Neave, 2012) but has since spread to many other European countries. Not that the state did not have evaluation mechanisms in previous years, but the evaluative state conceptualization signals a change in the state orientation towards universities, particularly in continental Europe, that arose out of crises and shifting priorities in individual countries and the influence of events at the regional or European level (Neave, 2012). It describes the policy shift from the "welfare state" and its associated forms of higher education coordination to market and professional self-regulatory forms of coordination. It also speaks to government-imposed controls (Sporn, 1999) under circumstances in which universities are under-resourced but the state simultaneously seeks to increase accountability requirements for academics (Milliken & Colohan, 2004).

At the nation-state level, committees and agencies established to scrutinize closely the achievements and performance of higher education institutions rely on formal mechanisms of performance indicators to determine a university's adherence to national priorities and agreed standards (Neave, 2012). In addition, reliance is also placed on instruments such as quality assurance and institutional accreditation. The state grants more managerial freedom to universities but also imposes new responsibilities such as the attainment of national strategic priorities and the implementation of external accountability mechanisms (King, 2007; Neave, 1998)—the notion of steering remotely from a distance.

The evaluative state is therefore a mechanism through which the contract conditions between a state and its universities are changed. This has had implications for institutional autonomy. Neave (2012) suggests that the evaluative state served as segue to the "re-engineering" of institutional autonomy. Neave argues that with the rise of the evaluative state, autonomy was no longer a guaranteed privilege for universities but was exercised on a conditional contract basis. Implicit in this is that performance feedback mechanisms became part of higher education. Hence, the evaluative state has transformed the operational space of universities in countries where it has taken root, such as France. However, the evaluative state system of governance has been implemented in different ways. Importantly, Neave argues that the evaluative state becomes a more dominant mode when responsibility for the evaluation of institutional performance is removed from central ministries and given to specialized agencies of public purpose, such as accreditation and quality assurance agencies.

Regulatory State

More recently, King (2007) describes the "regulatory state" as a particular form of university-state relationship, and he views the USA and the UK as important examples of this kind of state orientation. States that are considered regulatory have increasingly placed more emphasis on independent regulatory agencies and have delegated responsibility to these agencies to oversee the countries' economic and social affairs on behalf of the government. These agencies are granted statutory rights and duties to execute their responsibilities and be accountable to a particular branch of government (King, 2006).

For instance, higher education quality assurance agencies constitute regulatory bodies used by the government to hold higher education institutions accountable.

King argues that the regulatory state has different configurations, functions differently in different countries, and has varying levels of support. For example, he points out that in continental European systems of higher education, the regulatory state has replaced the more intrusive and micro-administrative approach of previous years and has gained more acceptance in the academy. On the other hand, in Anglo-Saxon countries such as the United Kingdom, Australia, and New Zealand, the regulatory state has diminished the level of autonomy and self-rule previously experienced by higher education institutions in these countries and the government is now seen as more interventionist (King, 2006). King views the rise of the regulatory state as part of a broader focus on market mechanisms to govern state entities and represents "the deliberate increase in the use of the market as a public policy instrument, in order to reduce forms of direct state administration" (King, 2007, p. 413). There is an implicit duality of expectations with the regulatory state. In one way, it is ostensibly granting more authority and control to universities in those countries that were tightly state-centric but simultaneously subjecting them to market mechanisms of control. In another way, it is being more directive in countries that previously had more governing latitude while simultaneously promoting market mechanisms as a means of governance and control. A distinctive features about the evaluative and the regulatory state are that the evaluative state relies more on a posteriori or ex post governing mechanisms while the regulatory state relies more on ex ante mechanisms. Most countries have some combination of both but some emphasize one more than the other.

OTHER STEERING MODELS

Steering models refer to "the approaches governments used to control and influence specific public sectors. . . . [and] to the institutional context of policy processes" (Gornitzka & Maassen, 2000, p. 268). They reflect policy objectives and contexts. Gornitzka and Maassen contend that the state steering models are characteristic of a system-level institutional context within which policies are promulgated. These steering models mediate, constrain, and facilitate policy formation and the way in which higher education institutions respond. This is facilitated through a set of rules and regulations. Gornitzka and Maassen refer to these rules as interaction rules and context rules. Interaction rules structure interaction behaviors of policy actors. They determine, for example, the roles of different policymakers, the exchange of information, and who should be involved in policy decisions (Gornitzka & Maassen, 2000). Context rules, on the other hand, refer to the regulation of the context in which the interaction occurs. These rules address issues such as the extent of government involvement and how authority is organized. The way these rules are applied depends on the type of models adopted by the public sector or government.

Van Vught (1989) advanced the rational planning and control model and the self-regulation model as public sector regulatory models. The rational planning and control model relies on stringent rules and regulations imposed by the government to assert control over entities, and it places faith in the ability of government actors to obtain comprehensive and reliable knowledge to make decisions. This is typical of state-centric and highly bureaucratic countries. With the self-regulation model, the government plays a monitoring role and oversees the way in which autonomous players in a system use the "rules of the game." Government intervenes only when the rules are perceived as not achieving their intended purpose (Gornitzka & Maassen, 2000). These two models are in consonance with the state-control model and the state-supervising model found in higher education (Neave & van Vught, 1991). However this dual model approach has been challenged. It is argued that it limits the range of models needed to adequately conceptualize the policy context of state steering (Neave, 1998).

Olsen (1988) identifies four state steering models that allow a more sophisticated analysis of changes occurring in state-university relationships: the sovereign, rationality-bounded steering model; the institutional steering state model; the corporate-pluralist steering model; and the supermarket steering model. Gornitzka and Maassen (2000) argue that Olsen's models provide a richer analytical framework to understand and address issues such as the policy conditions under which governments grant more or less autonomy to universities. Hence, policy movements that shape state-university governance are captured better using these models since they are linked to the ways in which policy changes are unfurling (Olsen, 1988).

The Sovereign, Rationality-Bounded Steering Model

The sovereign, rationality-bounded steering model is associated with state-centric countries in which the state controls how higher education is administered and for what purpose. In these environments, heavy emphasis is placed on accountability to the political directorate (Gornitzka & Maassen, 2000). Higher education is seen by the government as an instrument for the attainment of its political and policy agendas. The political effectiveness of universities is closely scrutinized. Because the state is so heavily involved, decision-making processes are highly centralized, top-down, and follow a chain of command. Hence, interaction rules between the state and universities are based on a superior-subordinate model (Gornitzka & Maassen, 2000). In terms of context rules, the government is at the heart of deciding on the goals of universities.

Institutional Steering State Model

Under this model, academic freedom and the traditions of universities are protected from political interference. State university relationships have unwritten conventions and there is a shared understanding about the extent to which the state becomes involved. Gornitzka and Maassen (2000) point out that the relationship between the state and traditional elitist universities provides the best example of this kind of steering model. Thus, norms and traditions play important roles in the way in which university leaders derive their authority. University autonomy is protected, and this autonomy provides the professoriate with the freedom to independently engage in the transfer and pursuit of knowledge.

Corporate-Pluralist Steering Model

This approach to steering embraces the multiple stakeholder concept in which multiple voices are granted authority, including the government and its education ministry. This approach allows a more broad-based network of policy-making in which the interests of multiple stakeholders with a right to participate are represented. With this model, negotiation and consultation play a major role in the decision-making process.

Supermarket Steering Model

With the supermarket steering model, the market plays an important and central role and the universities adopt organizational forms similar to corporations. The system is highly decentralized and individual institutions set their own priorities and make their own decisions, with survival as a leading goal. Emphasis is placed on efficiency, effectiveness, and economy, and the state is assumed not to be good at achieving these outcomes. The state plays more of an oversight role in assisting universities so that they have the capacity for self-regulation. Gornitzka and Maassen (2000) note that while both the supermarket model and corporate-pluralist model have similarities in stakeholder involvement, a defining difference resides in the fact that with the corporate-pluralist model stakeholders are institutionally legitimized. Hence, their status is determined a priori. On the other hand, with the supermarket model, stakeholders participate by virtue of their financial ability.

SUMMARY

This chapter has focused on system governance and the relationship between universities and the state, and we have introduced a number of key concepts, models, and approaches that can be used to understand and analyze university-state governance. As we have noted, there is considerable variation in the role of the state within different countries, and these variations underscore at least some of the quite different ways in which higher education is governed. There are also important differences in the perceived role of higher education in relation to the society in which these institutions function. In terms of the higher education sector within public policy, there is a growing complexity of mechanisms and approaches used by governments to "govern" what is increasingly viewed as a key public sector within modern society. In the next chapter we will apply some of these ideas and concepts in our review of system-level governance arrangements in selected countries in order to illuminate some key themes and trends.

DISCUSSION QUESTIONS

1. What are some of the assumptions that might underscore a government's decision to treat higher education as a quite distinct sector within public policy? What are some of the assumptions that might underscore the view that higher education should be treated just like every other sector of public policy?
2. What is the relationship between institutional autonomy and academic freedom? Is the former a requirement in order to protect the latter, or are there other ways of protecting academic freedom within a higher education system?
3. Consider state-university governance in your country. Which two concepts introduced in this chapter seem to be most applicable or meaningful in terms of describing the governance arrangements in your system?

REFERENCES

Berdahl, R. (1999). Universities and governments in the 21st century: The US experience. In D. Braun & F-X. Merrien (Eds.), *Towards a new model of governance for universities? A comparative view* (pp. 59–77). London, England: Jessica Kingsley.

Bleiklie, I. (1998). Justifying the evaluative state. New public management ideals in higher education. *European Journal of Education, 33*(3), 299–316.

Bleiklie, I. (1999). The university, the state, and civil society. *Higher Education in Europe, 24*(4), 509–526.

Bleiklie, I. (2000). Policy regimes and policy making. In M. Kogan, M. Bauer, I. Bleiklie, & M. Henkel (Eds.), *Transforming higher education: A comparative study* (pp. 53–87). London, England: Jessica Kingsley.

Braun D., & Merrien, F-X. (Eds.). (1999). *Towards a model of governance for universities? A comparative view*. London, England: Jessica Kingsley.

Breneman, D. W., Pusser, B., & Turner, S. E. (2006). The contemporary provision of for-profit higher education: Mapping the competitive environment. In D. W. Breneman, B. Pusser, & S. E. Turner (Eds.), *Earnings from learning: The rise of for-profit universities*. Albany, NY: State University of New York Press.

Burke, J. C. (2005). The many faces of accountability. In J. C. Burke & Associates (Eds.), *Achieving accountability in higher education*. San Francisco, CA: Jossey-Bass.

Castells, M. (1996). *The rise of the network society: The information age: Economy, society and culture*. Cambridge, MA: Blackwell.

Cerny, P. G. (1996). Paradoxes of the competition state: The dynamic of political globalization. *Government and Opposition, 32*(2), 251–271.

Clark, B. R. (1983). *The higher education system: Academic organization in cross-national perspective*. Berkeley, CA: University of California Press.

De Boer, H., & File, J. (2009). *Higher education governance across Europe*, ESMU Project. Brussels, Belgium: European Centre for Strategic Management of Universities.

Deem, R. (1998). "New managerialism" and higher education: The management of performances and cultures in universities in the United Kingdom. *International Studies in Sociology of Education, 8*(1), 47–70. doi.10.1080/0962021980020014

DeLeon, L. (2005). Public management, democracy and politics. In E. Ferlie, L. Lynn, & C. Pollitt (Eds.), *The Oxford handbook of public management*. Oxford, England: Oxford University Press.

Dill, D., & Sporn, B. (1995). *Emerging patterns of social demand and university reform: Through a class darkly*. Oxford, England: Pergamon Press.

Dobbins, M., & Knill, C. (2009). Higher education policies in Central and Eastern Europe: Convergence towards a common model? *Governance: An International Journal of Policy, Administration, and Institutions, 22*(3), 397–430.

Emerson, R. M. (1962). Power-dependence relations. *American Sociological Review, 27*, 31–40.

Etzkowitz, H. (1999). Bridging the gap: The evolution of industry-university links in the United States. In L. Branscomb & F. Kodama (Eds.), *Industrializing knowledge: University-industry linkages in Japan and the United States*. Cambridge, MA: MIT Press.

Etzkowitz, H., & Leydesdorff, L. (2000). The dynamics of innovation: From national systems and "Mode 2" to a triple helix of university-industry-government relations. *Research Policy, 29*, 109–123.

Ferlie, E., Musselin, C., & Andresani, G. (2008). The steering of higher education systems: A public management perspective. *Higher Education, 56*, 325–348.

Ferlie, E., Musselin, C., & Andresani, G, (2009). The governance of higher education systems: A public management perspective. In C. Paradeise et al. (Eds.), *University governance: Western European comparative perspectives* (pp. 1–19). Dordrecht, The Netherlands: Springer.

Filippakou, O., Salter, B., & Tapper, T. (2012a). Higher education as a system: The English experience. *Higher Education Quarterly, 66*(1), 106–122.

Filippakou, O., Salter, B., & Tapper, T. (2012b). The changing structure of British higher education: How diverse is it? *Tertiary Education and Management, 18*(4), 321–333.

Fowles, J. (2014). Funding and focus: Resource dependence in public higher education. *Research in Higher Education, 55*(3), 272–287.

Fulton, O. (2002). Higher education governance in the UK: Change and continuity. In A. Amaral, G. A. Jones, & B. Karseth (Eds.), *Governing higher education: National perspectives on institutional governance* (pp. 187–211). Dordrecht, The Netherlands: Kluwer.

Gibbons, M., Limoges, C., Nowotny, H., Schwartzman, S., Scott, P., & Trow, M. (1994). *The new production of knowledge: The dynamics of science and research in contemporary societies*. Thousand Oaks, CA: Sage.

Gornitzka, A. (1999). Governmental policies and organisational change in higher education. *Higher Education, 38*, 5–31.

Gornitzka, Å., & Maassen, P. (2000). Hybrid steering approaches with respect to European higher education. *Higher Education Policy 13*(3), 267–285.

Gu, J., Li, X., & Wang, L. (2010). *Higher education in China*. Hangzhou, China: Zhejlang University Press.

Harvey, L. (2005). *A brief history of neoliberalism*. Oxford, England: Oxford University Press.

King, R. (2006). *Analysing the higher education regulatory state*. London, England: London School of Economics and Political Science.

King, R. P. (2007). Governance and accountability in the higher education regulatory state. *Higher Education, 53*, 411–430.

Lane, J., & Kivisto, J. (2008). Interests, information, and incentives in higher education: Principal-agent theory and its potential applications to the study of higher education governance. In J. C. Smart (Ed.), *Higher education: Handbook of theory and research* (Vol 23, pp. 141–174). Dordrecht, The Netherlands: Springer.

Lane, J. E. (2007). The spider web of oversight: An analysis of external oversight of higher education. *The Journal of Higher Education 78*(6), 615–644.

Levy, D.C. (1980). *University and government in Mexico: Autonomy in an authoritarian system*. New York, NY: Praeger.

Maassen, P., Moen, E., & Stensaker, B. (2011). Reforming higher education in the Netherlands and Norway: The role of the state and national modes of governance. *Policy Studies, 32*(5), 479–495.

Marginson, S. (1999). After globalization: Emerging politics of education. *Journal of Education Policy, 14*(1), 19–31.

Martinez, M. (2002). Understanding state higher education systems: Applying a new framework. *Journal of Higher Education, 73*(3), 349–372.

McDaniel, O. C. (1996). The paradigms of governance in higher education systems. *Higher Education Policy, 9*(2), 137–158.

McGrew, A. (1992). A global society? In S. Hall, D. Held, & A. McGrew (Eds.), *Modernity and its futures* (pp. 62–113). Cambridge, England: Polity.

McLendon, M. (2003). State governance reform of higher education: Patterns, trends, and theories of the public policy process. In J. C. Smart (Ed.), *Higher education: Handbook of theory and research* (Vol. 18, pp. 57–144). Boston, MA: Kluwer.

McNay, I. (1999). The changing cultures in UK higher education. In D. Braun & F-X. Merrien (Eds.), *Towards a new model of governance for universities? A comparative view* (pp. 34–58). London, England: Jessica Kingsley.

Milliken, J., & Colohan, G. (2004). Quality or control? Management in higher education. *Journal of Higher Education Policy and Management, 26*(3), 381–391. doi.10.1080/1360080042000290221

Mok, K. H. (2005). Fostering entrepreneurship: Changing role of government and higher education governance in Hong Kong. *Research Policy, 34(4)*, 537–554.

Mok, K. H. (2009). Globalisation and higher education restructuring in Hong Kong, Taiwan and mainland China. In M. Tight, K. H. Mok, J. Huisman, & C. Morphew (Eds.), *Routledge international handbook of higher education.* Abingdon, England: Routledge.

Neave, G. (1988). On the cultivation of quality, efficiency and enterprise: An overview of recent trends in higher education in Western Europe, 1986–1988. *European Journal of Education, 23,* 7–23.

Neave, G. (1998). The evaluative state reconsidered. *European Journal of Education, 33,* 265–284.

Neave, G. (2012). *The evaluative state, institutional autonomy and re-engineering higher education in Western Europe: The prince and his pleasure.* Hampshire, England: Palgrave Macmillan.

Neave, G., & van Vught, F. A. (1991). *Prometheus bound. The changing relationship between government and higher education in Western Europe.* Oxford, England: Pergamon.

Nybom, T. (2007). A rule-governed community of scholars: The Humboldt vision in the history of the European university. In P. Maassen & J. P. Olsen (Eds.), *University dynamics and European integration* (pp. 55–80). Dordrecht, The Netherlands: Springer.

Ogul, M. S. (1976). *Congress oversees the bureaucracy.* Pittsburgh, PA: University of Pittsburgh Press.

Olsen, J. P. (1988). Administrative reform and theories of organization. In C. Campbell & B. G. Peters (Eds.), *Organizing governance: Governing organizations* (pp. 233–254). Pittsburgh, PA: University of Pittsburgh Press.

Ordorika, I. (2003). *Power and politics in university governance: Organization and change at the Universidad Nacional Autonoma de Mexico.* New York, NY: RoutledgeFalmer.

Orr, D., & Jaeger, M. (2009). Governance in German higher education: Competition versus negotiation of performance. In J. Huisman (Ed.), *International perspectives on the governance of higher education: Alternative frameworks for coordination* (pp. 33–51). New York, NY: Routledge.

Paradeise, C. (1998). Pilotage institutionnel et argumentation: Le cas du département SHS au CNRS. In A. Borzeix, A. Bouvier, & P. Pharo (Eds.), *Sociologie et connaissance—Nouvelles approches cognitives.* Paris, France: CNRS Editions.

Paradeise, C., Reale, E., Goastellec, G., & Bleiklie, I. (2009). University steering between stories and history. In C. Paradeise et al. (Eds.), *University governance: Western European comparative perspectives* (pp. 227–290). Dordrecht, The Netherlands: Springer.

Pfeffer, J., & Salancik, G. R. (2003). *The external control of organizations: A resource dependence perspective.* Stanford, CA: Stanford University Press,

Pusser, B. (2008). The state, the market and the institutional estate: Revisiting contemporary authority relations in higher education. In J. C. Smart (Ed.), *Higher education: Handbook of theory and research* (pp. 105–139). Dordrecht, The Netherlands: Springer.

Reale, E., & Poti, B. (2009). Italy: Local policy legacy and moving to an "in between" configuration. In C. Paradeise et al. (Eds.), *University governance: Western European comparative perspectives* (pp. 77–102). Dordrecht, The Netherlands: Springer.

Rebora, G., & Turri, M. (2009). Governance in higher education: An analysis of the Italian experience. In J. Huisman (Ed.), *International perspectives on the governance of higher education: Alternative frameworks for coordination* (pp. 13–32). New York, NY: Routledge.

Rhodes, R. A. W. (1997). *Understanding governance: Policy networks, governance, reflexivity and accountability.* Maidenhead, England; Philadelphia, PA: Open University Press.

Richardson, R. C., Reeves-Bracco, K., Callan, P. M., & Finney, J. E. (1999). *Designing state higher education systems for a new century*. Phoenix, AZ: American Council on Education/and Oryx Press.

Salazar, J., & Leihy, P. (2013). Keeping up with coordination: From Clark's triangle to microcosmographia. *Studies in Higher Education, 38*(1), 53–70.

Sawyerr, A. (1994). Ghana: Relations between government and universities. In G. Neave & F. van Vught (Eds.), *Government and higher education relationships across three continents: The winds of change* (pp. 22–53). Oxford, England: Pergamon.

Schuetze, H. G. (2012). University governance reform: The drivers and the driven. In H. G. Schuetze, W. Bruneau, & G. Grosjean (Eds.), *University governance and reform: Policy, fads, and experience in international perspective* (pp. 1–9). New York, NY: Palgrave Macmillan.

Shattock, M. (1996). The creation of the British university system. In M. Shattock (Ed.), *The creation of a university system* (pp. 1-27). Cambridge, MA: Blackwell.

Shattock, M. (2008). The change from private to public governance of British higher education: Its consequences for higher education policy making 1980–2006. *Higher Education Quarterly, 62*(3), 181–203.

Sirat, M., & Kaur, S. (2010). Changing state-university relations: The experiences of Japan and lessons for Malaysia. *Comparative Education, 46*(2), 189–205.

Skocpol, T. (1985). Bringing the state back in: Strategies of analysis in current research. In P. B. Evans, D. Rueschemeyer, & T. Skocpol (Eds.), *Bringing the state back in*. Cambridge, England: Cambridge University Press.

Slaughter, S., & Leslie, L. L. (1997). *Academic capitalism*. Baltimore, MD: Johns Hopkins University Press.

Sporn, B. (1999). *Adaptive university structures: An analysis of adaptation to socio-economic environments of US and European universities*. London, England: Jessica Kingsley.

Tandberg, D. A. (2013). The conditioning role of state higher education governance structures. *Journal of Higher Education, 84*(4), 506–543.

Tapper, T. (2007). *The governance of British higher education: The struggle for policy control*. Dordrecht, The Netherlands: Springer.

Taylor, J. (2003). Institutional diversity in UK higher education: Policy and outcomes since the end of the binary divide. *Higher Education Quarterly, 57(3)*, 266–293.

Trakman, L. (2008). Modelling university governance. *Higher Education Quarterly, 62*(1–2), 63–83.

van Vught, F. (1989). *Governmental strategies and innovation in higher education*. (Higher Education Policy Series no. 7). London, England: Jessica Kingsley.

van Vught, F. (1993). *Patterns of governance in higher education*. Paris, France: UNESCO.

Vidovich, L., & Currie, J. (2011). Governance and trust in higher education. *Studies in Higher Education, 36*(1), 43–56.

Waters, M. (2001). *Globalization*. London, England: Routledge.

Wolf, A. (2002). *Does education matter: Myths about education and economic growth*. London, England: Penguin.

Zha, Q. (2009). Diversification or homogenization: How governments and markets have combined to (re)shape Chinese higher education in its recent massification process. *Higher Education, 58*, 41–58.

CHAPTER 5

State-University Governance in Selected Countries

This chapter examines external or system-level governance, drawing on examples from North America, Continental Europe, the UK, and Asia to understand the variations and transitions in structures and practices across systems. The chapter explores the governing state-university relationship in countries selected from these regions. A body of higher education scholarship exists which suggests that there has been a shift in the balance of authority relations in higher education systems, particularly between states and universities, and that the shift may be linked to other changes in the national and international political economy of higher education (Pusser, 2008). The systems chosen reflect variations in governing state-university relations that are rooted in different national histories, political orientations, and traditions but in the last three decades have shown a pattern of convergence, though the pace of change varies by country.

Although the US, UK, and Continental European governance models historically have been viewed as the three most prominent models, other countries have had different traditions and political orientations that are reflected in their governance. China, for example, was historically influenced by the planned economic and central control practices of the former Soviet Union, but more recently has adopted market-based approaches in its macropolicies. Differences in historical practices of governance exist even among the UK and Continental systems. UK universities have traditionally been more self-directed, with minimal influence or interference from the state, but have in more recent times experienced increased government intervention and regulation (Shattock, 2008).

In Europe, the state traditionally played a more influential and regulatory role, and in many jurisdictions faculty were considered public (civil) servants. However, over the last two decades or so there have been tremendous pressures on higher education systems to change. The drivers of change have primarily been the enormous increase in costs to finance an expanding higher education sector and the increasing ideological acceptance of the principles of new public management (Capano & Regini, 2014). Emerging in these countries and regions are expansions in enrollment with the attendant focus on the 3Es (efficiency, effectiveness, and economy), more institutional autonomy being granted by the state, and a closer alignment of the institutional/

academic estate to practices of the commercial market. In addition, Capano and Regini suggest that there is evidence of policy convergence among European countries and it is reflected in the EU pressures toward the modernization of European universities' institutional governance. This policy convergence, they posit, originated from the Lisbon Agenda, which was launched in 2000. Hence, there is a legitimized shared template of higher education governance among European countries.

State-university governance also intersects with the concept of institutional diversity (van Vught, 2008). In some systems the emergence of quite different institutional types and categories has long historical roots. This systemic and institutional diversity, to use Birnbaum's (1983) terminology, is often associated with explicit differences in institutional mission, regulation, and, in some cases, system-level governance arrangements. Different institutional types are assigned different roles within the higher education system and may be governed differently. As you will note in our brief review of different systems, universities are sometimes component parts of systems that also include other institutional types (such as in France and the United States), and sometimes there are different types of universities with different system governance arrangements within the same country (as in China, for example). While we will not provide a detailed discussion of systemic and institutional diversity in this volume, it is important to recognize that institutional diversity adds another layer of complexity to system-level governance and public policy for higher education (Codling & Meek, 2006).

In this chapter, we discuss six different systems, their historical origins, and current practices. Among the European countries, we examine the United Kingdom, France, and Germany, since they typify different ways in which higher education is organized in Europe. And although countries are at different stages and speeds of development and it is difficult to generalize, there are patterns and trends in higher education and in the way governance is being organized in East Asian countries (Mok, 2007). Thus, from among the East Asian countries, we discuss Japan and China. Along with these systems, we examine the United States largely because of its size, complexity, and perceived success. Examining the histories and traditions of higher education systems in these countries allows comparisons between the past and the present and it also allows contemporary higher education governance, specifically state-university relations, to be contextualized.

GOVERNANCE IN THE UK

History and Tradition

UK higher education has undergone significant transformation in the last three decades, although the changes have not been uniform across all categories of HEIs. Major differences in the type and extent of theses change exist between the traditional universities such as Oxford and Cambridge, the "redbrick" civic universities that were founded in the late 19th and early 20th centuries, and the "new universities" that emerged following the 1992 reforms. The primary thrust of the changes in the UK suggests an attempt by the British government to use policy instruments to secure greater control over higher education and relate to universities as they would with any other public sector entity (Shattock, 2006). Central to this policy approach is greater accountability for universities and less autonomous self-governance.

UK universities have traditionally been funded by government, and thus there has always been some level of accountability by HEIs to the state. Yet over the years, these institutions maintained significant independence and strategic and operational autonomy from the state. This is unlike other public sector entities such as schools and hospitals, largely because higher education institutions are not constitutionally part of the "public sector" (Deem, Hillyard, & Reed, 2007). This practice was reflective of a private self-governing model which may be viewed as an example of British exceptionalism among European countries (Shattock, 2008). In other words, unlike most European countries in which the state machinery played an integral and direct role in the governance of HEIs, British higher education was the exception because of its independence from the state. Shattock (2008) argues that since World War II, and more specifically, since the arrival of the Thatcher conservative government in 1979, British higher education has shifted from a privately governed to an explicitly publicly governed model in which the state plays a central role in the governance process. With such state encroachment, the governance of British universities began to look more like other European countries. Taylor (2013) points out that during the postwar period until the advent of Thatcherism, both de jure and de facto academic power were vested in the university senate. The commonly accepted view was that supremacy in the university resided in its academic body and that there was no other entity or governing body as qualified as the senate to regulate the work and affairs of scholars (Moodie & Eustace, 1974). Taylor argues that the assumed supremacy of the senate was the result of the accommodating relationship that existed between universities and the UK University Grants Committee. However, Thatcherism brought about major changes in this relationship and a shift in the locus of power (Taylor, 2013), effectively breaking from tradition. To get a good picture of how this change occurred, we must examine two important things: (1) how the roles and functions of the University Grants Committee (UGC) in the UK changed; and (2) the introduction of New Public Management (NPM) as a public sector management tool and policy instrument.

The Universities Grants Committee (UGC): Policy Changes

The Universities Grants Committee emerged following World War I. It was an agency of the state and the central instrument through which UK universities were funded for both recurrent expenditure and capital purposes. Its composition was primarily academics along with a minority lay membership drawn from secondary schools and industry (Fulton, 2002). The academics were viewed as more in touch with the realities of the academy, its interests, and management than lay-dominated governing bodies (Fulton, 2002; Kogan & Hanney, 2000; Taylor, 2013). A fundamental difference between the prewar and post-WWII period was the high level of state funding universities received in the postwar period (Taylor, 2013) because of post-WWII reconstruction. Higher education in Britain was viewed as a social good to be underwritten by the state (Filippakou, Salter, & Tapper, 2012) and consequently less emphasis was placed on fund-raising by lay governing bodies (Taylor, 2013). This certainly had implications for strengthening the power base of the senate, given the level of autonomy granted to universities.

Although the UGC was an agency of the state and its membership appointed by the government, it served as a buffer between the universities and the state (Shattock, 1994). Its central remit was (1) to interpret and implement broad government policy related to issues such as the size of the higher education system or the allocation of student enrollment between different categories—science versus non-science for example; and (2) to analyze and assess the cost and feasibility of universities' plans in the context of government policy (Fulton, 2002).

Prior to the 1980s, the UGC's function was largely oversight with deference given to university autonomy (Fulton, 2002; Shattock, 2013). It basically relied on goodwill and trust relationships with the universities and simply provided the government with estimates of university costs to be funded (Fulton, 2002). Fulton argues that the financial challenges of the British government following the oil crisis of the 1970s rendered this funding approach unsustainable. As a result, in the early 1980s the UGC became more purposeful as a planning body (Shattock, 2013) using more direct resource allocations and firmly capped budgets (Fulton, 2002). This represented an early phase in the evolution of the UGC and shifting governance practices in British higher education.

The UGC suffered its first major blow in 1981 when, in response to the government's requests for financial cutbacks to universities, it implemented resource cuts using an unpopular approach that infuriated the government (Kogan & Hanney, 2000). Fulton (2002) argues that this strengthened the Thatcherite argument about the model of planning and funding in the academy, which they viewed as "producer-dominated." In the midst of this were other financial episodes in British higher education that prompted concerns about universities' autonomy; for example, an ineffectual governing body at Cardiff University resulting almost in its bankruptcy (Shattock, 1994). But significantly, the neoliberal philosophy had begun to permeate the UK policy agenda and was taking root in state-university governance mechanisms.

The result was the Reform Act of 1988. Two of the key policy outcomes with governing implications to emerge from this were: (1) the financial autonomy of universities was reduced and, instead, governing boards were responsible for the financial credibility and viability of the university; and (2) the UGC was replaced by a Universities Funding Council (UFC) with increased lay membership. Here we see the shift towards expanding stakeholder involvement in governing higher education. Establishing the UFC allowed greater direct ministerial policy direction by the Secretary of State for Education in England, the Welsh Assembly in Wales, and the Scottish Executive in Scotland (Shattock, 2013). The UFC was subsequently replaced in 1992 by the Higher Education Funding Councils for England, Wales, and Scotland. What is evident in the UK's case is that the state implemented changes to the funding mechanisms as one way to enact the policy changes that were foremost on their policy agendas.

The aggregate of these changes was ostensibly to provide the universities with more freedom and autonomy to conduct their own affairs; in other words, liberating them from what was viewed as an unwieldy and outmoded planning system (Fulton, 2002). However, Fulton argues that the new structure of governance provided nominally increased autonomy to universities because governing bodies were now held fully accountable to the Funding Councils and had to demonstrate that they were undertaking sound financial management practices. Through this structure of governance, the political directorate assumed greater control of higher education policy and planning and universities were subjected to more public governance and more firmly absorbed into the machinery of the state (Shattock, 2013). This in essence represented a power shift within British higher education governance.

New Public Management (NPM) and UK Universities

New public management is about new administrative ways in which to organize and regulate public services (Deem & Brehony, 2005), and hence, it entails regulatory governance mechanisms of public services and public entities by state agencies (Hood & Scott, 1996). NPM therefore is more concerned with the technical and administrative management of public sector services and agencies. And it seeks to limit bureaucratic practices in public service organizations and advocates for quasimarket approaches to managing the sector (Deem & Brehony, 2005). A cognate to NPM is new managerialism (Deem et al., 2007). Deem and Brehony (2005) argue that new managerialism is an ideological configuration of ideas and practices related to the management and delivery of public services. It essentially legitimates the right to manage in an environment such as the public sector where discretion among professionals was traditionally the way in which the sector functioned.

The practices and activities of NPM and the ideology of new managerialism have been drivers of a new approach to governing public sector services and entities, including universities. These practices have firmly taken root in the UK. NPM practices and ideology were advocated by Margaret Thatcher, who was an ardent proponent of reforming the public sector and implementing neoliberal and pro-market practices. These ideas also became part of the modus operandi of the university sector. Universities adopted market or quasimarket principles as an approach to optimize resource allocation and usage, ostensibly to strengthen public accountability mechanisms, and to foster more corporate-like governance and management practices (Deem et al., 2007). This created a new way of governing in the academy. Under the NPM approach, universities were now included among public sector entities and subjected to a similar approach to governance and management. In the process, power shifted to the university governing boards. The shift in power reflected a new philosophical position on governance in which more corporate-like and private sector governance practices and approaches were preferred. Importantly, the state drove these changes in order to promote efficiency, effectiveness, and economy (3Es) and market competition in the academy, which are central to the neoliberal agenda and the output-driven economic rationalism model.

The corporate governance philosophy has also been accompanied and reinforced by the introduction of more recent policy changes related to substantial tuition fees (except for Scotland where universities do not charge fees to Scottish students) and changing government funding arrangements. Increases in tuition fees to UK and EU students have come at a time when there is a drive to expand higher education access and widen participation rates in the UK. In fact, this has been supported by the appointment of a regulator to monitor access and widening participation arrangements (Middlehurst, 2004). This would therefore suggest that while the state is pursuing the development policy agenda that is supported by increased access and participation rates, the burden of funding has been shifted to the individual. NPM is thus a critical factor undergirding the transformation of governance.

GOVERNANCE IN FRANCE

History and Traditions

The system of higher education and research in France has been described as unique and characterized as French exceptionalism. According to Neave (2012), "exceptionalism reaches deep into the organization, structure and status of French higher education" (p. 64). Its uniqueness and exceptionality reside in the manner in which higher education was originally structured and how these structures and practices evolved over the decades.

The French model of higher education governance is characterized by a history of direct government involvement in and control of universities, government's direct relationships with the academic profession, and a discipline-based approach to decision-making (Musselin & Paradeise, 2009). However, the sector has undergone significant changes in the last three decades. Before we discuss these changes and the current design of French higher education, it is important that we first examine its history and traditions in order to place contemporary French higher education and the changes that have occurred in context.

Higher education in France, and by extension its governance, has different characteristics and traditions than the rest of Western Europe. First, France did not adopt the Humboldtian model of the German research university, but it also did not adopt the teaching and research overlap typical of modern research universities (Merrien & Musselin, 1999). Unlike Germany, teaching and research were segmented. Segmentation became even stronger during the post-World War II period because the state viewed research as a full-time endeavor that would provide a wealth of power to the nation, and that research needed to be separated from university activities to achieve this (Merrien & Musselin, 1999). Merrien and Musselin argue that this approach promoted a hierarchy of knowledge and power in which fundamental research was at the top of the pecking order.

The second distinctive element was that the French system was built around a tripartite institutional stratification—*Grandes Écoles*, university institutes of technology, and universities. Universities were viewed as serving the French middle class and the masses and had a legal obligation to admit all holders of an upper secondary school-leaving certificate (Neave, 2012). The *Grandes Écoles* were considered highly selective institutions that educated French elites and constituted the elite sector of the French higher education system. Neave describes the *Grandes Écoles* as having an a priori system of selection in which they had the mechanism to wholly control the quality of student flow. On the other hand, universities had an a posteriori mode of selection because of legal obligations to admit all students holding the *Baccalauréat*. Similar in selectiveness to the *Grandes Écoles* were the university institutes of technology. These two collectively have been described as a "closed" subsector of French higher education whilst universities constituted the "open" subsector of the system (Neave, 2012). What is therefore evident in France are systems design notions of segmentation and differentiation which were, and arguably still are, two of the defining characteristics of this system.

The third aspect of French higher education that is rooted in its history and traditions is the policy context within which the system operated. Up until the late 1970s,

France was a centralized state with significant direct government control, but a policy agenda of decentralization was launched in 1981 (Thoenig, 2005). Thus, French universities as public entities were historically governed in a highly centralized educational system. Issues such as staff recruitment, content of programs, and budgets fell under the purview of the central government (Kaiser, 2007). In fact, until 2007 the government, through the ministry in charge of higher education, was deeply involved in the financial administration of universities, including the management of salaries (Musselin & Paradeise, 2009). As a result, French universities were not autonomous institutions although this has changed somewhat in the last two decades as a result of decentralization. This was very different from the UK higher education system, in which universities had a significant degree of individual autonomy. One thing that must be noted here is that although higher education functioned in a centralized environment under a central government, there were and still are a number of ministries with responsibilities for different aspects of higher education, and thus the central government did not represent a monolithic entity (Kaiser, 2007). For instance, the *Grandes Écoles* are linked directly to the ministry responsible for the sector for which their graduates are being trained (Neave, 2012). Hence, sectors like defense and agriculture have governing authority over aligned *Grandes Écoles,* but universities fall under the general authority of the higher education ministry (Neave, 2012).

The fourth consideration relates to the role of the academic profession as a key player in state-university relationships. The French higher education system had a unique state-university-discipline-based model in which academic professionals co-managed higher education with the government. Musselin and Paradeise (2009) argue that this constituted a crucial element of French higher education governance and one that differentiated it from other systems. Merrien and Musselin (1999) describe this discipline-based approach as reflective more of an oligarchy than a bureaucracy when viewed through the lens of Clark's (1983) typology. Under this type of governance, faculties and chairs were independent actors in a system built on faculty supremacy, and universities (as entities) were of lesser significance in the state-university relationship. Thus, rather than universities serving as power entities managing or administering higher education teaching and research, they were seen as locations for assembling academics who were the direct powerbrokers with the state. Decision-making between the ministry and academics in faculties was through the dean, and universities functioned as weak administrative bodies in which faculties were housed (Musselin & Paradeise, 2009). Essentially, the French academic profession drove developments in the system, and these developments and decision-making were discipline-oriented while the universities' administrative bodies within the institution were weak and almost irrelevant.

When the aforementioned elements of French higher education are considered together, the uniqueness of the system becomes quite apparent. These differences were even more pronounced about 50 years ago when the structure, characteristics, and practices of French higher education were so different from the UK and Germany that, according to Merrien and Musselin (1999), it was difficult to speak of universities in France in the traditional sense. Capano and Rigini (2014) describe pre-1970 French universities as a confederation of faculties. Musselin and Paradeise (2009) attribute this kind of weak institutional development of governance to the suppression of universities during the French Revolution and the subsequent development under Napoleon of the "Imperial University" with a faculty-based structure. However, the system has undergone some changes, driven in part by pragmatism. In particular, during the 1980s there was a strengthening of the institutional autonomy of French universities (Capano & Regini, 2014). In the next section we will examine these changes and the implications they have for governing French higher education.

French Reforms: Moving from Centralized to Decentralized Governance

Significant changes have occurred in the French higher education system, especially in the last four decades. Musselin and Mignot-Gerard (2002) describe the changes as "a transformation of rather anomic universities into institutions with their own identity, perspectives, and dynamics" (p. 64). Many of these changes were facilitated by a series of legal enactments. The Faure Act of 1968, for instance, was a starting point for the institutional advancement of universities, followed by the 1984 Savary Act and its 1989 update. One underlying development that was at the heart of these legal developments was the move towards mass higher education participation rates, although much of this expansion and attendant changes occurred in universities and not *Grandes Écoles*.

These reforms can be discussed in terms of three major changes. First, there was the development of universities as autonomous institutions driven largely by the implementation of contracts between universities and government. Second, the sharp distinction between organizations conducting research and universities started to blur. Third, decentralization took root in the French education system, and as a result some powers and responsibilities traditionally held by state departments were devolved to territorial authorities (Kaiser, 2007), thereby creating a new system of partnership between the state and the regions (Neave, 2012).

The introduction of the contract model was a major change in French higher education. In 1988, the financing and budgeting policies for universities shifted from fixed-term criteria to a framework of four-year contracts negotiated between each university and the ministry. Using this new model, universities developed four-year strategic plans and then negotiated annual budgets based on needs and objectives identified in the plan. The central administration used the contract model policy to reform higher education through the use of broad principles that created guidelines for universities rather than specific rules (Merrien & Musselin, 1999).

The contract policy effectively meant that the ministry had established a direct relationship with higher education institutions as opposed to the prior discipline-based approach that was driven by strong faculties and powerful deans (Musselin & Paradeise, 2009). The transition to contracts meant that universities needed to develop the capacity to develop multiyear strategic plans; they needed to be able to bring faculties together and make decisions on the future direction of the institution as a whole. The role and authority of university presidents increased. Rather than just acting as internal mediators and representing the university, presidents became managers of universities, playing a very influential role in decision-making and strategic direction, particularly with major decisions. French universities became managed enterprises with a collegial, democratic governance arrangement.

Evident in these changes is the rise of the evaluative state. It is, however, argued that the French construction of the evaluative state is quite different in motivation from the neoliberal ideology driving its advance in places like the UK and USA (Neave,

2012). Neave points out that the neoliberal notion of the market as an alternative to the state and the advocating of competition and privatization as instruments for reshaping the relationship between the government, society, and higher education are not driving forces in French higher education governance changes. In fact, French higher education governance is underpinned by a republican polity that upholds meritocracy, liberty, and equality but eschews neoliberalism (Neave, 2012; Musselin & Paradeise, 2009). The Savary Act of 1984, which was an essential element in the transformation of French higher education, was therefore not just a legal framework for advancing the evaluative state but also had the long-term effect of ensuring a clear promulgation of French values and beliefs that underlie what is meant by French public service, retention of the academics' status as public servants, and maintenance of the role of universities as a public service (Neave, 2012). Therefore, although we see the restructuring of governance that may appear to be similar to what is happening in other countries where neoliberalism has been embraced, the French changes are driven by a different reality, history, and tradition.

In conclusion, the French higher education system has been reformed over the last four decades. It has moved from highly centralized and government-controlled to a more decentralized and autonomous enterprise. Universities are more self-governed and are no longer viewed as weak entities. They now have the opportunity to develop their strategic priorities and articulate their institutional identity, and this has created diversity in the system (Musselin & Mignot-Gerard, 2002). Musselin and Mignot-Gerard (2002) point out that this does not negate the very important role the ministry still plays, but the ministry is no longer central to the changes occurring in universities, and it is no longer the principal agent for determining system policies. While these changes in the French higher education system suggest a movement towards a more managed enterprise, they have not been driven by the ideological shifts associated with new public management or new managerialism found in some other countries. Instead, they represent pragmatic attempts to improve the efficiency and effectiveness of the French higher education system while at the same time maintaining basic French values and societal beliefs.

HIGHER EDUCATION GOVERNANCE IN GERMANY

History and Traditions

German higher education comes from a tradition of state centeredness. This centrist character has its roots in the importance ascribed to the state and the type of state-sponsored system of welfare that was developed in the 19th century and supported within Germany's constitution (Pritchard, 2006). Coupled with the centrist model, its system of higher education was circumscribed by Humboldtian ideals about the importance of research, freedom in research and teaching, and the notion of research as germane to teaching (Enders, 2001). This highly influential Humboldtian university model, essentially the creation of the modern research university, was implemented by a Prussian authoritarian state in which universities were granted significant autonomy with the proviso of their subordination to the state (Schimank, Kehm, & Enders, 1999). Through this arrangement, the state financed universities, as a matter of duty, asserted significant control over academics and simultaneously allowed them their freedom to teach and research.

Schimank et al. (1999) see within such a structure a duality in which, on the one hand universities are institutions of public law, and on the other hand they are autonomous corporations. Clark (1983) describes this system of higher education as having a combination of state-political-regulatory forces and a strong professional self-regulated academic oligarchy. In other words, the German higher education system was a combination of strong state regulation and strong academic self-governance (de Boer, Enders, & Schimank, 2007). The power to self-govern resided in a confederation of chair-holders within institutions (Capano & Regini, 2014; Schimank, 2005). Full professors were the cornerstone of the oligarchs. Under this system of governance, individual full professors received funding from the state to be allocated within their institute as a condition for their professorial appointment—the notion of organizing an institute around a professor (Enders, 2001). This system of governance not only allowed professors to enjoy high levels of institutional power, prestige, and autonomy as civil servants with tenure but also was a pathway for the state bureaucracy to have control over staffing and resources (Enders, 2001). Thus, the structure of higher education governance in Germany was in some regards directly connected to the employment relationship between the professor and the state and in this respect is similar to the French model.

In the pre-WWII period, the structure and values of German university system governance were shaped by the Humboldtian tradition which was advanced close to the beginning of the 19th century. A central aspect of this tradition was the unity or the inseparability of teaching and research, along with the freedom of academics and students to freely engage in the common pursuit of knowledge (Karran, 2009). This model recognized the importance of academic freedom to the advancement of science and knowledge. This was coupled with a political system of direct involvement and control and a system in which universities were embedded in the nation-state but simultaneously given freedom to engage in autonomous research and teaching—the notion of a university as a cultural institution. There was, therefore, detailed procedural steering by the state coupled with a high degree of substantive autonomy granted to the faculty (Stucke, 1999).

The Federal Republic of Germany was established as one of the two German nations emerging from the Second World War. The federalism of Germany meant that states were authorized to enact their own laws independent of the federal government of West Germany, and consequently there was no national legislative harmonization including laws governing higher education. However, in 1976 the federal government passed the Federal Framework Act as a unifying legislation that was needed to create some measure of harmonization across the federal states (Länder). Prior to the passage of this law, individual states were granted the right and duty to structure higher education within their jurisdiction without interference from the federal government, and this was guaranteed by the constitution (Stucke, 1999). Thus, state-university relations were structured at the state and not the federal level, except for a few basic federal laws that were the basis of the "framework law on universities." Moreover, the Länder are responsible for their universities, especially for their basic funding.

Under the current governing arrangements, the states still have the authority to enact their own higher education laws, but it is now undertaken within the parameters of the Federal Framework Act (Pritchard, 2006). Stucke (1999) notes that although the German system functions on the basis of cooperative federalism and there is joint state/

federal policymaking, federal states still have the legal authority, using the experimentation clauses within the provision, to "experiment" with policy pertaining to higher education institutions within their jurisdiction. Stucke suggests that reforms that grant greater organizational independence and more managerial authority to universities have been implemented at the state level using this provision.

Since the passage of the Framework Act of 1976, there have been modifications and amendments to the Act that were intended to reform Germany's higher education system; most notable is the Fourth Amendment. Some of these amendments were intended to allow states to reframe their higher education governance in order to align the system more closely to local, national, and international demands. Thus, changes in German higher education may be linked in part to increased enrollment, which was on an upward trajectory from the 1960s onwards, and to a desire to make German universities internationally competitive. In the next section we will examine the changes to Germany's higher education that have been occurring in the last three decades.

Reforming the German Higher Education System

Since the mid-1970s, student enrollment in German universities has increased significantly, and in some regards this is driving the reform of the system. The ensuing period, particularly between the 1990s and 2006, saw a number of constitutional amendments that have refashioned German higher education by granting significant control to the Länder governments (Capano & Regini, 2014). This, according to Capano and Regini, has led to the German university system having 16 independent, subnational systems with universities being guided by Länder legislation. For instance, an outcome of the Fourth Amendment was the Federal Framework Act. The Act was intended to introduce market principles to German higher education and enhance universities' international competitiveness by using the tools of deregulation and performance-oriented funding (Pritchard, 2006). The Fifth Amendment addressed governance structures at the mesolevel. One of the changes was the introduction of the junior professorship and another was the abolition of the postdoctoral thesis requirement as a prerequisite to becoming a professorial chair. There were also Sixth and Seventh Amendments. The Sixth Amendment introduced elements of the Anglo-American model and the Seventh Amendment granted universities more freedom over student enrollment (Pritchard, 2006).

Orr and Jaeger (2009) adopted three of Guy Peter's four models of governance to capture the reforms taking place in Germany: namely, deregulated governance, market governance, and participative governance. *Deregulated governance* characterizes reduced regulations and the detailed level of HEI steering by the state. In this regard, Orr and Jaeger highlight the introduction of university boards of governors and also the shifting of administrative authority, previously the purview of the ministry, to universities, including the recruitment of professors and staff payment, and also a shift from line item budgeting to a global one-line budget. With the introduction of the board of governors, the state supervising authority is now devolved to an external governing organ whose membership represents university stakeholders and is intended to create a closer linkage between universities and their wider societies (Orr & Jaeger, 2009). Orr and Jaeger note that in practice governing boards generally have a limited scope of responsibility and in many cases play a consultative role to the president.

Market governance is related to the broader debates occurring in Germany about the desire to have universities function more efficiently and be more entrepreneurial. Two important elements of this are the introduction of new report systems and performance-based allocations of state grants. The new report system is designed to address the need for more information on demand and supply issues resulting from a shift from input-led steering to an emphasis on targets and results (Orr & Jaeger, 2009).

With the performance-based allocation of state grants, the majority of states rely on performance indicators such as teaching performance as the basis for allocating grants to universities. In other words, some states use a formula for allocating funds. In other states, the formula is supplemental to established contracts and agreements, while others use a combination of formula-based and discretion allocations. The bottom line here is that states have governing authority over higher education within their jurisdiction and are free to decide on the type of funding arrangement independent of the federal government. In addition to performance-based allocations and new reporting systems, tuition fees were also introduced. When these policies are viewed collectively, it becomes clear that they are focused on creating a market-driven and competitive university system. However, tuition fees were and still are so unpopular in Germany that they were abolished again after only a few years.

Participative governance is associated with contract-like forms of steering (Orr & Jaeger, 2009). With this governance regime, target agreements exist between the state and universities in which there is agreement on budget allocations; they also exist between university leadership and departments within the university. Orr and Jaeger point out that initially some states opted for either formula-based funding or target-based agreements, but by 2006 almost all states were using a combination of the two as complementary instruments of university steering.

New Public Management (NPM) and German Universities

A deeper examination of the reforms in Germany suggests the influence of new public management (NPM). NPM became a part of the German public sector landscape in the 1980s and spread to the university sector in the 1990s. Although, when compared to England, the Netherlands, and Austria, Germany has been more "conservative" and a latecomer in adopting NPM (de Boer et al., 2007). The adoption of NPM in German higher education suggests that states/Länder want universities to become more managed enterprises. Hence, governance is structured around notions of greater institutional autonomy supported by enhanced hierarchical management by deans and rectors, more autonomy over financial and human resource management, greater external stakeholder involvement, increased competition among universities for resources, and funding based on lump sum budgeting (Schimank & Lange, 2009). In this context, more procedural autonomy is granted by the states to universities to manage their daily affairs while political actors engage in more mission-based negotiations (Schimank et al., 1999). Schimank and Lange (2009) draw a distinction between traditional German higher education governance and the NPM model. They highlight five distinguishing features: bureaucratic deregulation and managerial self-governance, external guidance, academic self-governance, hierarchical management, and competitive pressure.

Bureaucratic deregulation: Deregulation and allowing more flexibility to institutions and their faculty in the management of financial and other resources are measures that have been taken to improve the efficiency of universities. Hence, the traditional ear-marked budgeting was abandoned and replaced by a lump sum budgeting in order to give universities more freedom to manage their resources (Schimank & Lange, 2009). Schimank and Lange (2009) note that some states allow universities to choose their legal status, either opting to be public institutions or to be foundations of civil law. This allows universities more organizational autonomy and control in their financial management. These changes are accommodated by relaxing bureaucratic regulations. Relaxing bureaucratic regulations is a feature of NPM and it runs contrary to the traditional tightly controlled model of state governance.

External guidance: This is achieved through the use of university boards in which there is external stakeholder membership. The composition varies by state, but a wide cross-section of influential representative stakeholders from the government, civil society, and the private sector are board members. These boards provide their universities with advice and are instrumental in setting goals for their attainment. By using mission-based contracts, target agreements are negotiated between the university and the state, and included in these contracts is an agreement to identify strengths and weaknesses. Universities are then contractually obligated to address weaknesses, and this provides an avenue for external influence.

Increased competition: A primary objective of the reform of the German system is to increase competition among and within universities for resources, students, and reputation. This is central concept within NPM. The aim is to reform the traditional system that is controlled by a state-regulated profession and to introduce quasimarket or market-driven governing mechanisms (Schimank & Lange, 2009).

Hierarchical management: The role of university leaders, specifically rectors and deans, has changed in many states. They now have more managerial authority. This approach supports strengthening universities' competitiveness and is consistent with the NPM model. Deans and rectors have more authority in decision-making and goal-setting and "could decide many issues without a majority of the university senate or the faculty council" (Schimank & Lange, 2009, p. 65). Schimank and Lange point out that deans are also seen as representing the interests of their faculty to the rectors and are instrumental to the implementation of the rector's policies.

Academic self-governance: Academic self-governance has been a cornerstone of the Humboldtian model. However, in the current German higher education environment, in which efficiency and competitiveness are key focal points, academic self-governance has been formally weakened (Schimank & Lange, 2009). Schimank and Lange contend that it continues to function informally due to the existing culture of collegiality and consensus among academics. Hence, although there has been a strengthening of hierarchical management, the practice of governance still revolves around the concept of *primus inter pares*. Rectors and deans therefore still seek consensus from the academic peers.

GOVERNANCE IN THE USA

History and Traditions

Any analysis of higher education governance in the USA must be grounded in conceptualizations that draw on formative cultural, political, socioeconomic, and historical underpinnings of the country. It is a country characterized by antistatism, individualism, populism, and egalitarianism (Skolnik & Jones, 1992). The USA displays a distrust of the federal government and even state-level government to a level unseen in most countries—the antistatist culture—and a focus on individualism. An important element of this culture is grounded in the Constitution and Bill of Rights, which emphasize protection of the individual from encroachment by the state.

At the institutional level, higher education in the USA has been heavily influenced by the German Humboldtian ideals, particularly among research universities. In fact, in 1876 Johns Hopkins became the first American university to offer graduate studies based on the Humboldt model, and this has become the model for the modern American research university (Karran, 2009). It is against this backdrop that we can better examine the history and traditions of higher education governance in the USA and investigate the changes that are currently taking place.

To begin, there is no national higher education system. Responsibility for higher education resides with the states rather than the federal government largely because the US Constitution does not mention education. The Tenth Amendment to the Constitution granted powers not delegated to the federal government to the states, and so states assumed responsibility for higher education. (Berdahl, 1999). However, the federal government still plays an indirect role through student financial assistance, research grants, and funding incentives that create a relationship to institutions.

State-university relations are therefore at the "state" level of government and the nature of these relationships depends significantly on the policy environment and the underlying philosophical orientation of each state. Each state has its own unique history, politics, economics, and demography, and these factors influence higher education policy and governance (Richardson, Bracco, Callan, & Finney, 1999). Hence, state-university governing relations are influenced by and are reflections of the characteristics of respective states and their legal framework. Consequently, the USA has a plurality of higher education systems. As Berdahl (1999) writes:

> [w]ith the exception of a few federal military service academies, all institutions, public and private, must operate in the context of state law; so some form of state legal recognition and authorization constitutes a minimum threshold of any university or college existence . . . [but] public sector institutions have their legal structures and modes of governance determined by state law.
>
> (p. 69)

To get a better picture of the patterns of state-university governance that exist in the USA, it is useful to sketch the evolution and history of its higher education systems. In the early 1800s, there were few public colleges and universities in the USA. In fact, some universities predate the creation of the states they now reside in. Once states were established, funding for these universities was provided by these early state governments, but universities still functioned as independent enterprises and not state entities (McLendon & Hearn, 2009). That is, they had great freedom and autonomy from their state. McLendon and Hearn observe that legal interpretations by courts strengthened the autonomy of universities and created a governing framework that became the guiding principle for the governance of new institutions. A landmark decision by the United States Supreme Court that heavily influenced how states interacted with universities was in the *Dartmouth College v. Woodward* (1819) case. In this case, the Court limited outright state control of state-chartered institutions with their private boards. Hence, what were formerly considered rather informally as state-owned colleges became private colleges subject to limited state authority. Consequently, the states began to create their own truly public colleges as new entities. Prior to the Dartmouth decision, there were strong but largely unexamined overlaps between the states, their colonially associated church affiliations (e.g., the Quaker church in Pennsylvania), and the colleges. After the decision, those formerly unquestioned assumptions and associations no longer held.

This was an important development because as the century progressed and more people enrolled in higher education institutions, states built more and different types of universities and colleges (Richardson et al., 1999). Federal legislation was also passed to facilitate expansion (Berdahl, 1999). For example, the Morrill Federal Land Grant Act of 1862 was a major legislative enactment that led to the emergence of "land-grant" universities and the expansion of access.

State policymakers created *statewide higher education systems* to manage and coordinate the growth and expansion of higher education institutions within individual states. These state systems functioned through statewide governing boards, which are essentially the consolidation of local governing boards of individual institutions into a single state-level board. These governing boards were granted decision-making authority over higher education institutions within their jurisdiction. In 1905, Florida established the first statewide governing board for its four-year institutions (Richardson et al., 1999). By 1932, 11 states had statewide governing boards. Other states like Oklahoma established state-level coordinating boards as early as 1941.

As enrollment expanded, state expenditures on higher education increased but the autonomous and decentralized model continued. In essence, although expending heavily on higher education, state governments remained noninterventionist. Unlike other public sectors, states frequently granted universities a high level of autonomy, a form of "self-denying ordinance" (Berdahl, 1999). In some instances, states inserted language in their constitutions to create a buffer for public universities from government interference and control (McLendon & Hearn, 2009). In fact, the desire to ensure that universities remained as highly autonomous entities was manifested in some states by granting "constitutional autonomy" to their flagship universities (for example, the University of Michigan). However, over time the level of constitutional autonomy faded due to later court rulings that narrowed the scope of university autonomy, and universities simply surrendered some of their autonomy in exchange for increased state funding (McLendon & Hearn, 2009).

As enrollment in higher education continued to grow, some states expanded their funding to universities by allocating lump-sum appropriations to institutions, but this came with more direct state oversight and control. As McLendon and Hearn (2009) note, the pendulum swung decidedly in the early part of the 20th century in the opposite direction from what had previously obtained. During those earlier periods, universities functioned almost as private corporations, with each campus having its own local, lay-member governing board, but later state actors sought to create different governing arrangements to achieve greater control (McLendon, 2003) and to address the demand for greater public responsiveness from higher education institutions (Layall, 2001). Hence, there were policy and legislative attempts to make higher education institutions more accountable. The change occurred at a time when state government too was expanding, becoming more complex, and legislators were concerned about efficiency and spending levels (Richardson et al., 1999).

Further expansion in higher education in the aftermath of World War II was driven by the federal government through the enactment of the Serviceman's Readjustment Act of 1944 (also referred to as the G.I. Bill). Through this bill, the federal government financed higher education for returning veterans (Berdahl, 1999). There was a significant increase in demand for higher education in the ensuing years. As enrollment continued to swell, state legislators became more concerned about funding levels and the strain on state budgets, efficient management of resources, and about improving accountability. Legislatures became more interventionist and most states shifted responsibility from that of resource provider to institutional regulator (Richardson et al., 1999) with the intention of bringing greater order, efficiency, and equity to the system (McLendon, Hearn, & Deaton, 2006).

McLendon, Deaton, and Hearn (2007) point out that the modern system of governance is an artifact of the late 1950s when states redesigned their governance systems. Some states continued to consolidate their system by strengthening governing boards while others pursued a statewide coordination approach. Based on the redesigns of governments in the post-1950s, Bracco, Richardson, Callan, and Finney (1999) created a generally accepted taxonomy of three basic state structures: consolidated governing boards, coordinating boards, and planning agencies. A statewide governing board has responsibility for operational activities in, and also has line authority over, higher education institutions. States with this kind of structure pursued a very centralized mode of state-university governance. A statewide coordinating board is a centralized agency whose function is mainly to facilitate communications, coordination, and research efforts across a state's institutions but, in the case of the more powerful coordinating boards, may provide some measure of oversight to individual institutional governing boards within a state. A state planning board/agency has limited statewide coordinating authority and serves largely as an advisory body (McGuinness, 1997). Marcus (1997) suggests that the choice of statewide structure depended on the state's history.

Coordinating boards are intermediary bodies that create an extra layer between the state political actors and universities but nevertheless constitute a form of external control. They are tasked with the responsibility for statewide planning of higher education and provide advice to the legislature on statewide resource needs. But the level of authority associated with these boards varies by state, with some granted statutory responsibility and regulatory power over an entire state public higher education sector, some with jurisdiction over four-year colleges only, while others serve an advisory function and make recommendations to elected officials (Marcus, 1997; McLendon & Hearn, 2009).

While coordinating boards are viewed by some as professional entities having the requisite skills to support the efficient and effective management of universities and the system (Glenny & Bowen, 1977), McLendon and Hearn (2009) view them as a mechanism that shifted some of the authority previously vested with the campuses closer to the state governments. Hence, through this structure, state policy-makers assumed more control over institutions as opposed to previous decades when they funded institutions but kept a comfortable distance from them. This model of state-university governance persisted from shortly after World War II until the 1980s, when there was a distinct philosophical shift in the approach to public management to a market-oriented philosophy. From this point onwards, governance became a balance between state action, market forces, and institutional autonomy (Pusser, 2008). It is important to note that states systems are uniquely designed to be responsive to the idiosyncrasies of the state, but they change over time as the circumstances in states change, and this in turn influences the state-university relationship. And as Marcus (1997) points out, times and politics in a state change and so too does the conception of what constitutes a rational statewide system of higher education. Thus, different states implemented different versions of deregulated, decentralized, and market-oriented governance.

Reforms in US State-University Relations

The 1980s saw a swinging of the pendulum from a more centralized and regulatory governing relationship to a more "decentralized" and ostensibly more autonomous relationship. At the heart of the reforms was the adoption of neoliberal market principles as the most efficient means of allocating scarce resources. State-university relations moved towards deregulation, decentralization, and devolution of decision-making authority to the campuses and away from the coordinating state agencies (McLendon & Hearn, 2009), although states have sought to maintain control of some aspects of higher education activity while decentralizing. Berdahl (1999) insightfully suggests that the core element of the reforms was granting procedural autonomy to universities but retaining substantive autonomy. This was intended to grant flexibility to universities in the management of their budgets, personnel, and other financial affairs, and it came at a time when states were beginning to experience financial shortfalls in their own budgets. The underlying intent was to incentivize universities to find more operationally efficient ways to manage their daily and financial affairs (Hyatt & Santiago, 1984).

The reforms involving "decentralization" were of three types: deregulation of state procedural controls, loosening of state government regulation and statewide coordination, and the advent of charter colleges and universities (McLendon & Hearn, 2009). The decentralization of the state procedural controls was largely the result of fiscal stresses on state budgets and consequent shortfalls in appropriations to state universities. The result of this was university leaders making a case to state legislatures to grant them the flexibility to manage their own financial affairs, including authority to set tuition fees. States across the country devolved tuition-setting authority to universities, albeit with some variation in how this was administered by states. However, it represented a clear shift in policy and the decentralization of procedural control.

The loosening of state government regulation and statewide coordination is a relaxing of regulatory control of the system by the state (McLendon & Hearn, 2009). It was the means by which some authority that was previously the purview of state regulatory bodies was granted to institutions. This usually occurred following the dissolution and/or the reconstituting of the state agency in which there was a reduced regulatory reach. To illustrate this point, McLendon and Hearn cite the case of New Jersey, in which the legislature abolished its coordinating board and delegated authority over academic programs and budgets to the campuses.

Charter/enterprise colleges have agreements with the state in which authority and responsibility are delegated by the state with the precondition that institutions operate in a manner consistent with the state charter granted. For universities, these charters provide managerial discretion, essentially redefine the relationship between universities and the state government, and create a different operating framework (McLendon & Hearn, 2009). A notable recent case of this is in the state of Virginia in which the University of Virginia, the College of William and Mary, and Virginia Tech sought chartered status from the State Council of Higher Education for Virginia.

The Policy Environment

Bracco et al. (1999) point to the policy environment and the system design as two important dimensions of US state governance structures. They contend that focusing on policy environment highlights the role state governments play in balancing competing conceptions of professional values on the one hand and the market on the other. The authority relationship between the state and higher education underscores this. Authority relationships reflect policy priorities that are informed by competing interest groups inside and outside of government and the role the state plays to accommodate changing and competing claims among state, market, and academic interests (Williams, 1995). Hence, the state plays the roles of: a provider to institutions; a regulator of the relationship between institutions and the market; a consumer advocate channeling resources to students to create market options and choices for them; and a steering agent by influencing higher education market activities to create outcomes that are consistent with government priorities (Bracco et al., 1999). Bracco et al. argue that all states exhibit elements of these four policy roles but, depending on the state, one of these roles is typically more dominant than the others. Bracco et al.'s conceptualization brings us closer to understanding how policy agendas are influencing and shaping state-university relations and systems of governance.

System design involves decisions about the structure and organization of the system (Bracco et al., 1999). Bracco et al. argue that in order for a system to work effectively, there must be compatibility between the system and the policy environment. Three higher education systems are advanced in their model for the US: segmented, unified, and federal systems. In segmented systems, there are multiple governing boards in a state and each board has responsibility for one or sometimes more institutions. Typical of this is the state of Michigan in which four universities have their own governing boards. Michigan, coming from a history of constitutional autonomy, has therefore maintained the autonomy and independence of each public university.

In unified systems, there is a single governing board with responsibility for all higher education institutions and the board functions as the voice of the institutions in interactions with the legislature. An example of this is the state of Georgia in which there is a single Board of Regents, established in 1931 as a part of a reorganization of Georgia's state government, which has responsibility for two- and four-year institutions. Bracco et al. conclude that the regulatory role of the state (the policy environment) is consistent with the unified model.

Federal systems are somewhat similar to unified systems in that they have a state-wide board with responsibility for financial, administrative, and academic affairs. However, unlike the unified systems, there is separation of powers between activities undertaken by the coordinating board (the state level) and by the institutional governing boards (the institutional level). Bracco et al. (1999) point out that the federal system is better suited for a steering environment but not in a policy environment in which the state plays a provider role. An example of a federal system is the state of Illinois, which was designed as a federal model in 1961; while important changes were made in 1995, its federal character still persists.

What the foregoing highlights is that at the state level, the policy environment, the system design, state histories, and politics are interwoven and they shape state-university relations. There is a line of scholarship that clearly makes the connection between state level policy development and state level higher education governance (Bracco et al., 1999; Richardson et al., 1999). It also shows how the reforms are undertaken within the contextual framework of individual states, and even though there is some overall convergence, reforms are still undertaken within the state's larger policy frameworks. Although these reforms are initiated in the macropolicy environment, they have significant implications for governance at the institutional level. For example, the role of governing boards at public universities has changed from advocacy to a greater focus on oversight and public accountability (Layall, 2001). The members of many lay governing boards are usually appointed by, and view themselves as, representatives of the state legislature, and in more recent times some boards have shown a willingness to become more activist and extend their reach deep into the fabric of institutions by addressing curriculum matters and sometimes engaging presidents in contentious battles. These activist governing boards tend to be associated with trying to implement business models within higher education systems (Bastedo, 2009) and in the process can create organizational governing cultures and practices that are very distinct from what obtains with traditional boards (Bastedo, 2005).

In the current ethos of marketization and corporate practices in higher education, authority relations within universities have also changed. There is an emerging body of professional managers within the administrative estate that may be deemed by academic faculty as encroaching on their authority. Hines (2000) suggests that there is an increased number of "claimants to authority" (p. 105; cf. Pusser, 2008) in the academy. Hence, there is a rebalancing of authority and power in which the administrative estate has gained more prominence. Just like the UK, the USA has seen a strengthening of power at the center for institutions. This is the result of: (1) cuts in funding levels from the state; (2) a focus on greater efficiency and effectiveness resulting in the hiring of "high quality managers;" and (3) a CEO-type leadership (Middlehurst, 2004). University presidents have become much more powerful actors in the academy and it is argued that in the process there is a chipping away of collegiality. In particular, university presidents now have a greater external role and spend a significant amount of their time engaging external stakeholders and fund-raising. This is all subsumed under an entrepreneurial culture which is now widespread in higher education and associated with a different way of governing. Middlehurst points out that the core activities and the value-base of a university are inextricably linked to its internal governance arrangements. Hence, the driving ideological and policy directions that are dominant in the external environment and the prevailing financial circumstances of higher education institutions are major factors shaping the core activities and the value system of institutions. By extension, these factors are causing internal governance restructuring and a reforming of the relationship between US institutions and external stakeholders, including the state.

GOVERNANCE IN JAPAN

History and Traditions

In examining governance in the Japanese higher education system, in particular the state-university relationship, two pertinent factors must be considered. First, it must be noted that higher education in Japan is highly diversified, with both public and private providers of higher education. Christensen (2011) describes it as a higher education system that is even more diverse than the USA's. Unlike some other countries in East Asia, some of the Japanese private universities are highly ranked in the system and the state provides incentives to them (Sirat & Kaur, 2010). The system also includes Imperial universities, which traditionally held a privileged status.

Second, just like China, Japan's higher education is shaped by the Confucian Model (Marginson, 2011) or, as Marginson (2014) subsequently indicated, the Post-Confucian Model. Marginson (2014) suggests the Post-Confucian Model of higher education as practiced in East Asia has exceptional dynamism and clearly distinguishable relations between the state, family/society and higher education (Marginson, 2014). He indicates that the Post-Confucian Model of higher education has a different dynamic from what obtains in Western Europe, the UK, and the USA. Important features of the model, Marginson asserts, are strong nation-state steering policies involving close supervision and control, emphasis on strong top-down driven educational priorities and research, and the shaping of executive agendas. In other words, under the Post-Confucian model, the state is very involved. What is also occurring under this model is the rapid growth in higher education participation rates and the acceleration of research output (Marginson, 2011). The high participation rates encouraged by the state are driven by broader macro-desired outcomes, such as economic growth and global competitiveness.

The history and tradition of higher education in Japan, particularly up until World War II, reflected the German model in which there was strong faculty autonomy over sacredly held domains such as curriculum, degree offerings, and appointments and promotions (Christensen, 2011). In the postwar period, higher education in Japan shifted more towards the American model but retained elements of the German model. However, the Ministry of Education tightly controlled national universities, including their structure and operations, causing them to function as branches of the Ministry (Christensen, 2011; Yamamoto, 2005). Thus, up until the 2004 reforms, the system included a steering bureaucracy in which Japanese national universities were under the direct administration of the Ministry of Education, Culture, Sports, Science, and Technology (MEXT) and part of the national government (Oba, 2007).

Policy Shifts and Governance Changes

Despite the ministry's direct involvement, there were signs of reform prior to 2004. For example, between the 1960s and 1970s, more emphasis was placed on higher education as an engine of economic growth. As a result, Japan created a mass higher education system by expanding enrollment, and they placed more emphasis on graduate education (Itoh, 2002). In the 1980s, efficiency and value-for-money considerations were focal points of interest (Yamamoto, 2004; Itoh). Like other East Asian jurisdictions, such as China, Hong Kong, and Malaysia, Japan embarked on a restructuring of its higher education system and university governance. These changes were linked to strengthening global competitiveness, fostering economic expansion, and the view that higher education is instrumental to these outcomes (Mok, 2007). Universities have therefore adopted the third mission of promoting economic and social development. Along with this was disaffection with the conventional "state-oriented" and "highly centralized" model. Hence, state-university relations that were based on the state-controlled model began changing. With enrollment expansion and the rising cost to the state, notions of deregulation and autonomy began to take root. In Japan, as in other East Asian countries, there was a move towards "corporatization" with the intention of turning state/public universities into independent legal entities and granting them more flexibility and autonomy in running and governing their own affairs (Mok, 2007). As a result, the 1990s saw a gradual decrease in ex ante oversight (Christensen, 2011).

Although changes were being made, Japan was considered a "reluctant reformer" (Christensen, 2011). The minister still retained significant power. This often created tension between universities and the ministry in which deregulation and greater autonomy were at odds with the ministry's desire to regulate and direct. But in 2004, faced with a social, political, and economic crisis for which some blame was attributed to the universities, major governance reforms were implemented. New public management (NPM) reforms were adopted with the intention of making universities more efficient and internationally competitive (Hatakenaka, 2005). It clearly signaled that as a post-Confucian state, Japan had embraced neoliberal philosophies and forms of modernization. Universities were expected to take greater responsibility for their financial affairs and become more entrepreneurial (Marginson, 2011). National universities became National University Corporations (NUCs). These corporations are independent agencies with much greater autonomy and are also more result- and performance-oriented (Eades, Goodman, & Hada, 2005).

One important outcome of this change is that the staff at national universities are no longer public servants under the direct administration of the government. However, the state still assumes responsibility for financing these national university corporations, albeit based on a third-party evaluation (Huang, 2006). Huang argues that the incorporation of these universities fundamentally shifted the state-university relationship and patterns of institutional governance, and the government adopted an ex post facto approach to these entities.

What do these changes mean for the university-state relationship? The notion of corporatization of universities suggests granting wide-ranging institutional autonomy from the state in day-to-day administration and decision-making. For example, university presidents were granted more power under the NUC arrangements. However, NUCs are still subject to ministerial control and scrutiny, and there is more external stakeholder participation on university boards and councils. For example, university presidents had previously been elected by academic staff members, endorsed by the council, and appointed by the minister as a formality. Although the minister of education still appoints a president, the selection is made by a committee comprised of just as many external experts as internal representatives (Oba, 2007). And although variations exist across universities in the application of this approach, the important point here is that external experts (external stakeholders) are now key participants. The board of directors and the administrative council are now required to have external experts as members, a change designed to support the efficient management of universities (Oba, 2007). This change presumes that decision quality can be enhanced by drawing on diverse expertise that may not be easily found within universities.

The new governance environment in Japan also focuses on transparency and accountability to the Ministry of Education and the public at large. Christensen (2011) contends that the incorporation of universities may be a rhetorical measure intended to convey a message of more university autonomy and less state control, but in fact may be part of an alternative strategy to control and reregulate universities. In addition to the wider stakeholder participation, another manifestation of governmental supervision is in the funding arrangements in which audits and evaluations have been implemented (Yamamoto, 2004). Seen through another lens, these changes may represent a hybrid form of governance in which the state attempts to balance central control with institutional autonomy in a post-Confucian system, but with the Ministry generally still having significant control.

GOVERNANCE IN CHINA

History and Traditions

To begin to understand higher education governance in China, it is important to briefly review the history of higher education in this country and its cultural traditions. China's cultural assumptions and traditions are shaped by Confucianism (Bell, 2008). In this tradition, hierarchy is valued as the means for establishing order, and its underlying philosophy is rooted in the idea of elite control as the best way to promote prosperity and harmony (Chou, 1996; Lui, 2012). Lui posits that along with this is a collectivist culture in which relationships among people are based on reciprocal responsibilities and a consensual moral and ethical orientation. These historical traditions and cultural complexities form the basis on which early Chinese higher education and governance structures developed.

During the early part of the 19th century, the focus of Chinese higher education was on training traditional Confucian scholars and there was very little influence from outside, particularly, from the West (Yang, Vidovich, & Currie, 2007). From around the 1860s, the influence of Western models and Western-style schools started to become a part of the Chinese higher education landscape, and by 1905, Chinese students were being trained in Japan, United States, and Europe (Bastid, 1988). The Chinese education system became even more aligned with the Western system and prevailing world trends largely due to the absence of a central government from 1911, following the revolution, until 1927 (Yang et al., 2007). This trend was augmented by the return of Chinese scholars from Japan and Western countries. According to Hayhoe (1996), they embraced Western-style university models and placed emphasis on values such as autonomy and academic freedom.

With the founding of the People's Republic of China in 1949 by the Chinese Communist Party (CCP), the structure and practices of higher education changed significantly to reflect that of the Soviet Union system (Zha, 2009). This was a philosophical shift driven largely by the rise of the CCP as the ruling party. China became a planned economy similar to the Soviet Union. After 1953, the higher education system and the associated policy formulation were controlled by the central government ministries and provincial governments using a very top-down approach and direct control governing mechanisms. The central government's remit included responsibility for resource allocation and the exercise of administrative controls in areas such as hiring teaching and research staff, developing curriculum, choosing textbooks, recruiting students, and assigning jobs to university graduates (Yang et al., 2007). An important feature of the governing structure was the alignment of universities to either the Ministry of Education or a ministry with responsibility for administering an industrial sector that was linked to an academic discipline (Zha, 2009). This means that Chinese universities were governed through sectoral ministries such as the "Ministry of Machine Building, Ministry of Agriculture, Ministry of Forestry, Ministry of Water Conservation & Power, Ministry of Metallurgical Industry, [and] Ministry of Justice" (Zha, 2009, p. 42–43) which resulted in discipline isolation by sector and very limited interdisciplinary engagement.

Driven by a combination of worldwide trends and socioeconomic factors within China, Chinese higher education has undergone major reform over the last three decades (Huang, 2005). Much of the reform is located within China's modernization agenda and the attendant changes that have accompanied the modernization thrust. Li (2010) highlights some of the structural changes in higher education associated with modernization as: an emphasis on cost effectiveness, market responsiveness as a core institutional goal, the use of measurable output indicators, and advancing institutional entrepreneurship. These factors are all circumscribed within China's broader policies on modernization and its pursuit of international competitiveness, which have led to the expansion of higher education, accompanied by decentralization; the introduction of market incentives, university mergers, and internationalization; and the introduction of quality assurance requirements (Li, 2010). In the next section we examine the Chinese modernization agenda and the policy shifts that are reshaping higher education governance.

Modernization and Policy Shifts

There was a fundamental shift in 1976 in China's public policy direction towards achieving its modernization agenda (Yang et al., 2007). Two key elements of this agenda were changing to a market economy and an opening up of China to the outside world (Zha, 2009). These changes resulted from the abandonment of the planned economy approach to managing the country (Mok, 2009). The new governing environment emphasized efficiency of operations and resource constraints. Accompanying this shift was a restructuring of government, including the dismantling of some central ministries and the removal of the remaining central ministries' authority over higher education institutions (Zha, 2009). Central to this was restructuring the education system, and that resulted in the renewal of some of the previous foreign practices and values (Reed, 1988). Mok notes that power was devolved, centralization and government controls were reduced, and universities were granted more autonomy. By adopting this approach, the Chinese central government shifted higher education from a state-controlled model to a state-supervised model, but the central government still exercised authority over important higher education policy (Yang et al.,

2007). Hence, despite decentralization and the devolution of authority, the State Education Commission (SEC) still guides and monitors the whole sector.

A study by Yang et al. (2007) found that there were still constraints imposed by the central government related to issues such as political education, sensitive areas of research, and the appointment of presidents and party secretaries. They also found that while the governance model had shifted to granting more autonomy to the universities, there was an increase in accountability requirements. Yang, Vidovich, and Currie argue that the Chinese central government is steering higher education from a distance, engaging with globalization, market competition, and market ideologies, but at the same time, it continues to play a significant role as a regulator, facilitator, and negotiator. The central government, sometimes through the State Council and very often through the Ministry of Education, prescribes and pushes reform agendas, especially regarding institutional governance structures, with the aim to increase autonomy and accountability. New initiatives that have been implemented or are beginning to roll out include, but are not limited to, creating a chief accountant position at the senior administrative level, piloting presidential selection protocols, prescribing the role and composition of academic councils, and drafting university charters. In this respect, the central government still assumes a very strong role in initiating systemic changes. These changes to higher education governance in China are directly linked to the modernization of the country, massification of higher education, the building of China's global competitiveness, and securing its leadership role on the world stage. The changes in China's higher education governance can thus be seen as being driven by the state's macrosocial, economic, political, and cultural policies.

Massification and Governance Changes

With the modernization of China came a deliberate policy to adopt a mass higher education strategy. The central government set the goal of increasing postsecondary education participation rates of relevant age cohorts from 9% in 1998 to 11% in 2000 to 15% in 2010 (Zha, 2011). This resulted in a significant expansion in higher education enrollment. This was accompanied by an embrace of competition and market ideology. It was all a part of the new reform thrust that was launched in the mid-1980s (Mok, 2009) which also included devolution and decentralization. In the restructuring of government, central ministries such as the Ministry of Machine Building, the Ministry of Agriculture, the Ministry of Forestry, and the Ministry of Justice were no longer permitted to run higher education institutions (Zha, 2011). These ministries had been previously responsible for the administration of universities that specialized in programs aligned with their specific ministry's human resource needs. This change in policy constituted a significant change in the governance of universities in China.

The central government devolved authority over the administration of many of these universities to local government, and in so doing, these higher education institutions became more provincial, both in terms of system governance and orientation. Zha (2011) posits that by transferring government authority to local government, the central government was relieved of the financial burden of these universities. Keep in mind that enrollment expanded rapidly with massification, in sharp contrast to the tightly controlled state enrollment quotas that were an important component of policy from the 1950s until the early 1990s. Zha also observes that another important policy change that propelled massification was charging student fees beginning in 1997. This effectively removed the enrollment quota system and instead enrollment was driven by the social demand for education. In addition, in the early 1990s university funding from the central government was changed from an incremental-based to a formula-based approach in which there was a block appropriation based on enrollment and an appropriation for special items. The enrollment approach to funding, Zha argues, has driven enrollment competition among institutions. This competition is in line with China's embrace of the market and it is reflected in the funding model.

Gradually the institutional funding burden shifted to the universities. The national government is no longer the sole provider of financing for universities in China. Universities are now required or expected to raise an increasingly large proportion of their operating funds from nongovernmental and market sources, and simultaneously there has been an increase in the amount of fees paid by individual students (Zha, 2011). Zha posits that these policy shifts in governing universities were all very strategic. The devolution of responsibility to local or provincial governments and universities having to fight for their own survival by securing some of their operating costs from nongovernmental sources meant that the state could focus attention on national elite universities as part of the global competitive strategy. These national universities are directly under the control of the Ministry of Education. They have higher status, significantly higher research budgets, significantly lower enrollment numbers than universities governed at the local level, and focus on achieving global excellence.

What is clear is that there are movements in the governance of higher education parallel to changes occurring in the way the Chinese economy is administered- a broad transition from central planning to a much more market-oriented approach. These changes are all linked to a new overarching approach to the expansion of China's role and status in the world and its competitiveness in a global knowledge economy. Worldwide trends of neoliberalism impacting higher education governance and policy are also impacting higher education in China. Lui (2012) argues that neoliberal ideas resonate with China's utilitarian approach. Neoliberalism and utilitarianism are taking root in China's higher education system, and there is an evolution in the practice of higher education governance, but Chinese culture, values, and traditions cannot be separated from its way of governing. Current experimentation with governance reforms at the institutional level, including new approaches to selecting presidents and the development of academic councils with some authority over academic matters, are balanced with the desire to retain the authority of the party in institutional affairs and the need to maintain central coordination of what is now the world's largest and perhaps most complex system of higher education. China's higher education governance therefore has to be understood as an integration of post-Confucian ideals, along with strong historical and cultural traditions expressed within the logic of developing a globally competitive country.

SUMMARY

The relationship between governments and higher education institutions continues to be of major significance in the evolution of higher education and its governance. What we have shown in this chapter is that the nature of this relationship continues to change over time and in different ways depending on the country and its history, traditions, and specific circumstances. For example, the circumstances in the USA after World War II were driven by a massive increase in predominantly publicly funded higher education institutions. With this came the desire by the government to demand that the state have greater influence in institutional affairs (McDaniel, 1996). This represents normalcy in a country like China that has been governed by a central planning state-centric model. For others, increased governmental involvement is construed as an attempt to expand the exercise of state power and infringe on academic freedom and institutional autonomy. What is also evident in the countries reviewed is a convergence of governance which is largely ideologically driven by NPM and a desire to control national higher education spending by forcing universities to be more efficient.

These requirements are being imposed at a time when countries have reduced their per student funding contributions to institutions, and universities are expected to secure funds from alternative sources, such as the commercialization of university teaching and research. Countries seemingly are converging towards what seems to have become a universal trend but they are coming from different directions. State-centric countries are moving more towards market-based approaches to governing but with the state maintaining some level of oversight, and noninterventionist countries are imposing more government controls while encouraging more corporatized and market-based approaches.

DISCUSSION QUESTIONS

1. Based on the foregoing discussion, how is state-university governance different across jurisdictions? And why is it different?
2. How would you compare the state-university governance in your country to the ones discussed in this chapter?
3. In some countries professors are employees of the state, while in other systems they are employed by the university. What are some of the implications of this difference for system-level governance? For institutional governance?

REFERENCES

Bastedo, M. N. (2005). The making of an activist governing board. *Review of Higher Education, 28*(4), 551–570.

Bastedo, M. N. (2009). Convergent institutional logics in public higher education: State policy-making and governing board activism. *Review of Higher Education, 32*(2), 209–234.

Bastid, M. (1988). *Educational reform in early twentieth-century China*. Ann Arbor, MI: Centre for Chinese Studies, University of Michigan.

Bell, D. (2008). *China's new Confucianism*. Princeton, NJ: Princeton University Press.

Berdahl, R. (1999). Universities and governments in the 21st century: The US experience. In D. Braun & F-X. Merrien (Eds.), *Towards a new model of governance for universities? A comparative view* (pp. 59–77). London, England: Jessica Kingsley.

Birnbaum, R. (1983). *Managing diversity in higher education*. San Francisco, CA: Jossey-Bass.

Bracco, K. R., Richardson, R. C., Callan, P. M., & Finney, J. E. (1999). Policy environment and system designs: Understanding state governance structures. *Review of Higher Education, 23*(1), 23–44.

Capano, G., & Regini, M. (2014). Governance reforms and organizational dilemmas in European universities. *Comparative Education Review, 58*(1), 73–103.

Chou, D. (1996). Administrative concepts in Confucianism and their influence on development in Confucian countries. *Asian Journal of Public Administration, 18*, 45–69.

Christensen, T. (2011). Japanese university reform—hybridity in governance and management. *Higher Education Policy, 24*, 127–142.

Clark, B. R. (1983). *The higher education system: Academic organization in cross-national perspective.* Berkeley, CA: University of California Press.

Codling, A., & Meek, V. L. (2006). Twelve propositions on diversity in higher education. *Higher Education Management and Policy, 18*(3), 1–24.

de Boer, H., Enders, J., & Schimank, U. (2007). On the way towards new public management? The governance of university systems in England, the Netherlands, Austria, and Germany. In D. Jansen (Ed.), *New forms of governance in research organizations: Disciplinary approaches, interfaces and integration* (pp. 137–152). Dordrecht, The Netherlands: Springer.

Deem, R., & Brehony, K. J. (2005). Management as ideology: The case of "new managerialism" in higher education. *Oxford Review of Education, 31*(2), 213–231.

Deem, R., Hillyard, S., & Reed, M. (2007). *Knowledge, higher education, and the new managerialism: The changing management of UK universities.* Oxford, England: Oxford University Press.

Eades, J. S., Goodman, R., & Hada, Y. (Eds.). (2005). *The "big bang" in Japanese higher education: The 2004 reforms and the dynamics of change.* Melbourne, Australia: Trans Pacific Press.

Enders, J. (2001). A chair system in transition: Appointments, promotions, and gate-keeping in German higher education. *Higher Education, 41*, 3–25.

Filippakou, O., Salter, B., & Tapper, T. (2012). The changing structure of British higher education: How diverse is it? *Tertiary Education and Management, 18*(4), 321–333.

Fulton, O. (2002). Higher education governance in the UK: Change and continuity. In A. Amaral, G. A. Jones, & B. Karseth (Eds.), *Governing higher education: National perspectives on institutional governance* (pp. 187–211). Dordrecht, The Netherlands: Kluwer.

Glenny, L. A., & Bowen, F. M. (1977). *State intervention in higher education.* Cambridge, MA: Sloan Commission on Government and Higher Education.

Hatakenaka, S. (2005). The incorporation of national universities: The role of missing hybrids. In J. S. Eades, R. Goodman, & Y. Hada (Eds.), *The big banging in Japanese higher education: The 2004 reforms and the dynamics of change.* Melbourne, Australia: Trans Pacific Press.

Hayhoe, R. (1996). *China's universities 1895–1995: A century of cultural conflict.* New York, NY: Garland.

Hines, E. (2000). The governance of higher education. In J. Smart (Ed.), *Higher education: Handbook of theory and research* (Vol. 15, pp. 105–155). New York, NY: Agathon.

Hood, C., & Scott, C. (1996). Bureaucratic regulation and new public management in the United Kingdom: Mirror-image developments? *Journal of Law and Society, 23*(3), 321–345.

Huang, F. (2005). Qualitative enhancement and quantitative growth: Changes and trends of China's higher education. *Higher Education Policy, 18*, 117–130.

Huang, F. (2006). Incorporation and university governance: A comparative perspective from China and Japan. *Higher Education Management and Policy, 18*(2), 36–49.

Hyatt, J. A., & Santiago, A. A. (1984). *Incentives and disincentives for effective management.* Washington, DC; National Association of Colleges and Universities Business Officers.

Itoh, A. (2002). Higher education reform in perspective: The Japanese experience. *Higher Education, 43*(1), 7–25.

Kaiser, F. (2007). *Higher education in France: Country report*. Enschede, The Netherlands: Center for Higher Education Policy Studies, Universiteit Twente.

Karran, T. (2009). Academic freedom: In justification of a universal ideal. *Studies in Higher Education, 34*(3), 263–283.

Kogan, M., & Hanney, S. (2000). *Reforming higher education*. London, England: Jessica Kingsley.

Layall, K. C. (2001). Recent changes in the structure and governance of American research universities. In W. Z. Hirsch & L. E. Weber (Eds.), *Governance in higher education: The university in a state of flux* (pp. 17–25). London, England: Economica.

Li, Y. (2010). Quality assurance in Chinese higher education. *Research in Comparative and International Education, 5*(1), 58–76.

Lui, J. (2012). Examining massification policies and their consequences for equality in Chinese higher education: A cultural perspective. *Higher Education, 64*, 647–660.

Marcus, L. (1997). Restructuring state higher education governance patterns. *Review of Higher Education, 20*, 399–418.

Marginson, S. (2011). Higher education in East Asia and Singapore: Rise of the Confucian model. *Higher Education, 61*, 587–611.

Marginson, S. (2014). Emerging higher education in the Post-Confucian heritage zone. In D. Araya & P. Marber (Eds.), *Higher education in the global age: Policy, practice and promise in emerging societies* (pp. 89–112). New York, NY: Routledge.

McDaniel, O. C. (1996). The paradigms of governance in higher education systems. *Higher Education Policy, 9*(2), 137–158.

McGuinness, A. C. (1997). *State postsecondary education structures handbook*. Denver, CO: Education Commission of the States.

McLendon, M. K. (2003). State governance reform of higher education: Patterns, trends, and theories of the public policy process. In J. C. Smart (Eds.), *Higher education: Handbook of theory and research* (Vol. 18, pp. 57–143). London, England: Kluwer.

McLendon, M. K., Deaton, S. R., & Hearn, J. C. (2007). The enactment of state level governance reforms for higher education: A test of political instability hypothesis. *Journal of Higher Education, 78*(6), 645–675.

McLendon, M. K., & Hearn, J. C. (2009). Viewing recent US governance reform whole: "Decentralization" in a distinctive context. In J. Huisman (Eds.), *International perspectives on the governance of higher education: Alternative frameworks for coordination* (pp. 161–181). New York, NY: Routledge.

McLendon, M. K., Hearn, J. C., & Deaton, S. R. (2006). Called to account: Analyzing the origins and spread of state performance-accountability policies for higher education. *Educational Evaluation and Policy Analysis, 28*(1), 1–24.

Merrien, F-X., & Musselin, C. (1999). Our French universities finally emerging? Path dependency phenomena and innovative reforms in France. In D. Braun & F-X. Merrien (Eds.), *Towards a new model of governance for universities? A comparative view* (pp. 220–238). London, England: Jessica Kingsley.

Middlehurst, R. (2004). Changing internal governance: A discussion of leadership roles and management structures in UK universities. *Higher Education Quarterly, 54*(4), 258–279.

Mok, K. H. (2007). Withering the state? Globalization challenges and the changing higher education governance in East Asia. In W. T. Pink & G. W. Noblit (Eds.), *International handbook of urban education* (pp. 305–320). Dordrecht, The Netherlands: Springer.

Moodie, G., & Eustace, R. B. (1974). *Power and authority in British universities*. London, England: Allen and Unwin.

Musselin, C., & Mignot-Gerard, S. (2002). The recent evolution of French universities. In A. Amaral, G. A. Jones, & B. Karseth (Eds.), *Governing higher education: National perspectives on institutional governance* (pp. 63–85). Dordrecht, The Netherlands: Kluwer.

Musselin, C., & Paradeise, C. (2009). France: From an incremental transitions to institutional change. In C. Paradeise et al. (Eds.), *University governance: Western European comparative perspectives* (pp. 21–49). Dordrecht, The Netherlands: Springer.

Neave, G. (2012). *The evaluative state, institutional autonomy and re-engineering higher education in Western Europe: The prince and his pleasure.* Hampshire, England: Palgrave Macmillan.

Oba, J. (2007). Incorporation of national universities in Japan. *Asia Pacific Journal of Education, 27*(3), 291–303.

Orr, D., & Jaeger, M. (2009). Governance in German higher education: Competition versus negotiation of performance. In J. Huisman (Eds.), *International perspectives on the governance of higher education: Alternative frameworks for coordination* (pp. 33–51). New York, NY: Routledge.

Pritchard, R. (2006). Trends in the restructuring of German universities. *Comparative Education Review, 50*(1), 90–112.

Pusser, B. (2008). The state, the market and the institutional estate: Revisiting contemporary authority relations in higher education. In J.C. Smart (Ed.), *Higher education: Handbook of theory and research* (Vol. 23, pp. 105–139). Dordrecht, The Netherlands: Springer.

Reed, L.A. (1988). *Education in the People's Republic of China and U.S.-China educational exchanges.* (ED304054). Washington, DC: ERIC.

Richardson, R., Bracco, K.R., Callan, P., & Finney, J. (1999). *Designing state higher education systems for a new century.* Phoenix, AZ: American Council on Education/Oryx Press.

Schimank, U. (2005). New public management and the academic profession: Reflections on the German situation. *Minerva, 43*, 361–375.

Schimank, U., Kehm, B., & Enders, J. (1999). Institutional mechanisms of problem processing of the German university system: Status quo and new developments. In D. Braun & F-X. Merrien (Eds.), *Towards a new model of governance for universities? A comparative view* (pp. 179–194). London, England: Jessica Kingsley.

Schimank, U., & Lange, S. (2009). Germany: A latecomer to Management. In C. Paradeise et al. (Eds.), *University governance: Western European comparative perspectives* (pp. 51–75). Dordrecht, The Netherlands: Springer.

Shattock, M. (1994). *The UGC and the management of British universities.* Buckingham, England: Open University Press.

Shattock, M. (2006). Policy drivers in UK higher education in historical perspective: "Inside out", "outside in" and the contribution of research. *Higher Education Quarterly, 60*(2), 130–140.

Shattock, M. (2008). The change from private to public governance of British higher education: Its consequences for higher education policymaking, 1980–2006. *Higher Education Quarterly, 62*(3), 181–203.

Shattock, M. (2013). University governance, leadership and management in a decade of diversification and uncertainty. *Higher Education Quarterly, 67*(3), 217–233.

Sirat, M., & Kaur, S. (2010). Changing state–university relations: The experiences of Japan and lessons for Malaysia. *Comparative Education, 46*(2), 189–205.

Skolnik, M., & Jones, G.A. (1992). A comparative analysis of arrangements for state coordination of higher education in Canada and the United States. *Journal of Higher Education, 63*(2), 121–142.

Stucke, A. (1999). Higher education policy in Germany: Is there any strategy? In D. Braun & F-X. Merrien (Eds.), *Towards a new model of governance for universities? A comparative view* (pp. 163–178). London, England: Jessica Kingsley.

Taylor, M. (2013). Shared governance in the modern university. *Higher Education Quarterly, 67*(1), 80–94.

Thoenig, J-C. (2005). Territorial administration and political control: Decentralization in France. *Public Administration, 83*(3), 685–708.

van Vught, F. (2008). Mission diversity and reputation in higher education. *Higher Education Policy, 21,* 151–174.

Williams, G. L. (1995). The marketization of higher education: Reforms and potential reforms in higher education finance. In D. D. Dill & B. Sporn (Eds.), *Emerging patterns of social demand and university reform: Through a glass darkly* (pp. 170–193). Tarrytown, NY: Elsevier Science.

Yamamoto, K. (2004). Corporatization of national universities in Japan: Revolution of governance or rhetoric for downsizing? *Financial Accountability & Management, 20*(2), 153–181.

Yamamoto, S. (2005). Government and the national universities: Ministerial bureaucrats and dependent universities. In J. S. Eades, R. Goodman, & Y. Hada (Eds.), *The "big bang" in Japanese higher education: The 2004 reforms and the dynamics of change.* Melbourne, Australia: Trans Pacific Press.

Yang, R., Vidovich, L., & Currie, J. (2007). "Dancing in a cage": Changing autonomy in Chinese higher education. *Higher Education, 54*(4), 575–592.

Zha, Q. (2009). Diversification or homogenization: How governments and markets have combined to (re)shape Chinese higher education in its recent massification process. *Higher Education, 58,* 41–58.

Zha, Q. (2011). China's move to mass higher education in a comparative perspective. *Compare: A Journal of Comparative and International Education, 41*(6), 751–768. doi.10.1080/03057925.2011.590316

CHAPTER 6

Academic Self-Governance
Concepts, Theories, and Practices

Academic self-governance refers to the internal governing mechanisms and bodies that shape the borders of authority and responsibility for academic activities within a university. It is associated with a collegial academic tradition in which the professoriate is granted authority and responsibility as individual professionals and through internal academic bodies such as senates, faculty boards, and curriculum committees. Since the professoriate plays such an integral role in academic self-governance, the processes involved in governing internally among faculty and the way in which these bodies relate to other governing bodies within the university are of critical importance to the overall governance of an institution. For example, the way in which an academic body such as the senate relates to executive management or a university's administration has an impact on the functioning of that university. How well governance is "shared" between these two pillars of the academy comes to the fore. The way in which students are allowed to participate in the governance process is also paramount. Just as important is the way in which these relationships are changing as universities position themselves to function in a knowledge-based economy and are expected to be market-driven and competitive entities.

Rowlands (2013) asserts that academic boards have "become key sites for the intersection between executive management and academia, and are, therefore, symbolic of the struggle between the multiple roles of universities as entrepreneurial businesses and places of intellectual endeavor" (p. 1274). Rowlands further points out that in the current environment in which universities are adopting—or have adopted—corporatized models, there is evidence that government and executive management are seeking to refashion the roles, functions, and composition of academic senates. This has implications for participation and collegiality in institutional governance. How well a university is functioning as a collegial institution is impacted by the level of participation by faculty. This view is in consonance with the assumption that faculty participation is a vital link in effective institutional decision-making (Birnbaum, 1988). It also holds true for the participation of students in the governance process, through, for example, student participation on university councils or academic boards.

This chapter examines and discusses academic self-governance. Specifically, it addresses concepts such as academic freedom, collegiality, tenure, and the functioning of academic governing bodies, along with their relationship to other governing bodies within institutions, student participation in institutional governance, and how these all come together to shape the university's internal governance. In addition, the chapter explores these various elements of academic self-governance within the context of broader global changes in higher education governance.

COLLEGIALITY

Collegiality has been the bedrock of university governance practice for centuries and has been touted as the vehicle of institutional effectiveness in the academy. It is a tradition that revolves around conferring, collaborating, and gaining consensus. It is also a collective process for decision-making in which academics play an integral role. An underlying assumption of collegiality is that conflict can be eliminated through consensus-based discussions (Baldridge, Curtis, Ecker, & Riley, 1978). Important therefore to collegiality are notions of professional equality and democratic engagement in which actors in the academy have a willingness to act with a sense of shared collective responsibility (Burnes, Wend, & By, 2014). However, it must be recognized though that democratic engagement and consensus-building are not the same across all universities (even in the same country), and that depending on institutional context, there are different practices of collegiality (Gaita, 1997). For example, Burnes et al. point out that in England different collegial practices exist as a result of the time period in which different universities were established, their intended purpose, and the institutions' underlying philosophies. For instance, there is a notable difference between the traditional Oxford and Cambridge universities and the newer Victorian civic universities. The former are more self-regulating communities of scholars and students who engage in learning for learning's sake while the Victorian civic universities were established as drivers of industrial development and heavily influenced by lay governing boards (Burnes et al., 2014). Nevertheless, collegial practices generally coalesce around a common set of themes which support a plurality of individuals' views in the decision-making process. It presumes a collectivist organization (Bess, 1998). Hence, universities have governing structures that bring together individuals from different units, departments, and faculties to engage in collective decision-making and policy development (for example, a university senate meeting or an academic board meeting).

Bess (1988) suggests that collegiality has three distinct components: culture or the normative framework, decision-making structure, and the process of behaving which is guided by the structure and culture. Culture in this sense relates to varying sets of beliefs about what is organizationally appropriate. Structure is about the formalization of rules for decision-making. Behavior is interpersonal and relates to governing individual actions and interactions which provide the basis on which faculty relate to one another and with administration (Bess, 1988). According to Bess, culture and decision-making structures are both relatively static but they impose constraints on the process of behaving, which is the dynamic component of collegiality.

Bess (1988) argues that there are two key beliefs that underlie how these three domains of collegiality function: the university itself (the depersonalized element) and its staff (the personalized element). A key element of the belief system of the university is the importance of rationality and order to the structure and process of deliberations and to university decision-making. Bess points out that this is a depersonalized view of a university's system of rules and relationships. It relates to individuals' satisfaction with the amount of information exchanged, the method employed to do so, and how well systems are structured to resolve disputation and foster engagements.

At the staff level, it is about trust among individuals and the belief that all staff are pursuing some common goal in a manner that strikes a balance between the achievement of individual and organizational goals. In addition, the functioning of collegiality at the staff level depends on the level of satisfaction with the importance assigned to issues of cooperation and competition (Bess, 1988). From this viewpoint, collegiality is more personalized and involves a belief in others.

Collegiality as Culture

In the academy, the collegial culture extends beyond any single university and incorporates the collective of professionals in the academy across institutions; this is based on the discipline-oriented approach to organizing academia (Clark, 1983). On one hand, this culture pertains to a set of values and beliefs within the academy that promotes the notion of participatory democracy and the right to be heard. On the other hand, it promotes a belief in professional courtesy that acknowledges that the right of participation must be sometimes yielded so that the rights of other professional peers are accommodated (Bess, 1988). This constitutes a fundamental social norm of reciprocity among peers. Bess believes that the collegial culture resides in both large and small universities in fairly similar ways, except that with smaller campuses the culture is one of consensus while with larger campuses it is democratic representative participation that serves as the guiding cultural principle.

One of the key cultural differences that can be found among systems and institutions relates to how peers and colleagues are defined; that is, who are the members of the collective that have the opportunity to engage in collegial processes? The hierarchical structure of academic positions and related cultural assumptions found in some systems, such as in the German tradition, suggest that only professors or holders of academic chairs are regarded as full members of the collective, and junior academic staff are largely excluded from collegial processes. Even in systems where there is a culture of inclusion and academics of all ranks are considered members of the collegium, such as in the United States and Canada, the focus has traditionally been on full-time academics. But how are contingent and part-time faculty defined for this purpose? Has there been a cultural shift on this matter? Should, for example, faculty teaching on short-term contracts, sometimes referred to as adjunct faculty, have a voice within the collegium? In short, there are important cultural differences in how the membership of the collegium is defined and understood (Locke, Cummings, & Fisher, 2011) and these definitions shape institutional collegiality.

The collegial culture also exists at the organizational level. How collegiality is practiced is a function of a university's cultural context, how concerned individuals are of building consensus as a way of organizational existence (Chaffee, 1983), or how equitably power is shared across departments and faculties (Bush, 1995). Burnes et al. (2014) suggest that in universities where there is inequitable distribution of power across units and departments, collegiality is limited and weaker compared to an environment in which the norm is for power to exist collectively among members and is expressed through a forum such as the senate. However, in a "hard" managerialist environment as is being observed in the current higher education ethos in some countries, power is concentrated more in the hands of a few senior managers and, as a result, traditional forms of collegiality are eroded. This has hampered the relationship between academics and senior managers within universities and has resulted in academics being disengaged from their corporate roles and governance involvement (Burnes et al., 2014; Deem, 2008). The exclusion of academics and others that were traditionally part of the decision-making process can negatively impact the quality of decision-making, organizational change initiatives, and job satisfaction (Bryman, 2007; MacFarlane, 2005). Evidence has emerged in support of this view; for example, the work of Bryman (2007) on UK, USA, and Australian universities and similar research conducted by Knight and Trowler (2000) on English and Canadian universities.

Collegiality as Structure

In a nutshell, structure in the academy represents the collection of academic units such as departments, faculties, institutes, centers, and so on and the way they are organized and coordinated. The structure of collegiality therefore refers to the way in which the various subdivisions are organized and regulated to facilitate institutional decision-making (Bess, 1988). Drawing on the work of Mintzberg, Bess contends that colleges and universities rely on the standardization of worker skills, mutual adjustment, and direct supervision as modes of coordination. Standardization of worker skills refers to a university's requirements for a prescribed set of homogeneous professional preparation standards expected of all faculty. Thus, a university may specify that all faculty must have a doctoral degree. Mutual adjustment is the coordination of work by the simple process of informal communications (Bess, 1988; Mintzberg, 1983). Direct supervision refers to the issuing of instructions by a "supervisor" and monitoring the work outcomes of supervisees through the use of a formal system of authority.

Bess (1988) argues that collegial structures in universities tend to have a recognizable pattern of authority as the basis for regulating their members and decision-making. But some decisions in universities flow through the informal structure and do not follow the formal collegial pathway. Also within the structure of collegiality are rules for the adjudication of disputes and sanctions for breaches of protocol. These kinds of decisions and many others generally follow a formal participative decision-making apparatus, and Bess argues that this is important in universities because it conveys the image of an institution that is both rational and trustworthy. Hence, the structure of collegiality defines participatory rights of members of the academy and reaffirms the values and beliefs in the system. In this regard, Bess suggests that the structure of collegiality is a manifestation of the culture of collegiality. In this sense, the culture of collegiality can be understood as "a nexus of beliefs and values embedded in the professional and corporate culture of an institution" and the structure of collegiality as "a framework for expressions of those beliefs and values" (Bess, 1988, p. 104).

In many countries, structures have been implemented to facilitate increased state regulation and a culture of marketization. These developments run counter to collegiality and are contributing to its decline. In other words, structures are viewed as fostering less of a framework that expresses values and beliefs in collegiality than was the case traditionally. However, Burnes et al. (2014) caution us against thinking that collegiality has totally disappeared from all universities or that there is an inherent desire among all university leaders to abolish it. But rather, in some cases, senior managers are caught in a dilemma of trying to achieve prescribed targets and outcomes while trying not to disenfranchise staff. In fact, while in some cases there is conflict and contestation between academics and senior management, there is still a strong collegial culture at the departmental level (Bryman, 2007; Currie, 1998).

Collegiality as Behavior

The behavior of collegiality refers to the ways in which faculty and administration in an institution conduct themselves in their respective roles within the context of the structure and culture of collegiality (Bess, 1988). As indicated earlier, both the structure and culture of collegiality shape behavior. Hence, within an institutional framework, faculty and administrators act out a range of behaviors either individually or collectively as they perform their various roles or engage in policymaking. Bess points out that collegiality as a behavior entails "the patterns of relationships and interactions among colleagues as they perform *[these roles]*" (p. 104). Therefore, in a university where collegiality is defined by a particular culture, Bess suggests that behavior would reflect the norms and values associated with the culture, including patterns of interactions among individuals. Behaviors would then reflect individuals' interpretations of the level of trust and rationality within an institution. Collegial behaviors would therefore be different across institutions depending on structural configurations and cultural practices.

ACADEMIC FREEDOM AND FACULTY AUTONOMY

Academic freedom is one of the philosophical cornerstones of the academy and one that has a long and contested history. It is central to the principle of free inquiry, which is key to the broader idea of a university as an institution of discovery. According to Altbach (2001) it is at the very core of the mission of the university and essential to teaching and learning. Academics generally agree on its importance and many have argued forcefully for its protection. There is evidence that regional and global institutions are also advocates of academic freedom. For example, in the European Union (EU), the Magna Charta Universitatum states that "*[f]*reedom in research and training is the fundamental principle of university life, and governments and universities, each as far as in them lies, must ensure respect for this fundamental requirement" (European Universities Association, 1988, p. 1). This statement is clearly reminiscent of the Humboldtian notion of academic freedom as important to teaching and research, and the very essence of the university.

Despite academic freedom being seen as fundamental to the work of academics, there is still no single definition that precisely captures this concept. Karran (2009) argues that the imprecision of the definition in part resides in the fact that the words "academic freedom" came out of a medieval intellectual tradition and the notion of freedom having a somewhat different conceptualization from modern usage. Hence, academic freedom can mean different things to different actors depending on their circumstances (Henkel, 2005). For instance, the way in which academic freedom is practiced in a secular university could be different from what obtains in a religious university. Academic freedom is also practiced differently in different parts of the world or at different universities, depending on the traditions to which they adhere. Stated differently, the meaning and institutionalization of academic freedom varies widely (Henkel, 2007). It is impacted by variations in the way that universities engage in teaching and research within institutions, and also by different policy approaches between universities and among nation-states (Karran, 2009).

Van Alstyne (1972) defines academic freedom as:

> a set of vocational liberties: to teach, to investigate, to do research, and to publish on any subject as a matter of professional interest, without vocational jeopardy or threat of other sanction, save only upon adequate demonstration of an inexcusable breach of professional ethics in the exercise of any of them.
>
> (p. 146)

Van Alstyne (1975) further indicates that the liberty to pursue one's vocation in an academic institution is personal. However, it is not an absolute freedom but one that is circumscribed by standards of professional integrity and guided by protocols of academic inquiry. Berdahl (1990) views academic freedom as the "freedom of the individual scholar in his/her teaching and research to pursue truth wherever it seems to lead without fear of punishment or termination of employment for having offended some political, religious or social orthodoxy" (pp. 171–172). This definition too conveys an individualistic conceptualization of academic freedom. This is important, since academic freedom is sometimes conflated with autonomy.

Berdahl draws an important distinction between academic freedom and institutional autonomy. He sees autonomy as institutional and related to universities having "power to govern without outside controls" (1990, p. 171), whereas academic freedom relates to the individual and the conduct of his or her research and teaching, without fear of sanction and reprisals, thereby fulfilling the social role of academic discovery and knowledge advancement. Henkel (2007) sheds further light on this by pointing out that individual academic freedom and university autonomy are distinct but connected ideas within the broader notion of academic autonomy; university autonomy being the right to institutional self-governance which may be enshrined in the granting of an institutional charter. This duality is a feature of Anglo-Saxon universities, whereas it is absent in the Humboldtian system since academic freedom of professors and chair-holders is protected by the state, given that they are civil servants and not employees of the universities (Henkel, 2007).

In the USA, academic freedom is sometimes expressed as a free speech issue and a First Amendment right. As a result, there is both a professional and constitutional definition of academic freedom. These definitions were framed in response to threats to professors from university trustees and threats to universities from the state (Rabban, 1990). On one hand, the American Association of University Professors (AAUP) focused attention on the protection of individual professors against lay trustees and framed academic freedom as a professional value important to critical inquiry in universities. This served to shape the governing relationship between academics and governing boards or trustees. On the other hand, the Supreme Court emphasized the constitutional protection of the entire university community against state intervention and defined academic freedom as an individual right of professors as well as an institutional right of universities (Rabban, 1990). Rabban argues that First Amendment values such as critical inquiry, the search for knowledge, and tolerance of dissent "justify protecting both the professional speech of faculty and the autonomy of universities to make decisions about educational policy" (p. 230). This conceptualization has to some extent shaped the state-university governing relationship in the USA. It is supported by the AAUP, which sees institutional academic freedom from the state as a necessary condition for the academic freedom of faculty. This perception has evolved somewhat among university administrators, who now view institutional academic freedom "not as an additional layer of protection for professors against the state, but as a bar to judicial review of claims against universities by professors alleging institutional violations of individual academic freedom" (Rabban, 1990, p. 229). Hence, although academic freedom is primarily individualistic, there is some consideration of academic freedom at the institutional level. Through court decisions, universities use constitutional protections to guard against state interference, but at the same time universities may use the same protections against claims from faculty of academic freedom violations.

Drawing on Polanyi's (1962) *Republic of Science*, Henkel (2007) locates the larger concept of academic autonomy within the definition of knowledge, beliefs about how it is produced, and the associated modes of governance. Thus, academic freedom is not just freedom from state interference but also the freedom of the individual to engage in scholarly research and knowledge creation (Akerlind & Kayrooz, 2003). This requires institutional policies or legal and constitutional frameworks to protect individual freedoms. This would suggest that a university should function as "a bounded territory, separate from other sectors of society, where autonomy means something close to sovereignty" (Henkel, p. 89) in order to ensure the protection of academic freedom.

While there are many countries in which academic freedom is still alive and well, history is replete with examples of countries that have circumscribed the scope of academic freedom or significantly limited it. For example, some countries have restrictions on what can be researched. Thus, critical to academic freedom is the ability of the academic organization to provide enabling opportunities and support for scholarly activities (Herbert & Tienari, 2013), although a university's ability to create unencumbered pathways for free scholarly expression is sometimes hamstrung by larger nation-state macropolicies. Some countries, for instance, are theocracies where certain questions cannot be asked and certain assumptions cannot be challenged. In these cases, universities lack the "institutional sovereignty" to protect academic freedom.

One institutional enabler of academic freedom is tenure. We will discuss tenure in more detail later in the chapter, but suffice it to note at this point that tenure provides job security to academic peers and provides a mechanism to protect scholars and their work (DeGeorge, 2003). In other words, tenure is an institutional protection of academic freedom. An attack on or a weakening of tenure could imply a weakening of academic freedom. Tenure as a basis of employment has been challenged and its value contested in some countries, for example the United States (Chait, 2002; Herbert & Tienari, 2013), and eliminated in others, such as the United Kingdom. Nevertheless, tenure remains an important element of academia and academic practices in many jurisdictions, and is a pillar for academic freedom.

With the increasing influence of managerialism and new public management (NPM) on higher education, there has been a rise in the use of limited-term contracts and other categories of nonpermanent faculty in some countries. This has implications not only for free scholarly expression but also for participation in governing bodies within universities, particularly given that faculty representation on academic boards and senates is frequently limited to full-time faculty.

Academic Freedom and New Public Management

In Europe, the prevalence of NPM and managerialism have brought about some challenges to academic freedom. Tierney and Lechuga (2010) contend that academic freedom has deteriorated as universities engage in managerialism and import private sector practices into the academy. Marginson (2008) examines academic freedom within the context of new public management and the way it is impacting the academy. Marginson uses the concept of "self-determination" to express the freedom of academics to initiate and control their work. Self-determination means that the research and scholarly activities in a university are conceived, directed, and executed by scholars and researchers themselves. Marginson locates this discussion within the notion of *radical-creative imagination* in which he sees self-determination as essential to academic creativity. However, he acknowledges that the self-determining freedom of researchers and scholars is subject to internal and external conditions such as laws and regulations, modes of governing and managing, administrative and financial systems, publishing requirements, and academic hierarchies.

To develop a more robust explanation of the impact of NPM on academic freedom, Marginson (2008) draws on the work of Sen (1985) on the constituent parts of freedom. Marginson believes that such an approach would produce a more fine-grained analysis that interrogates academic freedom and NPM beyond polemics and broad assertions about their incompatibility. Marginson examines the concept of freedom by focusing on notions of agency freedom, freedom as power, freedom as control, and freedom as the capacity for a radical-critical break. Agency freedom relates to the independence of an individual, with an identity and a will, to determine and implement what he or she would do in conformity with their conceptualization of "good." This is the freedom of an academic, who as an agent of a university, is self-determining, self-conscious, and self-producing. Since these qualities are central to innovation, an academic may choose a less financially rewarding university academic job which allows freedom to pursue his or her work preference (Herbert & Tienari, 2013). Freedom as power is about freedom from constraints. Thus, individuals are not restricted in either their power or capacity to select and determine the outcomes of their activities (Herbert & Tienari, 2013). Faculty control their work (Henkel, 2005). Freedom as control is about freedom from coercion and the ability to choose how particular outcomes are achieved (Herbert & Tienari, 2013; Marginson, 2008). Freedom as the capacity for a radical-critical break is "the availability of possibilities to create previously unimagined 'new' knowledge" (Herbert & Tienari, 2013, p. 159).

Marginson (2008) explains that as universities embrace NPM as a mode of governing and managing, the changes associated with it are imposed on academics and represent a violation of freedom from coercion. In other words, freedom as control is reduced. In the case of agency freedom, NPM, with its emphasis on competition, may cause a researcher to adjust his/her work to fit the requirements for available funding. Hence, although an academic/agent conceptualizes a research project, he/she loses some agency freedom as a result of market signals. Agency freedom could also be reduced when accountability requirements are imposed on faculty, for example, quality assurance requirements. Marginson suggests that NPM shifts the locus of control away from the academic agent and has the potential to limit radical-creative imaginations but may enhance radical-creative work that is controlled by external agents. NPM tends to be a top-down management approach in which the chief executive has strong controls. Taylor (2013) suggests though that "academic freedom is an integral part of generating academic success that cannot be commanded from the top down but must be nurtured from the bottom up" (p. 85). In the current NPM and managerialism environment, there is a reduction in academic freedom and, according to Marginson, this may negatively impact creativity in the academy and the radical breakthroughs that are germane to knowledge creation.

ROLE AND FUNCTION OF SENATES AND ACADEMIC BOARDS

We use the term "senate" to refer to the senior academic decision-making body of a university, recognizing that different terms are used in different jurisdictions and institutions. A university senate is a formal forum for academic decision-making, a venue of internal self-governance, and the main body through which faculty participate in institutional governance (Melear, 2013; Minor, 2004). In essence, the senate is a governing body. As such, it is defined by an institution's constitution and bylaws that are linked somewhat to its history and culture (Johnston, 2003). There may be major differences in the legal foundation of the senate; in some cases the senate is created and assigned a formal role in governance under the statute or institution-specific legislation that established the university (Jones, Sanan, & Goyan, 2004), while in other cases the senate has been created inside and under the authority of the university and its board, and its role and function are entirely shaped by decisions that have taken place within the internal governance structures of the university.

In large universities, the senate is usually a representative body, while at small universities its membership may include all faculty. In some instances, it is composed of faculty only, while in other cases it is composed of a wider group of stakeholders. Birnbaum (1991) used the terms "pure" and "mixed" to describe these differences in composition. A "pure" senate, therefore, is composed entirely of faculty, while a "mixed" senate consists of faculty, often holding the majority of seats, along with other campus constituencies such as administrators and/or students. In the latter sense, Melear describes it as the primary vehicle through which members of the professoriate join with administrators to discuss academic issues. This in essence captures the composition and role of a mixed senate. Whether it is mixed or pure, a university senate's primary responsibility is academic and it concerns itself mainly with academic affairs. For example, at The University of the West Indies, the statutes and ordinances state that, "The Senate shall be the academic authority for the University and shall have the control and general direction of research, instruction and examinations and of the award of Degrees, Diplomas, Certificates and other distinctions" and shall have powers "[t]o determine the academic policy of the University and to advise the [University] Council on the provision of facilities to implement that policy" (University of the West Indies, 2010, p. 36).

Birnbaum (1991) breaks down the role of the senate into four organizational frames: bureaucratic, collegial, political, and symbolic. These were further categorized into manifest and latent functions. The manifest functions and outcomes are considered planned and intended while latent functions and outcomes are unplanned and unintended. The bureaucratic, collegial, and political aspects of the senate are considered as manifest functions. The symbolic function is considered as latent. The senate is viewed as bureaucratic because of its decision-making, goal-setting, resource allocation, and evaluation activities. Birnbaum argues that the way in which these activities are undertaken in a senate is indicative of a hierarchical, rational organization where formal policies, rules, regulations, and procedures are developed through a rational process to address institutional problems. This is typical of a bureaucratic setting. The senate is therefore portrayed as an academic management board (Jones et al., 2004). It is collegial in the sense that it is a forum for consensus-building among faculty on institutional matters, particularly academic in nature, and a venue that fosters shared understanding. As a political system, "the senate is seen as a forum for the articulation of interests and as the setting in which decisions on institutional policies and goals are reached through compromise, negotiation, and the formation of coalitions" (Birnbaum, 1991, p. 11). Leadership in the political frame is exercised by mediation and strategy, rather than by the exercise of formal authority (Jones et al., 2004). These are all manifest functions, and usually critics of the senate contend that these functions are not fulfilled properly.

Birnbaum (1991) argues that since the manifest functions are not being properly fulfilled, then the persistence of the senate as a governing body would suggest that there are latent functions that are being fulfilled. These are symbolic functions. In this regard, the senate is analyzed as a symbol, a status provider, a garbage can and deep freeze (organizational storage of solutions and problems), an attention cue, a personnel screening device, an organizational conservator, as a ritual and a pastime, and as a scapegoat. These symbolic descriptions suggest that the senate is a cultural forum within the academy where people interact and try to construct and understand their reality, share meaning, and engage in sense making, sometimes at the expense of decision-making.

Minor (2004) presents four models of a senate in relation to the faculty: functional, influential, ceremonial, and subverted. The senate is functional in the sense that it operates "to represent and protect the interest of faculty in university decision-making" (p. 349). It serves as a safeguard of faculty rights from transgressive actions of administration and as a check and balance on administrative authority. Key functional areas are curriculum, promotion, tenure, and academic standards. The senate also plays an advisory role to administration by making recommendations. Minor argues that the senate is sometimes perfunctory in terms of the scope of its authority because in some cases, authority over some academic matters resides with the governing board, trustee, or council. Some of the work associated with the functional responsibilities of a senate is carried out by committees. For example, at the University of the West Indies, the statutes and ordinances state in part that the academic board is a "standing committee of the Senate" and has "such powers as may be delegated by the Senate" (p. 39).

An influential senate usually derives its authority from an institutional cultural tradition and is the locus of legitimate faculty power and authority. It influences academic and nonacademic decisions. Hence, the senate influences decisions that affect the entire university and views itself as a body with an institution-wide responsibility for quality and the institution's overall functioning. In some universities the senate plays an important role in establishing the future direction of the university through the institutional planning process or influencing resource allocation decisions through the budget process—its scope of authority may extend well beyond a narrow definition of what is "academic" (Pennock, Jones, Leclerc, & Li, 2015). The influence of the senate is rooted in its legitimacy as a bona fide governing body.

The senate is ceremonial to the extent that it relies on symbolism. Ceremonial senates are not usually involved in academic issues, and decision-making on academic matters rests with individual schools and colleges. This accords with Birnbaum's (1991) latent function description of the senate's role.

Subverted senates have formal proceedings, but the informal channels of faculty engagement are more effective in decision-making. This could significantly weaken the formal senate, especially in cases where the administration consults on faculty matters through another appointed committee. Subverted senates are seen as obstacles and can have a negative image and the appearance of not adding value to a university's welfare.

The Changing Higher Education Environment and the Senate

As stated previously, the practice of higher education worldwide has undergone significant changes in the last two decades. Governance practices too have changed. These changes have impacted the role and function of the senate. Rowlands (2013) argues that there has been a shift in the balance of power in favor of the governing board, resulting from universities shifting focus towards creating a more managed enterprise focusing on financial viability, efficiency, effectiveness, and public accountability. Collegial interaction at venues such as the senate has declined somewhat because of the refocusing of university governance towards a more streamlined management-led decision-making model (Bleiklie & Kogan, 2007; Rowlands, 2013). Taylor points out that in the UK, for example, prior to the 1980s, academic power was de jure and de facto invested in the senate, but power shifted during the 1980s towards university councils. According to Shattock (2003),

> the shift towards investing power in the university governing body was seen as closer to the board structure of a private company, with the chair of the council mirroring the chairman of the board of a private corporation and the vice-chancellor as the chief executive officer, even though there are fundamental differences between a company board and a university governing board.
>
> (pp. 47–48, quoted in Taylor, 2013)

This view captures the managerial and corporate-like reframing of internal university governance and is associated with the touted notion of having some degree of tension between senate and governing board and shifting the balance of power towards the governing board and university administration (Taylor, 2013). With reference to Australian academic boards or senates, Rowland (2013) concludes that the diminution of the role, power, and status of the senate relative to executive management has caused senates to have symbolic power rather than real power.

GOVERNING AUTHORITY AND THE FIDUCIARY RESPONSIBILITY OF THE BOARD OF TRUSTEES

Many universities have some form of governing body at their strategic apex, usually referred to as a council, the board of trustees, or a governing board (board of governors). They vary in nomenclature and function from country to country and, in some cases, from state to state or institution to institution within a single country (e.g., USA) or depending on the types of higher education institutions within a country. For example, the UK uses names such as boards of governors, councils, and courts. In a sense, this makes it difficult to define these entities (de Boer, Huisman, & Meister-Scheytt, 2010). Nevertheless, de Boer et al. use a simple but instructive definition for governing boards as "a governance body that supervises and/or controls the executive management of a higher education institution" (pp. 317–318). Importantly, these bodies have both strategic and supervisory functions and have many similarities to a board of directors in the corporate setting. In fact, de Boer et al. use the term "supervisory boards" to describe governing boards. Meister-Scheytt (2007) highlights the importance of governing boards' supervisory competencies, their far-reaching decision-making consequences, and their relationship to universities' leadership and senates as fundamental to universities' strategic development.

In American universities, governing boards are really lay governing boards that are in some states elected by private citizens while in others appointed by the governor (Kezar, 2006). This is not always the case in other jurisdictions. In many countries, the council or governing board has a combination of internal stakeholders (in most cases academics and sometimes students) and external lay individuals. They have the ultimate authority to make key decisions and policy, have a fiduciary responsibility, and also have an accountability/oversight function (Birnbaum, 1988; Kezar, 2006). Fiduciary responsibility here refers to board members being diligent in their duty to protect the integrity of a university (Hendrickson, Lane, Harris, & Dorman, 2013). The decision-making scope at some institutions includes hiring and evaluating the president of the university, and ensuring the university's mission is fulfilled. They therefore have a very important function, particularly given the emphasis on institutional entrepreneurship in universities, strategic decision-making, and the expectation that the board can be trusted to make quality, ethical decisions in the best interest of the institution and external stakeholders (Kezar, 2006).

In some other jurisdictions the scope of authority of the board is far more limited. There are many universities where there is a long tradition of electing a professor as president or rector. Candidates are nominated, they campaign for office, and decisions are made by a formal election involving a vote by the faculty (and sometimes representatives of students, staff, and other constituencies). Clearly the role of the governing board becomes very different in an environment where the senior officer of the institution is chosen by the major constituencies within the university rather than by the board itself. In other jurisdictions, the state continues to play a major role in the ongoing operations of the university, and the board is assigned a more limited scope of authority.

Although governing boards of some sort have become an important part of the higher education landscape in many countries, there is still a limited amount of theoretical research on their role and activities, although there have been descriptive analyses on, for example, board structure and composition. Some higher education scholars (e.g., Ehrenberg, 2004; Hermalin, 2004; Kezar, 2006) have suggested drawing on the corporate literature to understand higher education boards. From the corporate literature, Mintzberg (1983) proposes seven major roles of governing boards and Hung (1998) applies six different schools of thought. This combination provides a holistic picture needed to understand governing boards. The seven major roles Mintzberg identifies are:

- Selecting the chief executive officer (in higher education this would be the president, vice-chancellor, or rector)
- Undertaking direct control during periods of crisis
- Reviewing managerial decisions and performance
- Co-opting external influences
- Establishing contacts for the organization
- Enhancing the organization's reputation
- Giving advice to the organization

The schools of thought that are frequently used to analyze the work of boards are:

- Resource-dependency theory
- Stakeholder theory
- Agency theory
- Stewardship theory
- Institutional theory
- Managerial hegemony

With the exception of managerial hegemony, these theories were previously covered in chapter two. However, we revisit them briefly here to show how they help us understand governing boards.

Resource-dependence theory emphasizes an organization's interdependence with its environment for critical resources, including those from other organizations and stakeholders. Because governing boards are usually lay boards whose membership comes from the wider environment, they serve as a bridge between, for example, a university and its environment. Board members establish links to resources and build social relations with influential actors in the wider community to facilitate access to resources. By having these ties established with the external environment, a university could access significant grant funds, philanthropic contributions from organizations or individuals, and enhance its legitimacy. The governing board can also co-opt threats in the environment such as regulatory agencies (Ornstein, 1984).

Stakeholder theory assumes that an organization has multiple stakeholders in its external environment to whom it has to respond and to whom it is responsible. Whether individuals or groups, these stakeholders can help or hurt the organization because they have multiple and sometimes conflicting interests. The role of the governing board, from a stakeholder theory perspective, is to negotiate, bargain, and compromise with these stakeholders in the interests of the organization (Hung, 1998). A university's governing board would therefore be expected to think not only about the internal functioning of the institution but also about the interests of the university's wider external constituencies and make decisions and implement policies with these groups in mind.

Agency theory is about reducing agent opportunism; that is, it is about governance mechanisms to prevent agents from taking self-interested actions that are not in the best interests of the organization. Hence, governance is captured by the principal-agent relationship, and the role of the governing board is to ensure managerial compliance by agents. The governing board of a university would establish some level of control to ensure that internal stakeholders, such as administrators and professors, are acting in the best interest of the state and other external parties.

Stewardship theory assumes that managers want to do a good job and be effective stewards of the organization's resources. Governing boards work collaboratively with managers to pursue the same strategic outcome. In this regard, a university's governing board would guide management to achieve the institution's mission and objectives, review strategies that have been formulated by management, and participate actively in analyzing and articulating strategic plans, proposals, and suggestions (Hung, 1998).

Institutional theory asserts that organizations are constrained by social rules and follow taken-for-granted conventions that impact how they manage organizational affairs (Ingram & Simons, 1995). Ingram and Simons (1995) describe this function of a governing board as the maintenance role whereby the board seeks to maintain the status quo of the organization. One of the important functions of the board, according to this theory, is to analyze and understand the external environment and the institutional pressure faced by an organization, for example, a university. Thus, a university's governing board would attend to all social rules and requirements the institution is expected to follow and be in conformance with if it is to receive support and legitimacy (Scott, 2008).

Managerial hegemony refers to "the situation when the governing board of an organization serves simply as a "rubber stamp" and all its strategic decisions are dominated and preempted by professional managers" (Hung, 1998, p. 107). According to this perspective, organizations tend to resist involvement of governing boards in strategic decisions. The review function of the board is merely superficial and effective performance or organizational evaluations are only done during crisis periods (Clendenin, 1972; Hung, 1998). In this regard, the function of the university governing board is largely ceremonial in order to satisfy legal and statutory requirements. In many of these cases the governing boards rely heavily on information supplied by university administration to make decisions because they do not have the requisite information needed for effective decision-making (Hung, 1998).

The relationship between governing boards and university administration can sometimes be strained. Boards have been criticized for overstepping their authority and threatening shared governance, sometimes micromanaging, and on other occasions engaging in divisive politics (Kezar, 2006). Recently, the performance and effectiveness of these governing boards has been receiving more attention. Some paint a grim picture of their performance. In the USA, some boards have been described as activist (Bastedo, 2005). They are, however, central to a university's strategic direction and advancement, and improving their effectiveness becomes paramount. Baird (2006) argues that effective boards are expected to nurture a respectful "climate of trust" that permits challenge and dissent. This view pertains to building a performance culture that is based on good human relations within the board and among the various branches of the university.

SHARED GOVERNANCE

The term shared governance resonates differently in different countries, and in some jurisdictions the phrase is not used at all. It is a conceptualization of governance that is often viewed as unique to university environments (Hirsch, 2001). In the US, shared governance refers to a tripartite arrangement among three major stakeholders—governing boards, administration, and faculty. It may be considered as a type of shared authority and an institutional commitment to democratic ideals. Through shared governance, a university "assigns specific rights and responsibilities to its three stakeholders . . . [which] provides for a separation of powers, and establishes a structure and process for stakeholders to interact in specific undertakings" (Hirsch, 2001, p. 147). Birnbaum (2004) describes governance as the "structures and processes that academic institutions invent to achieve an effective balance between the claims of two different, but equally valid, systems for organizational control and influence" (p. 5). One system of control and influence comes from the legal authority granted to the institution which resides with governing boards/trustees and university administration. The other system is faculty-driven and revolves around faculty academic "sovereignty" and professional authority. This dual system conceptualization describes a bicameral system of governance that is also the standard model found in many UK universities. It is within this context, as expressed by Birnbaum, that there is a sharing of governing authority and it is the basis of shared governance. The two major parts of the system come together for consultation and decision-making purposes in order for an institution to function. Consultation, deliberation, and compromise are three essential elements of shared governance.

The AAUP (American Association of University Professors) advocates a shared governance model in which administrators, faculty, and trustees have shared but unequal decision-making responsibility. Shared governance therefore acknowledges a division of authority and decision-making responsibility based on distinctive expertise and a bilateral division of labor (Rhoades, 2005). Pertinent to this shared interaction is respect for the authority of each group's domain of expertise. For instance, the senate would be respected as the authority on academic matters.

The ways in which power is shared within the university vary considerably by jurisdiction. In most Canadian universities, for example, both the governing board and the senate are assigned specific areas of responsibility and executive authority under the institution's act of incorporation, and so the sharing of governance authority is legislated. In addition, universities have established their own internal mechanisms to delimit the respective responsibilities of the board, senate, and administration (Jones, 2002).

The shared approach to governing has been criticized for having extensive debate and discussion resulting in slow decision-making, not responding to the external environment in a timely fashion, and being ill-suited to making hard decisions when necessary. Birnbaum (2004) argues that these criticisms tend to focus on the faculty side of the system and the radical changes needed there but they do not challenge the roles of trustees and administrators in the process. Birnbaum makes a case for quality decision-making that results from thorough discussion and a ventilation of all the issues as opposed to a speedier system of decision-making that increases the risk of making costly mistakes.

Managerialism, new public management, and academic capitalism are all conceptualizations of the context within which contemporary higher education institutions conduct their affairs. The cultural context of these approaches to the governance of higher education institutions emphasizes revenue generation by academic institutions and efficiency, effectiveness, and economy in their management (Deem, Hillyard, & Reed, 2007; Slaughter & Rhoades, 2004). In the United States these approaches have given rise to strengthening the governance role of central academic managers vis-à-vis the faculty, an increase in contingent faculty and nonfaculty professionals, and a decrease in full-time and tenure-track professors (Rhoades, 2005). In search of a stronger voice in the decision-making process, many faculty in some countries have turned to unionization, a phenomenon that we will discuss later in the chapter.

In addition, academic managers have created mechanisms, such as centers and institutes which are governed outside of regular departments and faculties, ostensibly to respond with more alacrity to markets. Rhoades (2005) argues that these new modes challenge the traditional shared governance model by reducing the role of faculty governance, restructuring professional employment of faculty, and creating managed professionals over whom administration has more control. Rhoades further points out that in this process traditional structures of faculty governance, such as the senate, are not dismantled, but new ones are created that supersede existing structures and allow managerial professionals to govern outside of shared governance procedures.

In the UK, similar trends have been observed, with many of the changes occurring during and after the Thatcher years. The challenges to shared governance that arose were the result of Prime Minister Thatcher's advocacy for adopting the new public management ideology, with its attendant beliefs in the optimality of market solutions and the supremacy of a private sector form of governance (Taylor, 2013). Taylor indicates that, excluding the ancient UK universities, university councils were legislatively granted lay corporate responsibility for pre-1992 institutions, a development that weakened the senate by exclusion, although statutes and charters still described the senate as the supreme academic body. However, this policy approach essentially strengthened governing boards/councils. These bodies were further strengthened by the 1992 Higher Education Act that established a unicameral system in post-1992 universities, in which small governing boards have full authority and the academic body has been weakened.

Taylor (2013) advocates for a shared governance model in which there is closer consultation, engagement, and collaboration between the academic body and the governing body. Taylor describes the senate and council as conjoined by a committee structure and coordinated by the executive. Taylor believes that in such a model the precise duties of each body should remain vague and a culture should be developed that is based on tone and mutual respect between the academic and governing bodies. Interactions between these two bodies should occur within a spirit of mutual cooperation. The vice-chancellor or president, who occupies the executive office, serves as a mediator between the academic and governing bodies but with each body retaining ultimate authority over their respective domains. In this sense, the governing body has ultimate accountability for the administration, financial management, institutional viability, and strategy, and the senate has accountability for academic matters. However, the exercise of authority in respective domains by the two bodies should be based on mutual cooperation rather than official supremacy vested in them.

FACULTY UNIONIZATION

In some countries, for example the United States and Canada, unionization in the academy is on the rise—both for faculty and graduate students. For instance, in the United States 27% of all faculty and one fifth of graduate student employees are represented by collective bargaining agreements (Berry & Savarese, 2012). Bucklew, Houghton, and Ellison (2013) point out that this trend towards faculty unionization began in the late 1960s as a movement representing faculty issues and concerns such as salaries increases. In Canada, higher education is one of the most heavily unionized of all sectors, and the vast majority of faculty are members of recognized institution-based trade unions. In addition, sessional/adjunct faculty, teaching assistants, research assistants, support staff, and many other categories of workers may be members of separate labor unions at the same university (Jones, 2013). In some other countries, faculty are technically employees of government, and therefore subject to the conditions of work associated with civil servants. Thus, negotiations concerning the conditions of work for university faculty take place at the national or system level, rather than at the level of the individual institution. In the discussion that follows we focus on governance and faculty unionization at the institutional level.

Despite the enthusiasm engendered by the representation faculty unions provide, there continues to be some skepticism about unionization's fit within the university governance structure, specifically, the possible negative impact it would have on the system of self-governance and the role of the senate (Duryea & Fisk, 1973). Some feel that faculty unions effectively replace faculty senates or at least limit their influence, are instrumental in shaping institutional policy, and will lead to a refashioning of the faculty appointment process from peer review to automatic tenure and promotion (Bucklew et al., 2013; Yellowitz, 1987). Still others believe that unionization creates a climate of distrust between faculty and administration and engenders an adversarial relationship between the two constituencies, damages collegiality, and limits professional autonomy (Bucklew et al., 2013; Mintzberg, 1983). On the other hand, contemporary observers argue that unionization protects the freedom and autonomy of faculty, protects faculty members' due process rights in grievance procedures, and safeguards faculties' cherished rights to research and publish their findings (Bess & Dee, 2008).

While there have been positive and negative views about unionization in the academy, the reality is that it exists in many institutions and national contexts. The most critical issue therefore is the way in which it works with traditional internal government systems, such as the faculty senate. With regard to traditional faculty governance processes, Bucklew et al. (2013) contend that a symbiotic dual-track approach to governance is required where traditional labor issues—wages, benefits, working conditions, etc.—are the purview of the union, while the senate retains control over academic issues. However, Bucklew et al. acknowledge that this symbiotic relationship may sometimes be challenging, particularly in instances when the union encroaches on the territorial domain of the senate. In so doing, the senate's role is usually diminished (DeCew, 2002). Thus, governing becomes a delicate balancing act between the traditional collegial faculty governance and the faculty union.

Administrators frequently view unions and collective bargaining as a hindrance to problem solving in a shared governance environment (Benjamin, 2009). They argue that faculty unionization effectively supplants the academic and collegial shared governance model with a corporate and confrontational labor-management model (Lyne, 2011). But Rhoades (2011) points out that the primary driving force behind unionization in public research universities in the United States, for instance, is the view held by tenured and tenure-track faculty of their diminishing voice in shaping the direction of the academy. In fact, many faculty members believe that shared governance has waned and administrators have become arbitrary, autocratic, and more top-down (Rhoades, 2011). In such instances, faculty prefer governance by negotiated contractual obligations in which the union plays a key role rather than by relying on the faculty handbook that is sometimes overlooked by deans and administration. Nevertheless, the role of unions and collective bargaining in university governance is not uniform across institutions and practices vary. Where faculty unionization exists, it is an important element of the governance process, particularly in relation to the employment process.

STUDENTS AND INSTITUTIONAL GOVERNANCE

There is considerable consensus about the importance of student involvement in the governance and functioning of universities (Planas, Soler, Fullana, Pallisera, & Vila, 2013). In most universities, formal student organizations and associations represent students' collective interest and protect their welfare (Klemenčič, 2012). These organizations have varying nomenclature depending on the jurisdiction or the university but typically they are referred to as student unions, councils, parliaments, boards, guilds, or associations. They are collectively known as student government and represent a way of governing the student body itself through a system of rules, norms, and institutional practices (Klemenčič, 2014). Klemenčič (2014) further indicates that student governments provide a framework through which broader organized interactions occur between students and their universities and to varying degrees they participate in university decision-making on behalf of their constituencies. Thus, students participate in university governance, decision-making, and policy-making through their representative bodies. However, students are sometimes involved in university governance independent of the student government, for example, course and program representatives within a faculty or department.

The role that students play in university governance is to some extent shaped by the type of university and its traditions, the extent to which contemporary managerial forces are influencing an institution, and the way in which students are perceived by a university. According to Rochford (2014), the nature of the relationships between universities and student organizations vary according to legislative, historical, organizational, and cultural factors. How effective students are in the governance process is determined to some extent by their willingness to participate and their commitment to the mission of the university and its long-term interest.

Students' participation in institutional governance is also central to student engagement (Trowler, 2010). Such participation may be manifested in different ways (for example, through formal mechanisms for student representation in course and programming matters, curriculum development, quality assurance, and strategic decision-making). Trowler cautions against tokenistic gestures of participation in which students are consulted after decisions have been made as opposed to having a genuine participative and authoritative voice in institutional governance. This is consistent with the notion that universities and students are partners in the collective experiences of teaching, learning, research, and knowledge development and application. It is also consistent with the view that active participation of students in decision-making on matters that affect their education enhances the quality of the educational product offered by a university (Menon, 2005). Such an approach serves to shape the relationship between the institution and its students by creating an atmosphere of openness and trust, and a positive organizational climate (Menon, 2005).

The nature of student involvement and participation in institutional governance and decision-making are significantly determined by the institution's conception of its students and the definition of its student-university relationship. For example, in some universities students are perceived as co-producers while in others they are perceived as consumers. When an institution defines its students as co-producers, the model of governance is more cooperative and egalitarian and invokes notions of students as stakeholders with a strong sense of institutional ownership (Carey, 2013; Luescher-Mamashela, 2010). With the consumerist conception, students are viewed as clients and participate in governance as service-users. A number of arguments have been advanced—based on political-realism, consumerism, communitarianism, democracy, and consequentialism—for the inclusion of students in institutional governance.

Political-realism: This argument advances the notion of students as internal stakeholders and a politically significant constituency of the university that should participate in its governance (Luescher-Mamashela, 2013). The subtext of this argument lies in the idea of a university as an institution of competing internal stakeholders whose voices must be heard and not just a single group dominated by the professoriate (Olsen, 2007). In other words, the university should function as a representative democracy. Political-realism also highlights the disruptive power of university students as has been demonstrated on occasions in the form of, for example, student protests. The co-optation of students into institutional decision-making can serve as a means of minimizing radical impulses and moderating student activism (Thompson, 1972).

Despite widespread acceptance of student participation in institutional governance, there have been opponents to the inclusion of students as committee members. They argue that including students in the governance process in this way hampers the consensual culture of a university's governance by formalizing the permanent participation of an adversarial group (Luescher-Mamashela, 2013; Moodie & Eustace, 1974). Opponents also questioned the significance of including students in a governance system that is dominated and controlled by a university faculty and administration if the student participation is simply for token reasons (Mason, 1978).

Consumerism: As market models become more entrenched in the higher education discourse, students are being referred to more and more as clients and consumers. This essentially is the re-conceptualization of students from what is advocated by political-realism and it emphasizes the political economy of the student-university relationship (Luescher-Mamashela, 2013). Students are now seen as a special kind of consumer, or client, in a contractual relationship with a unique type of service provider, the university (Bergan, 2004; Boland, 2005). The arguments for including students as consumers in university governance point to students having rights to representation in order to safeguard their interests. Bergan contends that student interests extend beyond short-term pricing concerns and include their long-term interests in service quality.

Communitarianism: The communitarian view of students' involvement in university decision-making and governance is based on the role and status of students as members of an institutional collectivity. There should be shared authority and interdependent responsibility between students and other university internal stakeholders. In other words, students are members of a university community involved in a cooperative enterprise of knowledge coproduction (McCulloch, 2009). Because of this collective experience in which students and the university are seen as combining resources and both having a stake in the educational process, the communitarian view argues for equal voice and authority for students through the governance process (Luescher-Mamashela, 2013). Opponents of this view challenge it on the basis of students being transient members of the community, not deeply committed to its mission, and having limited knowledge and experience compared to other members of the community (Moodie & Eustace, 1974; Zuo & Ratsoy, 1999).

Democracy and consequentialism: This perspective of students' involvement in institutional governance is driven by the idea of universities playing a major role in advancing citizenship and democracy. In democratic societies universities are sites of democratic values and students' involvement in institutional governance and decision-making provides venues for students to engage with and practice these values (Boland, 2005). Hence, public universities are seen as instruments of democratic socialization and their governance as having a culture that is compatible with societal democratic values and practices (Bleiklie, 2001). Other benefits to be derived from students' participation in a university's governance and decision-making process, according to this perspective, are openness, a peaceful responsive academic environment, trust, improvements in the student experience, and a better quality of decisions (Luescher-Mamashela, 2013).

SUMMARY

In this chapter we have reviewed many of the key concepts associated with academic self-governance within universities. As we have noted, traditional forms of academic governance are based on notions of collegiality, academic freedom, and faculty autonomy, and in many systems the academic senate or council continues to play a major role. We review a number of key concepts and models related to the work of senates and governing boards. Traditional governance arrangements are currently being challenged by power shifts within the university and external pressures for more efficient and effective decision-making structures. Faculty unionization, the existence of tenure, and the increasing employment of other categories of academic workers, such as short-term contract faculty, also have important implications for traditional forms of academic self-governance. Students and student governments play major roles in academic self-governance in many countries, and we have discussed a number of concepts that can be used to define and understand these roles.

DISCUSSION QUESTIONS

1. At many universities there is a range of different categories of workers who are employed to fulfill "academic" tasks, such as individuals employed to teach a single course, student affairs professionals, educational developers, and teaching assistants. What are some of the reasons for including representatives of these other categories of academic workers on university senates? What are some of the reasons for only including traditional faculty?
2. This chapter provided a brief summary of six different schools of thought that have been used to understand and analyze the work of governing boards. What are some of the limitations or disadvantages associated with each school of thought?
3. What role do students play in the governance of your university? How would you interpret or analyze this role given the concepts discussed in this chapter?

REFERENCES

Akerlind, G., & Kayrooz, C. (2003). Understanding academic freedom: The views of social scientists. *Higher Research and Development, 22*(3), 327–344.

Altbach, P. (2001). Academic freedom: International challenges and realities. *Higher Education, 41*(1/2), 205–219.

Baird, J. (2006). Beyond professionalisation: Enhancing the governance culture for Australian university governing boards. *Tertiary Education Management, 12*(4), 297–309.

Baldridge, J. V., Curtis, D. V., Ecker, G., & Riley, G. L. (1978). *Policy making and effective leadership: A national study of academic management.* San Francisco, CA: Jossey-Bass.

Bastedo, M. (2005). The making of an activist governing board. *The Review of Higher Education, 28*(4), 551–570.

Benjamin, E. (2009). Academic bargaining in hard times. *Collective Bargaining in the Academy, 1*(1), 1–8.

Berdahl, R. (1990). Academic freedom, autonomy and accountability in British universities. *Studies in Higher Education, 15*(2), 169–181.

Bergan, S. (2004). Higher education governance and democratic participation: The university and democratic culture. In S. Bergan (Ed.), *The university as res publica: Higher education governance, student participation and the university as a site of citizenship* (pp. 13–30). Strasbourg, France: Council of Europe.

Berry, J., & Savarese, M. (2012). *Directory of faculty contracts and bargaining agents in institutions of higher education.* New York, NY: National Centre for the Study of Collective Bargaining in Higher Education and the Professions.

Bess, J. L. (1988). *Collegiality and bureaucracy in the modern university: The influence of information and power on decision-making structures.* New York, NY: Teachers College Press.

Bess, J. L. (1998). Contract systems, bureaucracies, and faculty motivation: The probable effects of a no-tenure policy. *Journal of Higher Education, 69*(1), 1–22.

Bess, J. L., & Dee, J. R. (2008). *Understanding college and the university organization: Theories for effective policy and practice.* Sterling, VA: Stylus.

Birnbaum, R. (1988). *How colleges work: The cybernetics of academic organization and leadership.* San Francisco, CA: Jossey-Bass.

Birnbaum, R. (1991). The latent organizational functions of the academic senate: Why senates do not work but will not go away. *New Directions for Higher Education, 75*, 7–25.

Birnbaum, R. (2004). The end of shared governance: Looking ahead or looking back. *New Directions for Higher Education, 127*, 5–22.

Bleiklie, I. (2001). *Educating for citizenship: Report submitted to the working party 'Universities as sites of citizenship' of the Council of Europe's Higher Education and Research Committee (CC-HER).* Strasbourg, France: Council of Europe.

Bleiklie, I., & Kogan. M. (2007). Organization and governance of universities. *Higher Education Policy, 20*, 477–493.

Boland, J. A. (2005). Student participation in shared governance: A means of advancing democratic values? *Tertiary Education and Management, 11*(3), 199–217.

Bryman, A. (2007). Effective leadership in higher education: A literature review. *Studies in Higher Education, 32*(6), 693–710.

Bucklew, N., Houghton, J. D., & Ellison, C. N. (2013). Faculty union and faculty senate coexistence: A review of the impact of academic collective bargaining on traditional academic governance. *Labor Studies Journal, 37*(4), 373–390.

Burnes, B., Wend, P., & By, R. T. (2014). The changing face of English universities: Reinventing collegiality for the twenty-first century. *Studies in Higher Education, 39*(6), 905–926.

Bush, T. (1995). *Theories of educational management.* London, England: Paul Chapman.

Carey, P. (2013). Student engagement: Stakeholder perspectives on course representation in university governance. *Studies in Higher Education, 38*(9), 1290–1304.

Chaffee, E. E. (1983). *Rational decision-making in higher education.* Boulder, CO: National Center for Higher Education Management Systems.

Chait, R. P. (Ed.). (2002). *The questions of tenure.* Cambridge, MA: Harvard University Press.

Clark, B. R. (1983). *The higher education system.* Berkeley, CA: University of California Press.

Clendenin, W. (1972). Company presidents look at board of directors. *California Management Review, 16*(3), 60–66.

Currie, J. (1998). Globalization practices and the professoriate in Anglo-Pacific and North American universities. *Comparative Education Review, 42*(1), 15–29.

De Boer, H., Huisman, J., & Meister-Scheytt C. (2010). Supervision in "modern" university governance: Boards under scrutiny. *Studies in Higher Education, 35*(3), 317–333.

DeCew, J. W. (2002). *Unionization in the academy: Visions and realities, issues in academic ethics.* Lanham, MD: Rowman & Littlefield.

Deem, R. (2008). Unravelling the fabric of academe: The managerialist university and its implications for the integrity of academic work. In J. Turk (Ed.), *Universities at risk: How politics, special interests and corporatization threaten academic integrity* (pp. 256–281). Ottawa, ON: James Lorimer.

Deem, R., Hillyard, S., & Reed, M. (2007). *Knowledge, higher education and the new managerialism.* Oxford, England: Oxford University Press.

DeGeorge, R. (2003). Ethics, academic freedom and academic tenure. *Journal of Academic Ethics 1*(1), 11–25.

Duryea, E. D., & Fisk, R. S. (1973). *Faculty unions and collective bargaining.* San Francisco, CA: Jossey-Bass.

Ehrenberg, R. G. (2004). Introduction. In R. G. Ehrenberg (Ed.), *Governing academia* (pp. 1–6). Ithaca, NY: Cornell University Press.

European Universities Association. (1988). *Magna Charta Universitatum.* Bologna, Spain: EUA.

Gaita, R. (1997). Truth and the idea of a university. *Australian Universities Review, 40*(2), 13–18.

Hendrickson, R. M., Lane, J. E., Harris, J. T., & Dorman, R. H. (2013). *Academic leadership and governance of higher education: A guide for trustees, leaders, and aspiring leaders of two-and-four-year institutions.* Sterling, VA: Stylus.

Henkel, M. (2005). Academic identity and autonomy in a changing policy environment. *Higher Education, 49*(1–2), 155–176.

Henkel, M. (2007). Can academic autonomy survive in the knowledge society? A perspective from Britain. *Higher Education Research & Development, 26(*1), 87–99.

Herbert, A., & Tienari, J. (2013). Transplanting tenure and the (re)construction of academic freedoms. *Studies in Higher Education, 38*(2), 157–173.

Hermalin, B. E. (2004). Higher education boards of trustees. In R. G. Ehrenberg (Ed.), *Governing academia* (pp. 28–48). Ithaca, NY: Cornell University Press.

Hirsch, W. Z. (2001). Initiatives for improving shared governance. In W. Z. Hirsch & L. E. Weber (Eds.), *Governance in higher education: The university in a state of flux* (pp. 143–154). London, England: Economica.

Hung, H. (1998). A typology of the theories of the roles of governing boards. *Scholarly Research and Theory Papers, 6*(2), 101–112.

Ingram, P., & Simons, T. (1995). Institutional and resource dependence of responsiveness to work-family. *Academy of Management Journal, 38*(5), 1460–1482.

Johnston, S. W. (2003). Faculty governance and effective academic administrative leadership. *New Directions for Higher Education, 124,* 57–63.

Jones, G. A. (2002). The structure of university governance in Canada: A policy network approach. In A. Amaral, G. A. Jones, & B. Karseth (Eds.), *Governing higher education: National perspectives on institutional governance* (pp. 213–234). Dordrecht, The Netherlands: Kluwer.

Jones, G. A. (2013). The horizontal and vertical fragmentation of academic work and the challenge for academic governance and leadership. *Asia Pacific Education Review, 14*(1), 75–83.

Jones, G. A., Shanahan, T., & Goyan, P. (2004). The academic senate and university governance in Canada. *The Canadian Journal of Higher Education, 34*(2), 35–68.

Karran, T. (2009). Academic freedom in Europe: A preliminary comparative analysis. *Higher Education Policy, 20,* 289–313.

Kezar, A. (2006). Rethinking public higher education governing boards performance: Results of a national study of governing boards in the United States. *The Journal of Higher Education, 77*(6), 968–1008.

Klemenčič, M. (2012). Student representation in Western Europe: Introduction to the special issue. *European Journal of Higher Education, 2*(1), 2–19. doi.10.1080/21568235.2012.695058

Klemenčič, M. (2014). Student power in a global perspective and contemporary trends in student organising. *Studies in Higher Education, 39*(3), 396–411. doi.10.1080/03075079.2014.896177

Knight, P. T., & Trowler, P. R. (2000). Department-level cultures and the improvement of learning and teaching. *Studies in Higher Education, 25*(1), 69–83.

Locke, W., Cummings, W. K., & Fisher, D. (Eds.) (2011). *Governance and management of higher education institutions: Perspectives of the academy.* Dordrecht, The Netherlands, Springer.

Luescher-Mamashela, T. M. (2010). From university democratisation to managerialism: The changing legitimation of university governance and the place of students. *Tertiary Education and Management, 16*(4), 259–283.

Luescher-Mamashela, T. M. (2013). Student representation in university decision making: Good reasons, a new lens? *Studies in Higher Education, 38*(10), 1442–1456.

Lyne, B. (2011). Campus clout, statewide strength: Improving shared governance through unionization. *Journal of Academic Freedom, 2,* 1–6.

MacFarlane, C. (2005). The disengaged academic: The retreat from citizenship. *Higher Education Quarterly, 59*(4), 296–312.

Marginson, S. (2008). Academic creativity under new public management: Foundations for an investigation. *Educational Theory, 58*(3), 269–287.

Mason, H. L. (1978). Shared authority, triparity, tripolarity: Cross national patterns of university government. *Polity, 10*(3), 305–325.

McCulloch, A. (2009). The student as co-producer: Learning from public administration about the student–university relationship. *Studies in Higher Education, 34*(2), 171–183.

Meister-Scheytt, C. (2007). Reinventing governance: The role of boards of governors in the new Austrian university. *Tertiary Education and Management, 13*(3), 247–261.

Melear, K. B. (2013). The role of internal governance, committees, and advisory groups. In P. J. Schloss & K. M. Cragg (Eds.), *Organization and administration in higher education*. New York, NY: Routledge.

Menon, M. E. (2005). Students' views regarding their participation in university governance: Implications for distributed leadership in higher education. *Tertiary Education and Management, 11*(2), 167–182.

Minor, J. T. (2004). Understanding faculty senates: Moving from mystery to models. *Review of Higher Education, 27*(3), 343–363.

Mintzberg, H. (1983). *Power in and around the organization*. Englewood Cliffs, NJ: Prentice-Hall.

Moodie, G. C., & Eustace, R. (1974). *Power and authority in British universities*. London, England: George Allen & Unwin.

Olsen, J. P. (2007). The institutional dynamics of the European university. In P. Maassen & J. P. Olsen (Eds.), *University dynamics and European integration* (pp. 25–53). Dordrecht, The Netherlands: Springer.

Ornstein, M. (1984). Interlocking directorates in Canada: Inter-corporate or class alliance? *Administrative Science Quarterly, 29*, 210–231.

Pennock, L., Jones, G. A., Leclerc, J. M., & Li, S. X. (2015). Assessing the role and structure of academic senates in Canadian universities, 2000–2012. *Higher Education*. doi.10.1007/s10734-014-9852-8

Planas, A., Soler, P., Fullana, J., Pallisera, M., & Vila, M. (2013). Student participation in university governance: The opinions of professors and students. *Studies in Higher Education, 38*(4), 571–583.

Polanyi, M. (1962). The republic of science: Its political and economic theory. *Minerva, 1*(1), 54–85.

Rabban, D. M. (1990). A functional analysis of "individual" and "institutional" academic freedom under the First Amendment. *Law and Contemporary Problems, 53*(3), 227–301.

Rhoades, G. (2005). Capitalism, academic style, and shared governance. *Academe, 91*(3), 38–42.

Rhoades, G. (2011). Faculty unions, business models, and the academy's future. *Change: The Magazine of Higher Learning, 43*(6), 20–26.

Rochford, F. (2014). Bringing them into the tent—student association and neutered academy. *Studies in Higher Education, 39*(3), 485–499.

Rowlands, J. (2013). Academic boards: Less intellectual and more academic capital in higher education governance? *Studies in Higher Education, 38*(9), 1274–1289. doi.10.1080/03075079.2011.619655

Scott, W. R. (2008). *Institutions and organizations: Ideas and interests*. Los Angeles, CA: Sage.

Sen, A. (1985). Well-being, agency and freedom: The Dewey Lectures 1984. *Journal of Philosophy, 82*(4), 169–221.

Shattock, M. (2003). *Managing successful universities*. Maidenhead, England: SRHE and Open University Press.

Slaughter, S., & Rhoades, G. (2004). *Academic capitalism and the new economy*. Baltimore, MD: Johns Hopkins University Press.

Taylor, M. (2013). Shared governance in the modern university. *Higher Education Quarterly, 67*(1), 80–94.

Thompson, D. F. (1972). Democracy and the governing of the university. *Annals of the American Academy of Political and Social Science, 404,* 157–169.

Tierney, W. G., & Lechuga, V. M. (2010). The social significance of academic freedom. *Cultural Studies–Critical Methodologies, 10*(2), 118–133.

Trowler, V. (2010). *Student engagement literature review.* York, England: Higher Education Academy.

University of the West Indies. (2010). *Statutes and ordinances.* Kingston, Jamaica: University of the West Indies.

Van Alstyne, W. W. (1972). The specific theory of academic freedom and the general issue of civil liberties. *The Annals of the American Academy of Political and Social Science, 404,* 140–155. doi.10.1177/000271627240400112

Van Alstyne, W. W. (1975). The specific theory of academic freedom and the general issue of civil liberties. In E. L. Pincoffs (Ed.), *The concept of academic freedom.* Austin, TX: University of Texas Press.

Yellowitz, I. (1987). Academic governance and collective bargaining in the City University of New York. *Academe, 73*(6), 8–11.

Zuo, B., & Ratsoy, E.(1999). Student participation in university governance. *Canadian Journal of Higher Education, 29*(1), 1–26.

CHAPTER 7

Governance as Politics and Processes

In one way, governance in higher education may be perceived as a set of static institutional arrangements that guide the functioning of and decision-making in colleges and universities. The parameters, jurisdictions, and authority of governing instruments such as committees, boards, senates, and councils constitute the institutional arrangements through which decisions are made. We contend that to understand governance functions and how decisions are made requires an examination of the basis through which action occurs in universities. For example, we believe that having a static instrumental view of internal governance limits our understanding of it and that these instruments/structures should be viewed as functioning through an institutional governance process. In other words, governance should not be viewed as a set of static arrangements, but as a process.

This chapter adopts a process approach to institutional governance to examine the functioning of governing instruments such as committees, boards, senates, and councils in the academy and the general overall processes by which universities are governed. Concepts such as bureaucracy, hierarchy, organized anarchy, and the legitimacy of decisions are discussed along with the garbage can model of decision-making. In addition, the chapter also discusses power, politics, and conflict.

GOVERNANCE AS A PROCESS

Governance is fundamental to the way in which decisions are made in universities. Governance allows us to answer questions such as: In which forum should a decision be made? Who are the legitimate members of the forum? What are the terms under which the decision is legitimated? The participative collegial model of decision-making is the traditional value system that is the subtext of the way in which these questions are answered (Dowling-Hetherington, 2013). But although it provides answers to these questions, governance is still not an end in itself. Rather, it is a process towards the end or towards the achievement of desired outcomes. And the end is legitimated through the process. Hence, legitimation through the correct process is the sine qua non of collegial governance, policy formulation, and decision-making in the academy. For instance, the governance of a university may spell out that a decision on the introduction of a new academic program has to be ultimately made by the senate. However, the university's governance may indicate that the recommendation for the new program first has to be approved at the department and faculty level and by the senate subcommittee on academic programming (if there is one) before it is finally tabled for discussion and approval by the senate. This indicates that there is an expectation of multiple participants engaging in different fora and at different levels in the decision-making process. Another classic example is the institutional governance of probationary appointments, reappointments, tenure reviews, and the promotion process. For example, in the USA, albeit not at all universities, decisions taken on any of these employment contracts within an institution proceed through a series of hierarchical processes beginning at the departmental level and moving to the college or faculty level, the dean, the institutional review or appointments committee, and in some cases to the president or provost. Omitting any of the steps in a prescribed governance process without the appropriate constitutional grounds would threaten the legitimacy of the final decision.

The process of governance allows various constituencies within the academy to participate in governing an institution. Even at the level of governing boards, there is a process that involves engaging members in discussions on matters pertinent to the institution. In fact, the collegial model allows institutional governance to function through a process of consultation, debate, feedback, consensus, and collective action. Such involvement and participation in the decision-making process and governance of an institution allows various groups at different levels in the academy to have a "voice" in the affairs of the institution (Middlehurst, 1993), particularly those deemed to have legitimate rights of participation (Bess, 1988).

In addition, in a loosely coupled environment such as a university, the engagement process builds and/or strengthens institutional identity. It is also known to enhance morale and job satisfaction among academics (Johnsrud & Rosser, 2002). Through engagement and consultation, there is greater acceptance and ownership of final decisions and increased institutional knowledge (Kezar & Eckel, 2004; Mortimer & McConnell, 1979). Kezar and Eckel argue that the consultative process allows for early input from the various constituencies, allows adequate time for response formulation on important issues, increases information availability, and provides adequate feedback and a forum for the communication of decisions. They contend that although this approach takes more time and decision-making can be more discursive, it can actually enhance the effectiveness of governance.

Arguably, this process has, in more recent times, been compromised by the tensions between collegiality and managerialism, with critics of collegiality advocating for a more managerialist approach. The growing prevalence of managerialism has led, in some contexts, to increased centralized decision-making and a move away from consultation with faculty. The argument for this is that collegiality has led to inadequate responses to environmental demands and a slow, inefficient pace of decision-making (Dowling-Hetherington, 2013; Johnsrud & Rosser, 2002; Sanyal, 1995). Institutional governance in many universities has moved towards a strong executive model that is corporate-like with more explicit management-oriented approaches to governing, and this model minimizes process. This "new way" can have negative consequences for cohesion between faculty and administration, create the appearance of a lack of transparency, and challenge the overall functioning of institutional governance (Bennett, Crawford, & Riches, 1992; Dowling-Hetherington, 2013). Some scholars believe that the current model of governance, which minimizes process, limits the dual conceptualization of managerial and professional responsibility associated with shared governance. Even in areas where the technical expertise of faculty and the management's fiduciary responsibilities intersect in the decision-making process, there has been a shift towards greater control and responsibility on the part of administration (Apkarian, Mulligan, Rotondi, & Brint, 2014), effectively shifting the legitimacy of governing authority. Despite dissenting voices, there is still an acknowledgment of the need for an approach to governing that would allow institutions to be adaptive to their environment while simultaneously retaining a collegial, processual, and devolved approach to governing in the academy (Dowling-Hetherington, 2013).

HIERARCHY

Hierarchy suggests a vertical relationship, and in the governance of universities the term has three conceptualizations. One relates to a system of universities within a specific state jurisdiction and the rank order position that the universities occupy (Bleiklie, 2003). This type of hierarchy normally has no statutory or legal basis, but rather it is more of a perceptual or reputational hierarchy. Hierarchy of this type can be a function of institutional classification (for example, doctoral-degree-granting institutions as opposed to primarily undergraduate institutions) or institutional stratification (differences in prestige associated with research productivity) within the higher education system. The second type of hierarchy is structured around the legal and institutional framework of system governance. It captures the relationship between a ministry and/or a higher education commission or system governing board and individual universities. In this case, the individual universities are at the lower end of the hierarchy. The third type of hierarchy relates to the internal governance functions of a university. In this section, we focus on the latter. Hierarchy in this sense suggests governing authority located at different vertical levels within the organization. Thompson (1965) describes this hierarchy of authority in terms of organizational roles assigned based on subordination and superordination as a chain of command.

The raison d'être of a university is to coordinate higher education activities such as teaching and research. The collective actions of members of the university should therefore be directed towards a common coordinated action. Brunsson and Sahlin-Anderson (2000) suggest that the coordination required to achieve such an outcome requires an authoritative center to direct the actions of organizational members and that this is achieved through the construction of hierarchies. Hence, as universities become managerialist, more centralized in their decision-making, and decision-making becomes more vertical and less horizontal, hierarchies are strengthened and the power to govern is concentrated in the hands of those entrusted with the power to manage. The recognition of this hierarchy is to a considerable extent a function of statutes and bylaws that define the responsibilities and authorities of different offices and councils. These de jure provisions leave some scope for variance and fluctuations in the de facto divisions of power. De Boer and colleagues (2007) describe the Dutch higher education system as a case in which there has been an abandonment of the principle of codetermination and the adoption of strong executive management for both academic and nonacademic matters—the strengthening of hierarchy.

Governance hierarchies are observed across the spectrum of the university (e.g., within departments or between a department and a faculty or college), and universities function on the basis of hierarchical authority relations to accomplish collective goals (Bess & Dee, 2008). For instance, there may be a hierarchical organization of faculty at the department level based on academic rank or prestige. Administratively, the departmental chair has responsibility for making the final decision on certain departmental matters but other decisions may be subject to approval by the dean of the faculty or may even require final ratification by the senate. Implicit in this scenario is the notion of process: the way in which a decision may have to go through multiple hierarchically arranged levels. Central to this conception are flows of information, both bottom-up and top-down, to locations within the university that allow decisions to be legitimately made and implemented.

Hierarchies also have implications for power and control. Embedded within hierarchical control is authority vested in positions and traditions and it is one way in which universities control the behavior of their members (Bess, 1998). For example, a dean has control over a faculty or college by virtue of position. And although the collegial model is based on the principle of first among equals, *primus inter pares*, the position of dean still has legitimate power and control. Hierarchy may therefore be viewed as an important aspect of a university's structural and governing integrity (Stephenson, 2005). However, hierarchy only captures part of the structural configuration of governance in higher education. This is largely due to the unique and bifurcated academic-administrative structure of universities, with administrative hierarchies being much taller while academic hierarchies are much flatter. The tradition that governs the academic side of departments is based on academic freedom, and in accordance with this principle, faculty members have professional authority over their work and are self-directed (Bess & Dee, 2008). Hence, the structural arrangements over academic matters tend to be flatter. However, while structurally the academic side is flatter, there is an increase in the power and control granted to those who manage, for example, deans. On the other hand, administrative hierarchies are much taller because structures are based on bureaucratic arrangements and there is a presumption of a need for more control over administrative staff.

There are important conceptual limitations associated with using hierarchy to explain the dynamic relations undergirding governance in colleges and universities. For instance, it does not explain the shared governing relationship between the academic and administrative branches of a university. It also fails to capture the loosely coupled arrangements between faculties and colleges at a university and the social networks that exist between individuals at the same level or at other levels of the institution (Manning, 2013). Stephenson (2005) advances the notion of heterarchy in which hierarchy and networks are combined, thereby emphasizing vertical and horizontal linkages. At the heart of these relationships is the trust on which networks are based and which drives collaboration and cooperation. The loosely coupled academic relationships across colleges and faculties are better understood through the application of this social network analysis. These relationships also help to explain how "rational-formal elements of organizations function alongside informal non-rationalized actions" (Gumport, 2012,

p. 26) in an environment in which both formal and informal relationships are central to governing in the academy. Governance may therefore be better understood by combining hierarchy and social networks—heterarchy. In so doing, the combination sheds light on the relationships and interdependencies (horizontal, vertical, formal, and nonformal) in universities that allow governance processes to function.

BUREAUCRACY

Bureaucracy is one way of viewing how universities function, and the concept has been applied over the last several decades to understand governance. The concept was advanced by German sociologist Max Weber, who developed a model based on rationality, impersonality, and objectivity in decision-making and the application of rules to the efficient functioning of organizations (Bess & Dee, 2008). Weber suggested that bureaucratically designed organizations should be structured hierarchically with formal chains of command and systems of communication connecting the various levels, and that these organizations should also be based on the principle of rational-legal authority (Baldrige, 1971). That is, bureaucratic organizations are "rationally ordered instruments for the achievement of stated goals" (Selznick, 2005, p. 125) with positional authority as the basis for decision-making.

Weber conceptualized bureaucracy as an "ideal-type" or an archetypal configuration as opposed to a desirable condition (Gumport, 2012). Pugh, Hickson, and Hinings (1969) later operationalized Weber's "ideal-types" as "full" bureaucracies. These "full" bureaucratic structures have the following characteristics:

1. *[They are comprised of]* persons who are linked formally into completely specified, standardized interdependencies;
2. Positions are arranged in a system of formal, hierarchical authority that purports to prescribe all organizational interactions; and
3. Impersonal rules *[govern]* all behavior.

(Bess, 1988, p. 20)

From these characteristics, scholars have argued that the nonacademic side of universities tends to resemble a full bureaucracy, given that considerable emphasis is placed on the positional authority of administrators (Bess, 1988; Gumport, 2012; Manning; 2013; Stroup, 1966). However, the academic side has peculiarities that render it different from a full or typical bureaucracy. For instance, academics have significant control over their work because of their expertise in respective disciplines and fields, and in this environment decision-making is highly decentralized. In other words, expert authority is a guiding governing principle on the academic side. In addition, many "academic communities are defined by broad participation, extensive collaboration, collective responsibilities, flatter hierarchies, conformity to norms, adherence to traditions, and egalitarian impulses" (Hearn & McLendon, 2012. p. 48). Hearn and McLendon contend that conceptions of colleges and universities as collegiums (communities of scholars) were in part the result of the explanatory limitations of the bureaucratic model, which did not capture the nonrational and symbolic side of governance in the academy. Mintzberg (1979) advances the notion of professional bureaucracy to describe the type of structural relationship among academics. Thus, colleges and universities are governed in a space where two different types of bureaucracies function side-by-side and also interact with each other to achieve shared organizational goals. Much of the interaction between the two groups occurs through the use of structures that facilitate joint participation in decision-making, such as committees and boards. For instance, the senate at some universities includes faculty from various academic units across the institution as well as academic librarians and staff representatives from student affairs and student service units (Jones, Shanahan, & Goyan, 2004).

Baldridge, Curtis, Ecker, and Riley (1978) present six important elements that define a university as a bureaucracy.

1. Public universities are complex organizations that receive their charter from the state—the state itself being a bureaucracy and universities reflecting this in their own structures.
2. Universities have a formal hierarchy that is guided by bylaws. These bylaws specify how interactions occur among and between offices.
3. Universities have formal channels of communication.
4. Universities have authority lines and structures and, although blurred and ambiguous in some cases, they specify who exercises authority over whom.
5. Universities have formal policies and rules that govern their work.
6. Universities routinize much of their work in an attempt to create efficiency. This is particularly noticeable in activities such as the processing of students' registration and graduation— "people processing." It is also seen in decision-making processes in which formal administrative responsibility is delegated to designated officials who routinely administer specific aspects of a university's activities: for example, graduation or financial matters.

Universities are governed within these parameters. However, Baldridge et al. (1978) point out that while the bureaucratic paradigm captures issues of authority and legitimates formalized power, it does not adequately address other forms of power— power based on nonlegitimate threats, power based on appeals to emotions, or power based on expertise. Neither does bureaucracy address governing issues related to organizational change or the process of policy formulation. Yet these elements are germane to understanding governance in higher education.

ORGANIZED ANARCHY

Organized anarchy is one of the traditional conceptual models of higher education governance. It was advanced by Cohen and his colleagues (Cohen, March, & Olsen, 1972; Cohen & March, 1974) and, like many of the other traditional models, it highlights the peculiarities of universities as organizations (de Boer et al., 2007). The basic thesis advanced by these scholars is that the university is "anarchic" in the sense that it has problematic goals (internal conflict about the appropriateness of goals), unclear technology, and fluid member participation (Cohen & March, 1986; Bess, 1988). They view universities and colleges as ambiguous entities. This traditional model of the university conveys an organization with a high degree of internal fragmentation in which divisions are loosely coupled and individual self-interest is strong among its academics. Bess rejects the notion of anarchy to describe the higher education environment because it conveys a dysfunctional system of governance. Bess argues that a duality exists in which universities are expected to be rational entities and create stable internal decision-making processes typical of a bureaucracy while simultaneously having a loosely federated structure that is responsive and adaptive to external conditions. Others see order in organized anarchies, albeit some processes do not follow conventional patterns (Olsen, 2001).

An important conceptual foundation of organized anarchy is that it departs from the rational assumption of bureaucracy—with its focus on simplicity, determinism, linear causality, and objectivity—and instead highlights complexity, indeterminism, and mutual causality as important to understanding higher education (Clark, 1985; Manning, 2013). The reason for this is that organizational goals and the means of achieving them are sometimes not in harmony, key individuals are not always involved in decision-making processes, problems and potential solutions are ambiguous and not well understood, and new demands limit the amount of time that should meaningfully be spent on an issue (Bess & Dee, 2008). This context is incongruent with rational decision-making and is better represented by the assumptions of organized anarchy. Manning views organized anarchy as a shift to a postmodern paradigm that assumes multiple realities, and hence better matches the lived reality of faculty, administrators, university leadership including governing boards, and external stakeholders. These multiple realities are however tempered by the culture, history, and tradition of the academy and its commonly shared realities (Manning, 2001). Cohen et al. (1972) developed the garbage can model to explain the processes of choice and decision-making in an organized anarchy such as a university.

THE GARBAGE CAN MODEL

The garbage can is another model or perspective that can be used to describe university governance (Olsen, 2001). The subtext of the model is grounded in ambiguity, contingent choice processes, and emergent social systems (Hearn & McLendon, 2012) and represents one of the ways choices are made in universities (Manning, 2013). It describes a less rational process of choice and decision-making when compared to the bureaucratic and rational models. Kezar and Eckel (2004) pointed out that Cohen and March combined the structural and human dynamics of governance in this model. Hence, the model overcomes some of the inherent limitations of rational models. Kezar and Eckel describe the model in this way:

> Garbage can decision making focuses on structural aspects of the environment, such as goals and technology, as well as human conditions, such as participation, motivation, leadership, communication, and information channels, which operate to problematize an idealized rational governance process, pointing to its ambiguousness and challenges.
>
> (p. 382)

The garbage can approach to decision-making is conceptualized as solutions looking for problems and with institutions having a repertoire of responses at their disposal.

Or stated another way, organizations are looking for problems to fit their preconceived solutions. As Peters (2012) puts it *"[t]he* argument of the garbage can is that institutions have a set of routinized responses to problems, and will attempt to use familiar responses before searching for alternatives that are further away from core values" (p. 36). The decision-making process occurs through the confluence of four independent and very loosely associated streams: streams of problems, solutions, participants, and choice opportunities. According to the theory, the intersection of these streams produces a decision.

Problems occupy the attention of university/organizational members and could include typical university issues such as personal matters, external environment changes, or working conditions (Bess & Dee, 2008). These problems linger in the system in search of a decision opportunity for them to be presented (Hearn & McLendon, 2012). Solutions are not ideas generated to solve specific problems but rather are "answers" that flow continuously throughout the university in search of problems to which they can attach. Cohen et al. (1972) describe a solution as "an answer actively looking for a question" (p. 3). Participants are organizational agents searching for issues that they can use to build their status and they involve themselves with issues that are convenient to their career advancement (Hearn & McLendon, 2012). Choice opportunities enable decisions to be taken. These opportunities include budget meetings and hiring decisions that are sometimes incongruent with the time that is needed to solve a problem (Bess & Dee, 2008). This creates ambiguity and uncertainty. Hearn and McLendon argue that the goal ambiguity and conflict that exist in universities result in decisions that are highly contingent, unpredictable, and seldom successful in solving problems. As Cohen and March (1974) express it,

> *[t]he* garbage can process is one in which problems, solutions, and participants move from one choice opportunity to another in such a way that the nature of the choice, the time it takes, and the problems it solves all depend on a relatively complicated intermeshing of elements. These include the mix of choices available at any one time, the mix of problems that have access to the organization, the mix of solutions looking for problems, and outside demands on the decision-makers.
>
> (p. 16)

Nevertheless, problems are solved and decisions are made, but according to the model it is the intersection of the streams that produces these random and unpredictable decisions. How the streams intersect depends on the timing of the arrival of problems, choices, solutions, and decision-makers (Bess & Dee, 2008). Hence, decisions are made based on what is appropriate given the availability of solutions at that point in time and the institutional core values within which they are advanced, but this limits the search range for policy alternatives on which the institution could rely (Peters, 2012). It is within this context that the garbage can model explains how higher education institutions are governed and the process by which decisions are made.

POWER, POLITICS, AND CONFLICT

The political perspective is yet another lens through which one can view and interpret university governance. Morgan (2006) views "organizations as systems of government that vary according to the political principles employed" (p. 150). Pfeffer (1981) pictures organizations as political arenas where control is kept in the hands of those in power. To do this, organizational members on a day-to-day basis engage in negotiations, coalition-building, mutual influence, and "wheeling and dealing" whereby individuals seek to advance their specific agendas and interests (Morgan, 2006). Pfeffer defines such organizational politics as "those activities taken within organizations to acquire, develop, and use power and other resources to obtain one's preferred outcomes in a situation in which there is uncertainty or dissensus about choices" (p. 7). Higher education organizations such as universities and colleges are similarly conceptualized as arenas of coalitional and negotiating activities in which individuals' and subunits' preferences, interests, and goals are advanced, there are struggles over resources, and powerful agents influence decision outcomes (Hearn & McLendon, 2012). Unlike the bureaucratic approach, which focuses on formal authority and rules, the political perspective looks at the ways in which individuals and groups attempt to further their interests through both formal and informal interactions. For instance, a group of professors from different faculties may have informal meetings and form a coalition with the intention of contesting an issue under discussion in a formal governance setting such as the senate. This is an example of the politicking and "wheeling and dealing" that occurs in the governance of higher education and how power and influence is created to shape outcomes in favor of dominant groups. In many cases these interactions are dynamic; groups may come together to form a coalition to address a particular issue and then disband after a particular outcome has been achieved.

Baldridge et al. (1978) were among the first to analyze the political dimension of higher education and its governance. Baldridge depicted an interest-articulation model based on conflict theory (Dahrendorf, 1959) and community action studies (Dahl, 1966). The model emphasized the importance of factions or institutional subgroups, interests, coalitional activities, and bargaining in shaping institutional governance processes and outcomes and highlighted the role of power and conflict in the decision-making process (Hearn & McLendon, 2012). Hearn and McLendon too suggest that the political model is distinctively important for understanding governance in higher education. They point out that the political model emphasizes governing through the coordination of conflict as opposed to vertical coordination as practiced within bureaucratic systems and horizontal coordination as occurs within collegial systems. Conflict in this sense suggests a colliding of interests (Morgan, 2006). According to Morgan,

> [c]onflict may be personal, interpersonal, or between rival groups or coalitions. It may be built into organizational structures, roles, attitudes and stereotypes or arise over a scarcity of resources. It may be explicit or covert. Whatever the reason, and whatever the form it takes, its source rests in some perceived or real divergence of interests.
>
> (p. 163)

As pointed out by Morgan (2006), resource scarcity can lead to conflict. This conflict may emerge because there is competition for limited resources. It is also well accepted that modern organizations encourage competition and collaboration simultaneously. Collaboration involves the pursuit of a common task, while competition involves the pursuit of limited resources, status, and career advancement.

One may be tempted to think of a university as functioning in a disruptive and unstable governance environment, but actually there is stability. One reason for this is that organizational membership is distributed across multiple groups. In other words, organizational members tend to belong to more than one group and consequently they provide a check against instability and counterbalance one another's influence in the larger system while at the same time dominant coalitions remain stable for extended periods (Baldrige, 1971; Bess & Dee, 2008). Thus, while one academic department may compete for scarce resources with other departments, some members of the various departments are also members of the senate or some other university-wide committee, for example, where they assemble not only to formulate policy but in many instances they build coalitions and relational cohesion that are the fabric of stable governance.

The political perspective also highlights the significance of power in governing higher education institutions. Power, according to Morgan (2006), is "the medium through which conflicts of interests are ultimately resolved. . . . *[and it]* influences who gets what, when, and how" (p. 166). Morgan describes 14 important sources of power and we briefly review 11 that we think are particularly pertinent to higher education governance and power relations:

1. Formal authority. It creates legitimized power by virtue of the position or office held; for example, a dean or provost. It is usually supported by a bureaucratic structure that allows a position to have rights and obligations that create a sphere of influence. On the academic side of higher education, much of the formal authority in a dean or a head of department is legitimated by faculty/departmental colleagues from "below."
2. Control of scarce resources. Critical organizational resources are usually scarce. The ability to exercise control over scarce resources is therefore an important source of power. Resources are not restricted to money but include highly valued skills such as an internationally recognized researcher and scholar, or a faculty member with a dense network of external influential individuals. Nevertheless, financial resources, particularly discretionary funds, and the exercise of influence or control over them create conditions that can affect change in a particular direction (Pfeffer, 1981).
3. Use of organizational structure, rules, and regulations. These are all instruments in organizations that allow various tasks to be undertaken but, as Morgan notes, these instruments are used for political purposes. For example, a dean may opt to restructure a faculty but may encounter significant resistance because power and status among the professoriate may be closely tied to the rules and regulations of the current structure. Hence, while the dean may have the legitimate governing authority to make changes, the existing structures, rules, and regulations may be used to hinder or limit change.
4. Control of decision processes. Control of three interrelated elements of the decision-making process—decision premises, decision processes, and decision issues and objectives—can be a source of power in an organization. By controlling the decision premises, one can control the decision agendas and influence the kinds of decisions that are made and that can best serve a specific preferred interest. Hence, the chairperson of a university committee or a forum such as the governing board might have the authority to determine the agenda for meetings, but the

chairperson may be influenced by other powerful actors, such as the president, about what should be included on the agenda. The president then gets to have influence over the decision premise.

Morgan (2006) explains that decision-making is guided by ground rules; for example, how should a decision be made? Who should be involved in the decision? Or how should the order of the agenda be decided? The answers to these questions tell us how the decision-making process works. Having control of the decision-making process is a source of power that may be used to an individual's advantage and to shape outcomes in a particular way. For example, an ad hoc committee may be formed by a university provost to address an issue, but its membership may be intentionally constituted in a way to effect a certain desired outcome.

Influencing the decision issues and objectives under discussion and the means of evaluating them can contribute to a person's power. According to Morgan, some people use eloquence, command of the facts, passionate commitment, or sheer tenacity and persistence on certain issues as sources of power.

5. Control of knowledge and information. A person who has control over important pieces of knowledge and information can control them in such a way as to create patterns of dependency and shape how organizational circumstances are defined. For instance, universities are becoming more data-driven in their decision-making and as a consequence are relying more and more on statistical analyses. Individuals who are adept at analyzing data and synthesizing facts could develop expert power by ensuring that decision-makers are always dependent on them. As Morgan points out, these individuals jealously guard or block access to crucial knowledge in order to enhance their indispensability.

6. Control boundaries. Leaders sometimes seek to create more autonomy for their departments by controlling the department's interface and transactions with the rest of the organization and its environment, encouraging some transactions while blocking others. This is called boundary management. In cases where there is significant interaction and interdependencies between the department and its environment (internal and external), power can be enhanced by creating dependencies.

7. Ability to cope with uncertainty. Uncertainty is the reality of organizational life. Uncertainty can be environmental or operational. Morgan explains that "an ability to deal with these uncertainties gives an individual, group, or subunit considerable power in [an] organization as a whole" (p. 178). Morgan asserts that the degree of power gained by an individual depends on (1) the degree to which his or her skills are substitutable, and (2) the importance of their function to the organization. For example, an important academic department that has demonstrated the ability to cope with difficult financial challenges could become more powerful. The central administration might position the department as exemplary, creating a power and status differential with academic units that have been less successful. The head of the department might be asked to advise other units or be promoted to a senior leadership position given the individual's ability to cope with a rapidly changing financial environment.

8. Control of technology. Technology is a powerful tool when used correctly and appropriately in organizations. How technology is employed influences patterns of inter-dependencies within an organization and shapes the power relations

between those who rely on it and those who control it. Morgan argues that power relations are usually on display when there is an attempt to change the type of technology used in an organization. They occur because new technologies can sometimes alter the balance of power and those who control the technology are more inclined to manipulate circumstances to ensure they do not concede power. For example, in universities where distance education and/or online learning is a major part of their programming, the department that controls the technology usage needed in this environment is usually quite powerful and it safeguards that power by retaining control of the technology, both in terms of what is purchased and how it is used.

9. Interpersonal alliances, networks, and the control of "informal organization." A university president or vice-chancellor sometimes develops an informal system of interlocking networks with powerful people. The network, sometimes referred to as "the old boys' club," creates a mutually beneficial exchange between the parties. Much of this coalition and alliance building occurs informally and "under the radar," but because it is significantly based on mutual dependency and exchange, it allows a president or a vice-chancellor to get things done. From this networking and coalition-building, power is derived. It is also seen in relationships with outsiders whereby sometimes a building or a department on a campus is named after a major benefactor or a wealthy donor is awarded an honorary doctorate or may become the chairperson of a powerful governing entity. Being able to undertake these kinds of exchanges is a source of power for university leaders, especially in tough financial times.

10. Control of counter-organizations. Counter-organizations are entities such as trade unions, social movements, or lobby groups that can be quite powerful. Hence, although an individual may not hold a formal position of authority within the university's organizational structure, he or she may gain power by aligning with and sometimes controlling counter-organizations. For instance, the leaders of student associations or staff unions can sometimes exercise considerable influence on university decisions.

11. Symbolism and the management of meaning. Organizational leaders have a form of symbolic power that they use to influence the way people perceive their realities, make meaning of the context, and shape how they act (Morgan, 2006). Morgan suggests that the use of imagery, theater, and gamesmanship are three important aspects of symbolic management. A new university president may use imagery to outline a goal of leading the university towards greater prestige and a much higher international ranking. This goal may be regularly articulated in speeches and reports and provide a rationale for major decisions. While the goal may be largely symbolic of the president's desire to improve the institution, the effective use of imagery can also increase the power of the president as a leader perceived to be successfully moving the institution forward. Organizations are theaters where people learn the importance of presentation in terms of things like codes of dress and office layout to the appearance of having power. Hence, the appearance of a president's office is symbolic of the power that comes with the position. Gamesmanship refers to the way in which people manage their craft—sometimes collaborating, sometimes competing, sometimes through contentious exchanges. These actions are selectively chosen for their symbolic value and to enhance power among other actors.

POWER, POLITICS, AND ORGANIZATION-ENVIRONMENT RELATIONS

As Hatch (2013) contends, theories of organization-environment relations can be applied to explain organizational power distributions. Hatch suggests that strategic contingencies theory and resource-dependence theory are appropriate in this regard and are explicit about the role organizational politics plays. Strategic contingencies theory, as advanced by Hickson, Hinings, Lee, Schneck, and Pennings (1971), suggests some level of organizational uncertainty and draws on Lawrence and Lorsch's (1967) definition of an organization as "a system of interrelated behaviors of people who are performing a task that has been differentiated into several distinct subsystems" (p. 3). According to Hickson et al. strategic contingencies theory of intra-organizational power recognizes interdependencies among subunits and uncertainty within an organization. It focuses on how coping with uncertainty can give rise to subunit or departmental power—the power-holder being a formal group that copes best in an open system where there are multiple goals. In the case of a university, the unit of analysis would be a department, an institute, or a unit.

Hatch (2013) argues that strategic contingencies theory helps to explain how power in a university department is derived from the ability to deal with uncertainty and provide the organization with critical needs. For instance, in times of financial uncertainty, departments with the highest levels of enrollment and with the greater ability to attract large sums of external funding enhance their power position (Hatch, 2013). In such cases, the governing dynamics can shift since these departments can assert significant influence over decision-making because of their acquired positional power. Hickson et al. (1971) add to this view by arguing that power is not simply linked to coping with uncertainty but also to the ability of a unit/department in a university, for example, to cope effectively with the sources of uncertainty, specifically those sources that are deemed as central to an organization's operations.

From a resource-dependence perspective, universities depend on the external environment for resources, and this sometimes creates uncertainty within. Pfeffer and Salancik (2003) view this as an opportunity for individuals or units to garner power by coping with uncertainty associated with the scarcest or most critical resources. Rewarding a department for effectively coping with environmental uncertainties by providing access to more resources, bigger budgets, and higher status effectively strengthens the department's power. Such resource power can in turn be used by the department to legitimize and institutionalize its power in the university, which is sometimes manifested in blocking any attempts at resource redeployment or limiting other departments' access to sources of power (Hatch, 2013). Hence, in universities one observes the actions of deans of powerful faculties or heads of powerful departments and the influence they have on university-wide decisions. In these cases, power is used to create "informal" authority which can then be used to advance the interests of the power-holder or to control other less powerful groups or departments.

SUMMARY

In this chapter we have focused on university governance as process, and we have illuminated a number of conceptual lenses or theories that can be used to understand and explore these processes. Hierarchy plays an important role in universities in that there are formal positions of authority, but also because decisions are often only viewed as legitimate if they have moved up the hierarchy of decision-making bodies from the local academic unit, to the administration and other committees, and finally to the senate or board. It is generally argued that university governance is becoming more centralized and hierarchical as a function of increasing managerialism.

Governance processes can also be analyzed under the lens of bureaucracy in order to explore the formal power and authority relationships within the institution and the important role of procedural rules and policies. In contrast, the political lens illuminates the importance of both formal and informal power relationships as individuals and groups seek to further their interests through lobbying and the development of coalitions. Organized anarchy provides a way of exploring the less rational elements of university governance processes, and garbage can decision-making raises a series of fascinating questions about how and why decisions are made within the highly complex environment of the modern university. Finally, the chapter discussed how power and authority relationships within the university can be influenced by the ability of actors to contend with the uncertainties of the university's environment.

DISCUSSION QUESTIONS

1. It is frequently argued that the concept of bureaucracy has limited utility in exploring academic governance processes, but is this situation changing? Using examples, discuss whether academic governance has become more bureaucratic at your university or college.
2. The bureaucratic, political, and organized anarchy views of university governance give us very different lenses through which to observe and analyze complex governance processes, and one could argue that we see very different things depending on which lens we use. What is the role of the university president in each of these three perspectives on governance processes?
3. Use the garbage can model to analyze an important university decision that you are familiar with. In what ways did the model contribute to your understanding of that decision process? What do you see as some of the limitations associated with the garbage can model as an analytical tool?

REFERENCES

Apkarian, J., Mulligan, K., Rotondi, M. B., & Brint, S. (2014). Who governs? Academic decision-making in US four-year colleges and universities, 2000–2012. *Tertiary Education and Management, 20*(2), 151–164.

Baldridge, J. V. (1971). *Power and conflict in the university: Research in the sociology of complex organizations.* New York, NY: John Wiley.

Baldridge, J. V., Curtis, D. V., Ecker, G., & Riley, G. L. (1978). *Policy making and effective leadership.* San Francisco, CA: Jossey-Bass.

Bennett, N., Crawford, M., & Riches, C. (Eds.). (1992). Introduction: Managing educational change: Centrality of values and meanings. In *Managing change in education: Individual and organizational perspectives* (pp. 1–16). London, England: Paul Chapman.

Bess, J. L. (1988). *Collegiality and bureaucracy in the modern university.* New York, NY: Teachers College Press.

Bess, J. L. (1998). Contract systems, bureaucracies, and faculty motivation: The probable effects of a no-tenure policy. *Journal of Higher Education, 69*(1), 1–22.

Bess, J. L., & Dee, J. R. (2008). *Understanding college and the university organization: Theories for effective policy and practice.* Sterling, VA: Stylus.

Bleiklie, I. (2003). Hierarchy and specialisation: On the institutional integration of higher education systems. *European Journal of Education, 38*(4), 341–355.

Brunsson, N., & Sahlin-Anderson, K. (2000). Constructing organizations: The example of public sector reform. *Organization Studies, 21*(4), 721–746.

Clark, D. L. (1985). Emerging paradigms in organizational theory and research. In Y. Lincoln (Ed.), *Organizational theory and inquiry: The paradigm revolution* (pp. 43–78). Beverly Hills, CA: Sage.

Cohen, M., & March, J. G. (1974). *Leadership and ambiguity.* New York, NY: McGraw-Hill.

Cohen, M., & March, J. G. (1986). *Leadership and ambiguity* (2nd ed.). New York, NY: McGraw-Hill.

Cohen, M., March, J. G., & Olsen, J. P. (1972). A garbage can model of organizational choice. *Administrative Science Quarterly, 17*(1), 1–25.

Dahl, R. A. (1966). *Who governs? Democracy and power in an American city.* New Haven, CT: Yale University Press.

Dahrendorf, R. (1959). *Class and class conflict in industrial society.* Stanford, CA: Stanford University Press.

De Boer, H., Enders, J., & Leisyte, L. (2007). Public sector reform in Dutch higher education: The organizational transformation of the university. *Public Administration, 85*(1), 27–46.

Dowling-Hetherington, L. (2013). The changing shape of university decision-making processes and the consequences for faculty participation in Ireland. *Tertiary Education and Management, 19*(3), 219–232.

Gumport, P. J. (2012). Strategic thinking in higher education research. In M. N. Bastedo (Ed.), *The organization of higher education: Managing colleges for a new era* (pp. 18–41). Baltimore, MD: Johns Hopkins University Press.

Hatch, M-J. (2013). *Organization theory: Modern, symbolic, and postmodern perspectives.* Oxford, England: Oxford University Press.

Hearn, J. C., & McLendon, M. K. (2012). Governance research: From adolescence toward maturity. In M. N. Bastedo (Ed.), *The organization of higher education: Managing colleges for a new era* (pp. 45–85). Baltimore, MD: Johns Hopkins University Press.

Hickson, D. J., Hinings, C. R., Lee, C. A., Schneck, R. E., & Pennings, J. M. (1971). A strategic contingencies theory of intra-organizational power. *Administrative Science Quarterly, 16,* 216–229.

Johnsrud, L. K., & Rosser, V. J. (2002). Faculty members' morale and their intention to leave: A multilevel explanation. *Journal of Higher Education, 73*(4), 518–542.

Jones, G. A., Shanahan, T., & Goyan, P. (2004). The academic senate and university governance in Canada. *Canadian Journal of Higher Education, 34*(2), 35–68.

Kezar, A., & Eckel, P. D. (2004). Meeting today's governance challenges: A synthesis of the literature and examination of a future agenda for scholarship. *Journal of Higher Education, 75*(4), 371–399.

Lawrence, P.R., & Lorsch, J.W. (1967). Differentiation and integration in complex organizations. *Administrative Science Quarterly, 12*, 1–47.

Manning, K. (2001). Infusing soul into student affairs. In M.A. Jablonski (Ed.), *The implications of student spirituality for student affairs practice (New Directions for Student Services, No. 95*, pp. 25–35). San Francisco, CA: Jossey-Bass.

Manning, K. (2013). *Organizational theory in higher education.* New York, NY: Routledge.

Middlehurst, R. (1993). *Leading academics.* Buckingham, England: SRHE and Open University Press.

Mintzberg, H. (1979). *The structuring of organizations.* Englewood Cliffs, NJ: Prentice- Hall.

Morgan, G. (2006). *Images of organization* (3rd ed.). Thousand Oaks, CA: Sage.

Mortimer, K., & McConnell, T. (1979). *Sharing authority effectively.* San Francisco, CA: Jossey-Bass.

Olsen, J.P. (2001). Garbage cans, new institutionalism, and the study of politics. *American Political Science Review, 95*(1), 191–198.

Peters, B.G. (2012). *Institutional theory in political science: The new institutionalism.* New York, NY: Continuum.

Pfeffer, J. (1981). *Power in organizations.* Boston, MA: Pitman.

Pfeffer, J., & Salancik, G. (2003). *The external control of organizations: A resource dependence perspective.* New York, NY: Harper & Row.

Pugh, D.J., Hickson, D.J., & Hinings, C.R. (1969). An empirical taxonomy of structures of work organizations. *Administrative Science Quarterly, 14*(1), 115–126.

Sanyal, B.C. (1995). *Educational management: A unified approach of education.* New Delhi, India: Global India.

Selznick, P. (2005). Foundations of the theory of organization. In J.M. Shafritz, J.S. Ott, & Y-S. Jang (Eds.), *Classics of organizational theory* (6th ed., pp. 125–134). Belmont, CA: Thomson Wadsworth.

Stephenson, K. (2005). Trafficking in trust: The art and science of human knowledge networks. In L. Coughlin, E. Wingard, & K. Hollihan (Eds.), *Enlightened power: How women are transforming the practice of leadership* (pp. 242–265). San Francisco, CA: Jossey-Bass.

Stroup, H. (1966). *Bureaucracy in higher education.* New York, NY: Free Press.

Thompson, V.A. (1965). Bureaucracy and innovation. *Administrative Science Quarterly, 10*(1), 1–20.

CHAPTER 8

Governing the Managed Enterprise

In earlier chapters we presented the idea that some contemporary universities might be described as managed enterprises, a description that suggests a movement away from the traditional collegial model and towards practices and governance arrangements that are more closely associated with business. While concerns that American universities have been increasingly adopting business-like practices can be traced back to at least the early 20th century (Veblen, 1918), the current discussion frequently links changes in university management practices to the prevailing neoliberal ideology. As we will discuss in more detail in this chapter, some observers have suggested that this ideology is influencing the cultural, socioeconomic, and political world order and has had a significant impact on public sector governance, including universities. The impact is seen in the emergence of new governing practices variously referred to as managerialism, new managerialism, and new public management.

The adoption of these practices is based on the assumption that private sector management and governance approaches are needed for the proper functioning of the public sector. In some countries these ideas have influenced higher education governance, for example Australia (Christopher, 2014; Vidovich & Currie, 2011), the United Kingdom (Deem, Hillyard, & Reed, 2007), and New Zealand (Brenneis, Shore, & Wright, 2005; Shore, 2010).

In this chapter, we delve more deeply into these concepts by first locating the discussion within broader public sector practices. Specifically, we discuss the philosophical and ideological ideas of neoliberalism and the practices of managerialism, new managerialism, and new public management. We then extend the analysis to managing and governing higher education organizations. We believe that a deep conceptual exploration of these concepts is needed because the neoliberal ideology and its cognate practices now play an important role in the analysis of, and research on, higher education governance.

NEOLIBERALISM AND THE PUBLIC SECTOR

According to Saad-Filho and Johnston (2005), "we live in the age of neoliberalism" (p. 1). Neoliberalism has become a ubiquitous set of practices built around a specific set of beliefs. Specifically, it addresses the role to be played by the state and private citizens within a framework that is driven by an ideology of free-market fundamentalism and economic neo-Darwinism. In other words, the ideology is constructed around a market-driven rationality with an emphasis on individualism and ruthless competition and with a subtext that promotes a logic of privatization, efficiency, flexibility, the accumulation of capital, and the minimization of state actions (Giroux, 2010). For public sector entities, it represents a dramatic ideological shift in the way in which they are governed and how they undertake their societal functions in the 21st century. As publicly funded entities and as service-oriented public institutions, universities too have been impacted by this belief system (Braun & Merrien, 1999). Olssen and Peters (2005) describe it as "a politically imposed discourse" (p. 314) in which a specific economic philosophy has become dominant, although not equally so in all countries. The basic tenets of neoliberalism as summarized by Nef and Robles (2000) are as follows:

1. Re-establishing the rule of the market
2. Reducing taxes
3. Deregulating the private sector
4. Reducing public expenditure
5. The privatization of the public sector
6. The elimination of the collectivist concept of the "public good"

Neoliberalism is not a totally new idea. The label first appeared around the 1950s, but it gained more prominence from the 1970s on. Prior to neoliberalism, there were classical liberalism and economic liberalism, with which it shares some similarities, and Keynesianism, with which there are important conceptual differences. It is important to be familiar with these earlier predecessor concepts in order to have a clearer understanding of neoliberalism.

First, classical liberalism promotes a minimalist view of the state, where state involvement should be restricted to the armed forces, law enforcement, upholding of public order, and other nonexcludable goods, while everything else should be under the purview of citizens engaging in free exchanges (Thorsen & Lie, 2006). Considerable emphasis is placed on individual liberty.

Second, economic liberalism is a belief that the state should abstain from intervening in the economy, but it should promote the liberty of individuals to participate in free and self-regulating market exchanges (Thorsen & Lie, 2006). Economic liberalism has much in common with classical liberalism and it also has some commonality with neoliberalism, in that all of these concepts include notions of the self-interested individual, free-market economics, a commitment to laissez-faire practices in the marketplace, and a commitment to free trade (Olssen & Peters, 2005). However, as Olssen and Peters indicate, there are differences that are critical to understanding "the distinctive nature of the neoliberal revolution as it has impacted on OECD countries" (p. 315) and beyond. Importantly, the neoliberal ideology advocates for the state to have a role in organizing the market, while classical and economic liberalism focus on the free participation of individuals in a market that is unfettered by the state (Burchell, 1996; Olssen & Peters, 2005). In the application of neoliberal ideology to the higher education sector, for example, the state plays a less central role in directing the affairs of universities and more of a regulatory and market facilitative role.

Third, Keynesianism dominated economic theory and policy-making in many countries during the period from about 1945 to 1970. During this period, economic planning and industrial planning were state-led, the state undertook resource redistribution policies, and it practiced a welfare mode of governing. In the welfare mode of governing, there was significant public spending, including significant public financial support for universities. This economic practice was subsequently replaced by a neoliberal monetarist view inspired by the ideas of Milton Friedman (Thorsen & Lie, 2006). According to this view, the market is a more efficient mechanism for the distribution of resources than the welfare-based distribution that was inspired by state-led planning (Olssen & Peters, 2005). Hence, as public sector entities, contemporary universities and their governance have to be understood within this fundamental shift that began in the1980s in places like the UK and New Zealand and has become influential in other countries.

NEOLIBERALISM AND HIGHER EDUCATION GOVERNANCE

Evidence is emerging about the influence of neoliberal ideas on public higher education and universities. This belief system has brought about a transition in the identity of universities and their role in society (Braun & Merrien, 1999). And with this has been a transformation of the governance of universities. The governance of these institutions now reflects an ideological shift that advocates for quasimarket principles, private or corporate sector management techniques, and a minimalist state but not a passive one. Consequently, the discourse on governance has assumed a corporate logic (Giroux, 2010) and education is viewed "as an input-output system which can be reduced to an economic production function" (Olssen & Peters, 2005, p. 324). In other words, education has become a quantifiable product produced by education organizations by minimizing inputs and maximizing outputs. The collective result of this new ethos, according to Giroux and Giroux (2004), is an environment in which universities have to confront the challenges of budget cuts, new funding mechanisms, the downsizing of faculty, the corporatization and militarization of research, and curriculum restructuring to create an alignment with labor market training needs. Along with these conditions are measurement and monitoring regimes that are linked to quality assurance requirements, performance management practices, and international benchmarking activities (Shore, 2010; Shore & Wright, 1999).

Within universities, one can also observe changes in the structure of relations arising from a neoliberal discourse on governance and the hierarchical chain of authority and command. This approach to governing stems from the principal-agent orientation and is typical of the private sector. Olssen and Peters (2005) argue that the hierarchical structuring of authoritative relations is detrimental to autonomy, which is one of the guiding principles of governance in the academy, and it can have negative consequences for the roles and functions of academics, for example, the de-professionalization of academic staff. Olssen and Peters suggest three ways in which neoliberalism is de-professionalizing the academy.

1. The shift from a flat collegial structure of individual professional control to a hierarchical model in which top management asserts more control and specifies job performance requirements that ought to be satisfied.

2. Management becoming more involved in workload and course content decisions and hence limiting professional autonomy.
3. Market pressures encroaching on and in some cases shaping the traditional conception of professionalism. In such cases, the rights associated with professionalism are eroded and the autonomy over work is subject to external control (for example, the pressure to acquire external research grants and the external influence that can have on decision-making).

Thus, in some national and institutional contexts one observes internal structural changes within universities, a shift in decision-making authority, and a recasting of the professional culture of the academy. Shore (2010) describes it as the "professoriate being proletarianized" (p. 16), particularly with the rising number of adjunct and short-term contract faculty whose influence in decision-making is minimal or nonexistent. US public universities provide a classic case of this occurrence.

The neoliberal revolution is not restricted to Anglo-Saxon and Anglo-American democracies. Some scholars note that neoliberalism is also restructuring higher education in East Asia, where global trends of privatization, marketization, massification, and commodification are now part of the higher education landscape. For instance, as Mok (2005) reports, China's economic reforms have embraced the market model and the ideas and strategies of neoliberalism. Mok contends that China has adjusted its economic planning and public policy norms, guidelines, and regulations to align itself with the practices advocated by global governing entities such as the World Trade Organization (WTO). Consequently, China has created neoliberal policies and pro-competition instruments in order to reform and restructure how education is governed internally. Chinese students now have to pay tuition fees, a policy designed to shift at least some of the financial burden to students. This change parallels the neoliberal view that university education is an economic investment in the individual, and a private good, rather than a "public good" geared to producing an educated citizenry (Shore, 2010), although in China's case, the state still provides the majority of funding for universities.

Singapore, a country with a strong state-led development model, has also reformed its higher educational policies and strategies to align more closely with the prevailing neoliberal ideology and the notion of higher education as a tradable service. For example, Singapore has opened up its borders to foreign education providers and consumers under its Global Schoolhouse policy initiative and has incorporated its public universities (Lo, 2014). The Global Schoolhouse initiative was launched by the government to bring about changes that would diversify the higher education sector and decentralize the governance system. Despite these changes, Singapore still holds fast to a state-led model and the state plays a strong role in steering the reform process and holding universities accountable for meeting the goals of national policies (Marginson, 2013). Hence, neoliberalism is implemented in a different way compared to countries like the UK, Australia, and New Zealand, where the government has generally retreated from its central role in higher education and universities are increasingly influenced by the market forces (Lo, 2014). Higher education governance in Singapore, in contrast, is characterized by a neoliberal discourse that is integrated with a state-led development model. Mok (2008) describes it as "an authoritarian mode of liberalism" (p. 150).

What is gleaned here is that neoliberalism is being experienced in higher education across a range of different economic regimes but nevertheless there are similarities in the ways it is being experienced, which would suggest a global diffusion of the ideology. Capano (2011) makes this point in his examination of higher education governance in four European countries: Germany, Italy, the Netherlands, and the UK. Capano found variations in these countries, but the common trend was towards government steering from a distance. In Germany, Italy, and the Netherlands, the shift was towards less procedural governing in which the state granted significantly more latitude to universities in determining the means towards achieving an outcome, but focused more on specifying the goals to be achieved by universities. The UK also showed a similar trend in which the state became more involved in the specification of goals, while simultaneously limiting self-governance. These occurrences and practices are all part of the neoliberal agenda.

In the next sections of the chapter, we will discuss cognate areas of neoliberalism—managerialism and new public management.

MANAGERIALISM, NEW PUBLIC MANAGEMENT, AND GOVERNANCE

One of the outcomes of neoliberalism is the rise of practices of managerialism, or new managerialism as it is sometimes called, and new public management (Davies & Petersen, 2005). It is necessary to examine conceptually these modes of public sector practices in order to understand how they are reshaping governance. We begin first with managerialism.

Managerialism is an influential ideological movement or a belief system that "regards managing and management as being fundamentally and technically indispensable to the achievement of economic progress, technological development, and social order within any modern political economy" (Deem et al., 2007, p. 6). In other words, "managing" and "management" are core themes of managerialism, in which managing is a set of sociotechnical practices for rationally coordinating and controlling collective action, while management is the collective agents and institutions responsible for enacting these practices. Deem and her colleagues, in their analysis of university governance in the United Kingdom, outline three forms through which managerialism has evolved: neo-corporatist managerialism, neoliberal managerialism, and neo-technocratic managerialism.

Neo-corporatist managerialism was prevalent from about World War I to the 1970s, and it was a blend of Keynesian economic policy, state welfarism, political pluralism, industrial tri-partisan, and Fordist-style management that derived its legitimacy from serving the producer-led industrial society (Deem et al., 2007). A key concern of neo-corporatism was the relationship between state and society, particularly the tripartite relation between the state, representatives of labor, and capital (Kickert, 1997). Thus, bureaucratic and state welfare models combined in a manner that sought to minimize tension between contending owner and producer classes. Deem et al. point out that this mode of governing led to the emergence of professional bureaucracy as the dominant organizational form and that the design, delivery, and development of public services were the responsibility of professionals who were considered experts. In the UK in particular, these bureaucratic professionals played a lead role in strategic policymaking and institutional and administrative management. However, under this form of managerialism, there were some market inefficiencies, technological rigidities, and organizational inflexibility that limited its governing capabilities. Consequently, neo-corporatist managerialism collapsed because of its inability to cope with the economic, technological, political, and cultural changes that were occurring in the international political economy (Deem et al., 2007); the collapse of neo-corporatist managerialism was also accelerated by the economic crisis of the welfare state.

Neoliberal managerialism emerged as a critique of neo-corporatist managerialism and took root in the late 1970s and early 1980s. Deem et al. (2007) describe it as having an organizational logic and underlying ideological principles that were anti-state/pro-market, anti-provider/pro-consumer, and anti-bureaucracy/pro-network. Neoliberal managerialism advanced the free market concept and touted private business as a superior organizational form over governmental agencies. The adoption of market mechanisms and private sector organizational disciplines in the design, delivery, and management of public services was viewed as a means of enhancing strategic effectiveness and operational efficiency (Du Gay, 2000). The concept of neoliberal managerialism played an important role in radical transformations in the public sector in many countries since this conceptualization challenged the established power structures and control relations underpinned by bureaucratic principles of the neo-corporatist world. It also emphasized more accountability and deemphasized regulations. Deem et al. and others (e.g. Pollitt, 1993; Pollitt, Birchall, & Putman, 1998; Ferlie, Hartley, & Martin, 2003) posit that neoliberal managerialism was the ideological springboard from which NPM became a policy paradigm and mode of governance.

Neo-technocratic managerialism is the latest evolution of managerialism that is redefining policy priorities, organizational forms, and managerial practices in the continued organization of public sector organization (Deem et al., 2007). Deem et al. suggest that neo-technocratic managerialism relies more on metrics and less on markets to drive the delivery, organization, management, and governance of the public sector. It attends more to work-based performance management and control, places significant emphasis on consumerism, and reduces the technical expert to being a service provider.

NEW PUBLIC MANAGEMENT

The World Bank and other international organizations are proponents of the view that having sound or good governance is vital to economic development and societal advancement, and that the public sector should function on the basis of good governance. New public management (NPM) is a vehicle through which this good governance philosophy has been introduced to public sector organizations, including universities (de Boer, Enders, & Schimank, 2005). As a new paradigm for public management and governance, it promotes a modernization agenda and has reformed how the public sector functions in many countries. It has become a common dominant trend in OECD countries (Kickert, 1997), initially gaining traction in the UK and later in New Zealand, Australia, the US, Europe, and beyond. Some countries, like France for instance, have adopted NPM reforms without using the label to describe the reforms (Ferlie et al., 2009). The trend can also be found, for instance, in former Soviet countries such as Lithuania.

The practices associated with NPM include performance measurement, customer and bottom-line orientation, the revising of incentive schemes, deregulation, outsourcing, and privatization (Kersberger & Waarden, 2004). And although the public sector reform movement has varied in depth, scope, and success depending on the country, Kaboolian (1998) argues that the goals associated with public sector reforms have been quite similar. NPM is therefore seen as "a general structural prescription, spreading from OECD or Anglo-American countries as an instrumental 'super standard' or collection of structural standards for coping with problems common to public organizations" (Christensen & Laegreid, 1999, p. 171).

Diefenbach (2009) provides a more fine-grained conceptualization of NPM as:

> a set of assumptions and values statements about how public sector organizations should be designed, organized, managed and how, in a quasi-business manner, they should function. The basic idea of NPM is to make public sector organizations . . . much more "business-like" and "market-oriented" that is, performance-, cost-, efficiency-, and audit-oriented.
>
> (p. 893)

From this, one can readily glean three key elements: businesslike management, client-centeredness, and market-like competition. These are all private sector adaptations because NPM relies on theories and techniques from private sector management. In particular, it is conceptually influenced by organizational economics and draws on the principal-agent theory to give prominence to incentives and performance (Ferlie et al., 2009). NPM is associated with the notion of "hollowing out of the state" and the view that the state should be "steering" and playing a key role in policy decisions but not "rowing" and getting heavily involved with service delivery (Dent, Howorth, Mueller, & Preuschoft, 2004; Kersberger & Waarden, 2004; Osborne & Gaebler, 1992). The main idea behind it is for public sector organizations to have a new orientation, change the way they operate, and come in line with the larger epochal developments of globalization and neoliberalism.

NPM AND UNIVERSITIES

Public universities in some jurisdictions have also been affected by NPM. Critical observers in some countries have noted that universities have become managed entities in which the executive leadership is strengthened, and incentive steering, quality assurance, evaluation, and accountability have all taken root. For universities, it may be seen as an incompatible mix, given the prevailing assumptions about the university's basic characteristics. These characteristics include often being in pursuit of contradictory goals and being a deeply institutionalized entity with a strong collegial tradition (Leisyte & Kizniene, 2006; de Boer, Ender, & Leisyte, 2007). Nevertheless, changes spurred by NPM in the wider public sector have occurred, although in different countries at different times and to varying degrees. In countries like the UK and New Zealand where NPM has been significantly influential, universities have had to grapple with it much earlier than, for example, Germany. Consequently, there are significant variations in how NPM has influenced governance practices depending on the extent to which NPM is institutionalized, the different paths taken to implement it, and the different styles implemented (Leisyte & Kizniene, 2006). While these variations may have the appearance of a set of disorganized practices, de Boer et al. (2005) posit that "NPM is not just a bundle of loosely coupled or even disconnected changes, but rather an integrated approach towards an overall redirection of the entire university system" (p. 140). De Boer et al. note that proponents of NPM advocate that:

- The state should have less direct control of universities and focus more on goal setting.
- Market mechanisms should be used to increase efficiency and lower cost.
- Instead of having input controls, there should be ex post evaluations of performance.
- Universities should hire high quality managers and create the right environment for them to manage.
- Universities should compete for resources.
- Leadership should be strengthened.
- Stakeholder involvement should be an integral part of the long-term orientation to a university's competitive strategy.

Collectively, these principles constitute an integrated approach to governing universities. Although not all universities have adopted all these principles or in the same way, international research on university governance suggests that the academy as a managed enterprise is on the rise. For example, Meister-Scheytt (2007) indicates that "Austria's higher education institutions have undergone a process of profound change in the last decade from the classic Humboldtian type of institution to a 'modernized' and managed organization of knowledge production and dissemination" (p. 248). In this context, the practice of academic self-governance has been undermined and marginalized, specifically by labeling it as lacking in accountability to government and to society (Leisyte & Kizniene, 2006) and as not being efficient, effective, and cost containment focused. With specific reference to New Zealand, but equally applicable in some other countries, Shore (2008) summarizes the ethos of NPM and the contemporary context of university governance as:

> the transformation of the traditional liberal and Enlightenment idea of the university as a place of higher learning into the modern idea of the university as corporate enterprise whose primary concern is with market share, servicing the needs of commerce, maximizing economic return and investment, and gaining competitive advantage in the Global Knowledge Economy.
>
> (p. 282)

GOVERNANCE, QUALITY, AND QUALITY ASSURANCE

As stated earlier, much of the market development and the modes of governance associated with neoliberalism that have emerged over the last few decades have their foundation in the work of public choice theory, agency theory (discussed in chapter 2), and transaction cost economics as espoused by Oliver Williamson (1992). These theories emphasize efficiency and effectiveness. Governance, according to this logic, emphasizes compliance through mechanisms that are externally imposed and internally reinforced (Olssen & Peters, 2005). This is seen internally, for instance, with the rise of the audit culture that has become pervasive in some universities, ostensibly to enhance transparency and accountability (Shore, 2008), and externally, through the imposition of quality assurance requirements. In this section, we focus on quality assurance and how it is now a central instrument in governing universities.

Roger King (2007) discusses the rise of the higher education regulatory state in which there is an encroachment on the autonomy and the governing domain of higher education institutions by the state. Through regulatory mechanisms, such as quality assurance requirements and agencies, the state in many countries has sought to "undertake the classic regulatory functions of setting standards, monitoring activities, and applying enforcement to secure behaviour modifications" (King, 2007, p. 413). Jarvis (2014) reports that nearly half the countries in the world now have higher education quality assurance systems or quality assurance regulatory bodies and many of them have independent state bodies established to oversee and "ensure" quality in higher education. The worldwide spread of quality assurance in higher education can be further observed in the rapid growth in the membership of the International Network for Quality Assurance Agencies in Higher Education (INQAAHE).

In some instances, the regulatory bodies are national agencies but in others they are provincial (as in some parts of Canada), state (as in the United States), or regional (as in the Maritime Provinces of New Brunswick, Prince Edward Island, and Nova Scotia in Canada). In many cases, these quality assurance bodies are structurally separated from the traditional bureaucratic state governance so as to grant them independence and the level of authority required to oversee higher education institutions adequately. Engebretsen, Heggens, and Eilertsen (2012) describe the emergence of quality assurance mechanisms in Norway as a powerful new governance regime.

Despite the apparent global ubiquity of a focus on quality assurance, Jarvis (2014) points out that the nature of state-university relationships—specifically, their political and historical context, historical path dependencies, and institutional legacies—shape the way in which the governance of quality unfolds. In other words, there are cross-national variations in quality assurance practices and some important national exceptions (Weinrib & Jones, 2014). In some jurisdictions, the emphasis is entirely on public universities, while in other countries one of the key issues that quality assurance agencies are asked to address is whether private universities are maintaining appropriate standards. Despite these important differences, Jarvis (2014) argues that "there are discernible trends in regulatory approaches to quality assurance" (p. 159). A clear trend found in many countries is the re-assertion of the state over higher education (Dill & Beerkens, 2010). The quality assurance model in all these countries, be it the USA, the UK, Scandinavian countries, or China, is designed to force universities to be more accountable and to comply with the respective country's policy directions (Harvey & Newton, 2007). In particular, some governments have used quality assurance to reorient universities towards programming that is relevant to the contemporary workplace and that could enhance the countries' competitive position in world markets. Evidence of this approach can be observed through, for instance, the use of employer or industry assessments of graduates, levels of graduate employment, and reputational rankings of universities as indicators of "quality," indicators that might even be linked to performance funding. Hence, quality assurance has become an instrument of governance driven by neoliberal forces external to universities but institutionalized through internal structures.

Quality assurance as a governing instrument is also evident in the use of National Qualifications Frameworks (NQF). NQFs are regulatory in their logics. Jarvis (2014) points out that NQFs are used to standardize skills attainment, learning outcomes, program and course content, and metrics of academic credit or educational attainment and contends that they are increasingly being used as a metapolicy instrument for regulating higher education. These frameworks are not restricted to national jurisdictions but are also used in regional geographical spaces. For example, the Bologna agreement with a complement of 45 countries, including 25 European Union member states, stipulates that member countries should adopt a common qualifications framework. In addition, there are agencies with a quality assurance remit across Europe. For instance, the European Quality Assurance Register for Higher Education (EQAR) registers European quality assurance agencies and requires "substantial compliance with the Standards and Guidelines for Quality Assurance in the European Higher Education Area (ESG) before agencies can be admitted into the register" (ENQA, 2007, p. 6; Jarvis, 2014). Thus, at multiple levels—local, state, and regional—quality assurance regimes are spreading worldwide and, in many jurisdictions, they are system-level instruments of higher education governance. Jarvis argues that these quality assurance regimes are not benign managerial instruments, but rather, they constitute part of a larger neoliberal policy agenda that promotes market and economic rationalism. The adoption of these quality assessment mechanisms also has deeper implications for the governance of knowledge, in particular the type of knowledge the university is producing, for whom it is producing this knowledge, and how the knowledge disseminated is assessed.

LEADERSHIP POWER, AUTHORITY, AND INFLUENCE

Leadership is a multilevel activity. It occurs at the departmental level, faculty level, senate level, vice-chancellor or president level, or at the level of the governing board. It is incumbent upon university presidents, provosts, and vice-chancellors to govern, lead, and manage (Hearn & McClendon, 2012) in a manner that recognizes the multilevel nature and uniqueness of their institutions. The traditional university leadership-governance practice was based on a shared leadership and governance model in which there was vertical and lateral collegial interaction. That is to say, university leadership recognized the academy as having an institutionalized multilevel consensus-based decision-making model. However, in an environment of rapidly expanding enrolments, declining levels of public funding in some instances, stiff competition among institutions for public funds, and a strong emphasis on managing the academic enterprise, the leadership model and practices in universities have changed in some countries. The current neoliberal higher education environment is one in which universities are more and more pressured to adopt the logic of new managerialism (Blaschke, Frost, & Hattke, 2014) and adopt a stronger executive leadership model to support the rise of the entrepreneurial university (Clark, 1998). The current belief is that traditional modes of governing are inconsistent with the executive demands that are now placed on leaders.

The change can be observed in the strengthening of the leadership and management of universities' executive boards. For example, Shattock (2013) reports that university governing bodies in the UK were encouraged and empowered to undertake their responsibilities using a corporate board culture. Similarly referencing the UK, Middlehurst (2013) highlights the strengthening of the steering core in which there has been a broadening of the scope of the office of the vice-chancellor and a tightening of the linkages between the strengthened steering core and the academic heartland to create a more corporate institutional structure. In Australian universities, the vice-chancellor serves as the chief executive officer with an executive team (Rowlands, 2013), and this is also the case in other jurisdictions. Along with this has been the replacement of elected academic leaders with appointed managers, a development that has been described by Shattock (2013) as the "executivisation" of universities.

Thus, in the current higher education landscape, leadership and executive powers have been refashioned to align more closely with broader changes in the external environment, specifically increased responsibility and accountability superimposed on the need for strong fiscal and strategic management. With this has come a strong managerial governance culture in many universities along with changes in the distribution of power and influence in the academy. Such redistribution of power from intellectual capital (scholars) to academic capital (managers) (Rowlands, 2014) is sometimes at the root of contestation between the power of the scholar and the power of the manager/leader (Bourdieu, 1988; Rowlands, 2014). Managers sometimes exercise hegemonic authority supported by a consolidation of power within the office of the president, but there is also a corresponding diminution of the role of the academic board (Marginson & Considine, 2000; Rowlands, 2014). This has major implications for leadership in an environment that has traditionally been based on collegiality and the concept of *primus inter pares*.

In a study of three publicly funded Australian universities, Rowlands (2014) found that the locus of power resided with the vice-chancellor, who made key financial, strategic, and management decisions. Rowlands further found that these institutions used a top-down managerial style, the vice-chancellor and his executives dominated academic board meetings, and that they controlled the board agenda. Nevertheless, it was found that Australian universities still continued to practice collegial governance but in a modified form. Currie et al. (2003) posit that the future performance and success of universities will depend on "the ability to blend traditional academic values with new managerial values" (p. 78). It is therefore conceivable that governance and leadership would adopt hybridized models.

Variances exist in the extent to which there is executive domination of universities' decision-making and academic boards. While there seems to be general convergence towards a corporate governance model, there has been considerable resistance to these trends in some institutions, and there may be structural factors that have served to limit the adoption of a corporate model. In Canada, for example, the role and authority of university senates is enshrined in the charter legislation, and while there may have been shifts in the balance of authority between the senate, board, and administration, the senate continues to have the legal authority to determine academic policy for the institution, a structural reality that obviously limits the executive authority of the central administration (Jones, 2002; Pennock, Jones, Leclerc, & Li, 2015). Institutional cultures, traditions, faculty unions, and student activism can also stifle, or at least limit, the adoption of corporate-style administrative authority within a university.

GOVERNANCE IN A STRATEGIC CONTEXT

As early as 1983, Keller suggested that higher education governance needed to become more strategic. Keller was mindful of the weakness of the collegial model to cope with the changing external environment. Some scholars felt that the academy and strategic planning/management were incompatible (Birnbaum, 2000). This view was strengthened particularly by the uniqueness of higher education institutions—organizations with ambiguous goals (Cohen & March, 1974), loosely coupled structures (Weick, 1976), contradictory functions (Castells, 2001), a collegial academic community of scholars (Machado & Taylor, 2010), and a different structural configuration based on shared governance (Clark, 1983).

As we entered the 21st century, institutional accountability and responsibility significantly increased in many jurisdictions, and along with this there has been a greater emphasis on managing the higher education enterprise. Driven by pressure from governments, especially in the Anglo-Saxon countries, integrated performance management systems have crept into universities with a battery of performance indicators (Sarrico, 2010). These systems link organizational strategy and performance measurement. Consequently, strategic management and the associated governing instruments have become a day-to-day way of functioning within higher education institutions. Bouckaert and Halligan (2008) advanced the idea of governance for performance as the way universities should be governed in an enterprise- and performance-management environment. Many higher education institutions have granted governing authority to strategic management/planning units to oversee the planning process, monitor the progress towards attaining strategic plans, and evaluate overall outcomes. Often, the attainment of strategic outcomes is tied to funding and resource allocation levels.

A key element of strategic planning is ensuring that the organization's plans are in sync with the realities of the external environment. In the managed enterprise of higher education, universities too must attend to the external environments. Not only is this important for good strategic planning, but universities have to conform in order to secure and maintain their legitimacy (DiMaggio & Powell, 1991). This attention to the external environment has increased the influence of external stakeholders, largely through the greater involvement of external stakeholders in institutional governance processes such as advisory councils and governing boards. Given that public universities do not have shareholders, a strategic governing model for higher education institutions should recognize accountabilities to, and engagement with, their multiple stakeholders whose interests need to be understood and explicitly or implicitly taken into consideration.

Amaral, Meek, and Larsen (2003) point to the growing presence of external stakeholders in the governance of higher education institutions. This trend has continued. Some of these external stakeholders occupy positions on governing boards that usually sit at the nexus between the internal and external environment. And in addition to their oversight function, they sometimes serve to forestall threats and create access to opportunities for universities. In addition, the governing board usually approves the strategic plan of a university and subsequently monitors progress towards its attainment. Thus, governance becomes less internally and institutionally confined and instead involves a blurring of boundary lines between the internal and external environment.

POLICY NETWORKS AND NETWORK GOVERNANCE

Policy networks are another way of understanding governance processes and the influence of internal and external stakeholders. The concept of policy networks assumes that decisions do not emerge within a vacuum of an executive office, but rather through interactions within a complex network of interested parties and stakeholders (Padure & Jones, 2009). A government decision on higher education policy, for example, might have been made following extensive formal and informal interactions among the senior officials of the lead government agency, institutional leaders, student groups, business organizations, a professor who is an expert in this policy area, and a retired but highly influential former politician. The concept can also be used to explore the internal governance of institutions by recognizing that senior administrators do not work in isolation, but that key decisions may have emerged from interactions and consultations with a wide range of actors both inside and outside the university.

Klemenčič (2012, 2014) argues that the direction of higher education policy-making worldwide suggests a movement towards policy networks in which there is less hierarchy and policy decisions are being negotiated and mediated among several stakeholders rather than simply imposed by the authorities. In the current neoliberal environment, the state plays a less central role and political resources are distributed to a variety of public and private sector actors. This forces universities to include a wider array of actors in their decision-making process in order to demonstrate good policy formulation, secure legitimization of the adopted policy, and satisfy accountability expectations (de Boer, Enders, & Schimank 2007; Klemenčič, 2014; Olsen, 2005). Universities too have developed networks of relationships between themselves which allows for the sharing of information, benchmarking, and the development of new networks of senior academic leaders.

Network governance can be defined as the strategic use of networks as a governance mechanism and seen as an alternative approach to traditional public-sector governance. Network governance is a very different way of envisioning the implementation and management of public sector programs and services. Networks are made up of multiple organizations or entities which are tied by some form of structural interdependence in which one unit is not the subordinate of others by virtue of its formal position (O'Toole, 1997, p. 45). In other words, there is a peer-to-peer relationship through which these multiple actors coordinate their joint activities (Turrini, Cristofoli, Frosini, & Nasi, 2010). With network governance, more actors are involved compared with traditional bureaucratic practices and the power to coordinate is shared between actors, but the state plays a facilitative role rather than a directive one (Ferlie et al., 2009). Such governance entails more lateral and less vertical forms of management and the state is viewed as governing with the society and not above it.

SUMMARY

In this chapter, we discussed the rise of neoliberalism and the ways in which neoliberalism has impacted public policy and governance practices in higher education. Generally speaking, neo-liberalism positions higher education as primarily a private good that benefits the individual student, and the government steps back in order to increase the influence of the market. It is assumed that the efficiency and effectiveness of universities can be improved if they adopt the decision-making approaches of the private sector; they should be managed enterprises. We then reviewed a series of related concepts and ideas that help us understand the changes in administrative practices associated with neo-liberalism, including managerialism and new public management. As the state steps back from funding and broadly regulating higher education, quality assessment mechanisms have emerged as an important, and often quite powerful, governance instruments. Given the reduced role of government and the increasing role of the market, it becomes extremely important for universities to consider the external environment in their strategic planning and to involve and engage external stakeholders. The concept of policy networks provides a way of understanding the complex formal and informal interactions that may underscore governance and decision-making, while network governance is the strategic use of networks to engage stakeholders in governance processes.

DISCUSSION QUESTIONS

1. At some universities presidents are elected by their peers, while at other universities they are appointed by the governing board following a search process. What are the implications of each of these methods of selecting a president for the university as a "managed enterprise"?
2. Are world-class research universities more likely or less likely to adopt a strong executive governance model compared with lower status universities where teaching is viewed as its major function? Why?
3. Imagine that you are a recent doctoral graduate applying for your first academic position and you have two job offers. Would the level of "managerialism" or the culture of shared governance at each university have any bearing on your decision? Why or why not?

REFERENCES

Amaral, A. V., Meek, L., & Larsen, I. M. (Eds.). (2003). *The higher education managerial revolution?* Dordrecht, The Netherlands: Kluwer.

Birnbaum, R. (2000). The life cycle of academic management fads. *The Journal of Higher Education, 71*(1), 1–16.

Blaschke, S., Frost, J., & Hattke, F. (2014). Towards a micro foundation of leadership, governance, and management in universities. *Higher Education, 68,* 711–732. doi.10.1007/s10734-014-9740-2

Bouckaert, G., & Halligan, J. (2008). *Managing performance: International comparisons.* Abingdon, England: Routledge.

Bourdieu, P. (1988). *Homo academicus.* Cambridge, England: Polity Press.

Braun, D., & Merrien, F-X. (1999). Governance of universities and modernisation of the state: Analytical aspects. In D. Braun & F-X. Merrien (Eds.), *Towards a new model of governance for universities? A comparative view* (pp. 9–33). London, England: Jessica Kingsley.

Brenneis, D., Shore, C., & Wright, S. (2005). Getting the measure of academia: Universities and the politics of accountability. *Anthropology in Action, 12*(1), 1–10.

Burchell, G. (1996). Liberal government and techniques of the self. In A. Barry, T. Osborne & N. Rose (Eds.), *Foucault and political reason* (pp. 19–36). Chicago, IL: University of Chicago Press.

Capano, G. (2011). Government continues to do its job. A comparative study of governance shifts in the higher education sector. *Public Administration, 89*(4), 1622–1642.

Castells, M. (2001). The new global economy. In J. Muller, N. Cloete, & S. Badat (Eds.), *Challenges of globalisation: South African debates with Manuel Castells* (pp. 2–21). Cape Town, South Africa: Maskew Miller Longman.

Christensen, T., & Laegreid, P. (1999). New public management: Design, resistance, or transformation? A study of how modern reforms are received in a civil service system. *Public Productivity & Management Review, 23*(2), 169–193.

Christopher, J. (2014). Australian public universities: Are they practising a corporate approach to governance? *Studies in Higher Education, 39*(4), 560–573. doi.10.1080/03075079.2012.709499

Clark, B. R. (1983). *The higher education system: Academic organization in cross-national perspective.* Berkeley, CA: University of California Press.

Clark, B. R. (1998). *Creating entrepreneurial universities: Organizational pathways of transformation.* Oxford, England: Pergamon.

Cohen, M. D., & March, J. G. (1974). *Leadership and ambiguity.* New York, NY: McGraw-Hill.

Currie, J., DeAngelis, R., de Boer, H., Huisman, J., & Lacotte, C. (2003). *Globalizing practices and university responses: European and Anglo-American.* Westport, CT: Praeger.

Davies, B., & Petersen, E. (2005). Neo-liberal discourse in the academy: The forestalling of (collective) resistance. *LATISS: Learning and Teaching in the Social Sciences, 2*(2), 77–98. doi.10.1386/ltss.2.2.77/1

de Boer, H. F., Enders, J., & Leisyte, L. (2007). Public sector reform in Dutch higher education: The organizational transformation of the university. *Public Administration, 85*(1), 27–46.

de Boer, H. F., Enders, J., & Schimank, U. (2005). *Orchestrating creative minds. The governance of higher education and research in four countries compared.* Enschede, The Netherlands: CHEPS.

de Boer, H. F., Enders, J., & Schimank, U. (2007). On the way towards new public management? The governance of university systems in England, the Netherlands, Austria, and Germany. In D. Jansen (Ed.), *New forms of governance in research organizations: Disciplinary approaches, interfaces and integration* (pp. 137–152). Dordrecht, The Netherlands: Springer.

Deem, R., Hillyard, S., & Reed, M. (2007). *Knowledge, higher education, and the new managerialism: The changing management of UK universities.* Oxford, England: Oxford University Press.

Dent, M., Howorth, C., Mueller, F., & Preuschoft, C. (2004). Archetype transition in the German health service? The attempted modernization of hospitals in a North German state. *Public Administration, 82*(3), 727–742.

Diefenbach, T. (2009). New public management in public sector organizations: The dark sides of managerialistic "enlightenment." *Public Administration, 87*(4), 892–909.

Dill, D. D., & Beerkens, M. (2010). *Public policy for academic quality: Analyses of innovative policy instruments.* New York, NY: Springer.

DiMaggio, P. J., & Powell, W. W. (1991). *The new institutionalism in organizational analysis.* Chicago, IL: University of Chicago Press.

Du Gay, P. (2000). *In praise of bureaucracy.* London, England: Sage.

Engebretsen, E., Heggen, K., & Eilertsen, H. A. (2012). Accreditation and power: A discourse analysis of a new regime of governance in higher education. *Scandinavian Journal of Educational Research, 56*, 401–417.

ENQA. (2007). *Report to the London Conference of Ministers on a European Register of Quality Assurance Agencies.* Occasional Paper 13, Helsinki, Finland. Retrieved from http://www.enqa.eu/indirme/papers-and-reports/occasional-papers/ENQA%20occasional%20papers%2013(1)

Ferlie, E., Hartley, J., & Martin, S. (2003). Changing public service organizations: Current per-spectives and future prospects. *British Journal of Management, 14*, 1–14.

Ferlie, E., Musselin, C., & Andresani, G, (2009). The governance of higher education systems: A public management perspective. In C. Paradeise, E. Reale, I. Bleiklie, & E. Ferlie (Eds.), *University governance: Western European comparative perspectives* (pp. 1–19). Dordrecht, The Netherlands: Springer.

Giroux, H. A. (2010). Bare pedagogy and the scourge of neoliberalism: Rethinking higher edu-cation as a democratic public sphere. *Educational Forum, 74*(3), 184–196.

Giroux, H. A., & Giroux, S. S. (2004). *Take back higher education: Race, youth, and the crisis of democ-racy in the post-civil rights era.* New York, NY: Palgrave Macmillan.

Harvey, L., & Newton, J. (2007). Transforming quality evaluation: Moving on. In M. J. Rosa, B. Stensaker, & D. F. Westerheijden (Eds.), *Quality assurance in higher education: Trends in regulation, translation and transformation* (pp. 225–246). Dordrecht, The Netherlands: Springer.

Hearn, J. C., & McLendon, M. K. (2012). Governance research: From adolescence toward matu-rity. In M. N. Bastedo (Ed.), *The organization of higher education: Managing colleges for a new era* (pp. 45–85). Baltimore, MD: Johns Hopkins University Press.

Jarvis, D.S.L. (2014). Regulating higher education: Quality assurance and neo-liberal manageri-alism in higher education: A critical introduction. *Policy and Society, 33*, 155–166.

Jones, G. A. (2002). The structure of university governance in Canada: A policy network approach. In A. Amaral, G. A. Jones, & B. Karseth (Eds.), *Governing higher education: National perspectives on institutional governance* (pp. 213–234). Dordrecht, The Netherlands: Kluwer.

Kaboolian, L. (1998). The new public management: Challenging the boundaries of the manage-ment versus administration debate. *Public Administration Review, 58*(3), 189–193.

Keller, G. (1983). *Academic strategy: The management revolution in American higher education.* Balti-more, MD: Johns Hopkins University Press.

Kersberger, K. V., & Waarden, F. V. (2004). "Governance" as a bridge between disciplines: Cross-disciplinary inspiration regarding shifts in governance and problems of governability, accountability and legitimacy. *European Journal of Political Research, 43*(2), 143–171.

Kickert, W. J. M. (1997). Public governance in the Netherlands. An alternative to Anglo-American managerialism. *Public Administration, 75*(4), 731–753.

King, R. (2007). Governance and accountability in the higher education regulatory state. *Higher Education, 53*, 411–430.

Klemenčič, M. (2012). Student representation in Western Europe: Introduction to the special issue. *European Journal of Higher Education, 2*(1), 2–19. doi.10.1080/21568235.2012.695058

Klemenčič, M. (2014). Student power in a global perspective and contemporary trends in student organising. *Studies in Higher Education, 39*(3), 396–411. doi.10.1080/03075079.2014.896177

Leisyte, L., & Kizniene, D. (2006). New public management in Lithuania's higher education. *Higher Education Policy, 19*, 377–396.

Lo, W. Y. W. (2014). Think global, think of local: The changing landscape of higher education and the role of quality assurance in Singapore. *Policy and Society, 33*, 263–273.

Machado, M. L., & Taylor, J. S. (2010). The struggle for strategic planning in European higher education: The case of Portugal. *Research in Higher Education Journal, 6*, 1–20.

Marginson, S. (2013). The impossibility of capitalist markets in higher education. *Journal of Education Policy, 28*(3), 353–370.

Marginson, S., & Considine, M. (2000). *The enterprise university.* Melbourne, Australia: Cam-bridge University Press.

Meister-Scheytt, C. (2007). Reinventing governance: The role of boards of governors in the new Austrian university. *Tertiary Education and Management, 13*(3), 247–261.

Middlehurst, R. (2013). Changing internal governance: Are leadership roles and management structures in United Kingdom universities fit for the future? *Higher Education Quarterly, 67*(3), 275–294.

Mok, K. H. (2005). Globalization and educational restructuring: University merging and changing governance in China. *Higher Education, 50,* 57–88.

Mok, K. H. (2008). Varieties of regulatory regimes in Asia: The liberalization of the higher education market and changing governance in Hong Kong, Singapore and Malaysia. *The Pacific Review, 21*(2), 147–170.

Nef, J., & Robles, W. (2000). Globalization, neoliberalism, and the state of underdevelopment in the new periphery. *Journal of Developing Societies, 16*(1), 27–48.

Olsen, J. P. (2005). *The institutional dynamics of the (European) university*. Arena Working Paper No. 15. Oslo, Norway: ARENA.

Olssen, M., & Peters, M. A. (2005). Neoliberalism, higher education and the knowledge economy: From the free market to knowledge capitalism. *Journal of Education Policy, 20*(3), 313–345.

Osborne, D., & Gaebler, T. (1992). *Reinventing government: How the entrepreneurial spirit is transforming the public sector*. Reading, MA: Addison-Wesley.

O'Toole, L. J., Jr. (1997). Treating networks seriously: Practical and research-based agendas in public administration. *Public Administration Review, 57*(1), 45–52.

Padure, L., & Jones, G. A. (2009). Policy networks and research on higher education governance and policy. In J. Huisman (Ed.), *International perspectives on governance of higher education systems: Alternative frameworks for coordination* (pp. 107–125). New York, NY: Routledge.

Pennock, L., Jones, G. A., Leclerc, J. M., & Li, S. X. (2015). Assessing the role and structure of academic senates in Canadian universities, 2000–2012. *Higher Education*. doi.10.1007/s10734-014-9852-8

Pollitt, C. (1993). *Managerialism and the public services: Cuts or cultural change in the 1990s?* Oxford, England: Blackwell Business.

Pollitt, C., Birchall, J., & Putman, K. (1998). *Decentralising public management*. London, England: Macmillan.

Rowlands, J. (2013). Academic boards: Less intellectual and more academic capital in higher education governance? *Studies in Higher Education, 38*(9), 1274–1289.

Rowlands, J. (2014). Turning collegial governance on its head: Symbolic violence, hegemony and the academic board. *British Journal of Sociology of Education, 35*(1), 1–19. doi.10.1080/01425692.2014.883916

Saad-Filho, A., & Johnston, D. (2005). Introduction. In A. Saad-Filho & D. Johnston (Eds.), *Neoliberalism: A critical reader* (pp. 1–6). London, England: Pluto Press.

Sarrico, C. S. (2010). On performance in higher education: Towards performance governance. *Tertiary Education and Management, 16*(2), 145–158.

Shattock, M. (2013). University governance, leadership and management in a decade of diversification and uncertainty. *Higher Education Quarterly, 67*(3), 217–233.

Shore, C. (2008). Audit culture and illiberal governance: Universities and the politics of accountability. *Anthropological Theory, 8*(3), 278–299.

Shore, C. (2010). Beyond the multiversity: Neoliberalism and the rise of the schizophrenic university. *Social Anthropology, 18*(1), 15–29.

Shore, C., & Wright, S. (1999). Audit culture and anthropology: Neoliberalism in British higher education. *Journal of the Royal Anthropological Institute, 5*(4), 557–575.

Thorsen, D. E., & Lie, A. (2006). *What is neoliberalism?* Unpublished manuscript. Oslo, University of Oslo, Department of Political Science. Retrieved from http://scholar.google.ca/scholar?hl=en&q=classical+liberal+view+of+Hayek+%281976%29&btnG=&as_sdt=1%2C5&as_sdtp=

Turrini, A., Cristofoli, D., Frosini, F., & Nasi, G. (2010). Networking literature about determinants of network effectiveness. *Public Administration, 88*(2), 528–550.

Veblen, T. (1918). *The higher learning in America: A memorandum on the conduct of universities by businessmen.* New York, NY: B. W. Huebsch.

Vidovich, L., & Currie, J., (2011). Governance and trust in higher education. *Studies in Higher Education, 36*(1), 43–56.

Williamson, O. E. (1992). Markets, hierarchies and the modern corporation: An unfolding perspective. *Journal of Economic Behaviour and Organisation, 17*(3), 335–352.

Weick, K. E. (1976). Educational organizations as loosely coupled systems. *Administrative Science Quarterly, 21*(1), 1–19.

Weinrib, J., & Jones, G. A. (2014). Largely a matter of degrees: Quality assurance and Canadian universities. *Policy and Society, 33*(3), 225–236.

CHAPTER 9

New Issues and Challenges in Governance

Higher education in the 21st century looks very different from a few decades ago, with new issues and challenges reshaping the sector and its governance both at the institutional and system levels. The issues and challenges impacting the governance environment are significantly driven by factors such as the demands created by massification, changing economic conditions among the nation-states, the desires of national governments for higher education to respond holistically to the socioeconomic and cultural advancement of nations, more heterogeneous student bodies, new funding arrangements (both privatization of sources and performance-based funding), the expectations of students in a customer-oriented environment, and the clarion call for efficiency, effectiveness, and value for money. In the first part of this chapter we look at governance issues related to risk, trust, information technology, and multi-campus institutional arrangements. In the second half of the chapter we focus on the complex governance issues related to the glonacal, transnational, and regional dimensions of higher education.

GOVERNING RISK

Risk can be interpreted as a socially constructed concept that emphasizes the probability of a negative outcome. The Higher Education Funding Council for England (HEFCE) (2004) defines risk as "the threat or possibility that an action or event will adversely or beneficially affect an organization's ability to achieve its objective" (p. 24; cf. Huber, 2009, p. 86). The USA National Association of College and University Business Officers and PriceWaterhouseCoopers (2001) defines it as "any issue that impacts an organization's ability to meet its objectives. . . . [and] risks fall into five categories: strategic risk, financial risk, operational risk; compliance risk; and reputational risk" (p. 4; cf. Clyde-Smith, 2014, p. 328).

Risk management has for some time been an important aspect of the management of private firms and public companies. But in the aftermath of corporate scandals and collapses, there has been increased emphasis on this function as one means of improving corporate governance. Many corporate boards are now required to undertake risk management as part of their fiduciary duty of care (Ingley & van der Walt, 2008) and it has been accompanied by the implementation of risk management systems (Subramaniam, McManus, & Zhang, 2009). The audit committee is another mechanism relied on by boards in governing risk (Korosec & Horvat, 2005). More recently, the risk management committee (RMC) has emerged as yet another instrument used in corporate governance to assist boards in meeting their corporate risk management responsibilities (Subramaniam et al., 2009).

Risk management and governance has moved beyond the corporate sector and is now featured more prominently in universities (Huber, 2009). Much of the impetus for this came from the private sector and the collapse of a number of large-scale private enterprises such as Enron. However, Huber reports that as early as 2000 in England, the HEFCE introduced a mandatory risk management framework for higher education institutions. Other countries are pursuing similar policies and setting up governing mechanisms. For instance, the enterprise risk management (ERM) system has been adopted as a new paradigm in higher education for managing risk portfolios (University Risk Management and Insurance Association, 2007). One governing mechanism used for this purpose is the establishment of management audit departments or risk management and internal audit departments. For example, the University of Pretoria in South Africa uses the title Risk Management and Internal Audit and the department "provides. . . . services to support the University Council and University Management in executing its corporate governance responsibilities namely Risk Management support" (University of Pretoria, 2015). Risk governance has also become an integral element of the accreditation process in some higher education systems. In these instances, universities are required to report on the risk governance process in their accreditation review.

In addition, higher education institution leaders are concerned about the risk associated with natural hazards such as hurricanes, typhoons, and floods and, more recently, with issues of campus violence and possible acts of terrorism. While the concept of risk management is largely framed in financial terms, there is a growing awareness that university governance needs to address broader issues of community safety in the face of a catastrophic incident and personal and community support in response to crises. The issue of crisis preparedness—ensuring that there are policies and plans in place to deal with, for example, sexual assault, campus shooting incidents, and major natural disasters—has become a major governance challenge. Governance must now address issues of responsibility, relationships with local emergency services, on- and off-campus communication, and allow institutional support for the needs and safety of victims and community members.

GOVERNANCE AND TRUST

Trust is a complex phenomenon with different interpretations (De Boer, 2002; Lane, 1998). From a cognitive perspective, Zucker (1986) describes three forms of trust: characteristic-based, process-based, and institutional-based trust. Characteristic-based trust is derived from social similarity and cultural congruence in the sense that all parties belong to the same social group and background (De Boer, 2002). Process-based trust is the result of repeated interactions among parties. Institution-based trust is an impersonal form of trust that is related more to formal social structures. Arguably, these characteristics resonate with governance in the academy and at the system level.

Higher education scholars like De Boer (2002), Tierney (2006), and Vidovich and Currie (2011) have all shown an interest in looking at governance through the trust lens. They highlight the importance of trust to understanding, analyzing, and improving governance. Tierney (2006) for example focuses on trust and governance at the institutional level, Vidovich and Currie (2011) examine trust in Australian governance at the system level, and De Boer similarly investigated trust and system-level governance in the Netherlands. What is evident from these scholars is that trust is pertinent to governance both at the organizational and at the systems levels.

In defining trust, it is useful to juxtapose trust and distrust. Thus, according to Migliore and DeClouette (2011), "trust is the positive expectation that another's motives, behaviors, and competence levels will produce positive outcomes, and distrust is the negative expectation regarding another's motives, behaviors, and competence levels" (p. 321). Hence, trust increases when behaviors and outcomes from an individual conform to expectations, while distrust increases with the converse (Migliore, 2012). Goedegebuure and Hayden (2007) juxtapose compliance of higher education institutions with the state requirements to the notion of trust. They argue that compliance is the flip side of trust and note that some countries have lost the trust they previously had with key stakeholders, including the government. Goedegebuure and Hayden suggest that good governance is essential to regaining trust, which is an important element of institutions achieving their mission in competitive knowledge-based societies.

Building strong relationships leads to trust between parties, and trust too leads to good relationships (Kezar, 2004). Tierney (2006), in commenting on internal or institutional governance, uses the term *repeated interactions* between parties to describe one way of building trust, although mindful that one or a few bad interactions can destroy trust. Tierney suggests that "trust is inevitably social and relational" (p. 21) and that it is the social capital developed through "positive" *repeated interactions* that is the basis of trust. Tierney believes that faculty involvement in institutional governance and having repeated interactions is critical for building social capital and a culture of trust, and sees risk-taking and innovation as an important organizational outcome of building trust. Interactions also occur as governing boards undertake their governance responsibilities and engage with faculty and administration, particularly on issues of accountability. This too requires trust between parties or governing bodies. The governance-trust nexus is therefore a dynamic process whereby different parties are involved in a series of interactions in which some risk or faith is required on the part of one or all parties (Tierney, 2006).

Vidovich and Currie (2011) extend the trust concept to system-level governance in which the principal parties are institutions of government and universities. Trust is a prime consideration in jurisdictions where governments attempt to have greater regulatory control over higher education, albeit with context-specific differences. For example, the "Group of Eight" research-intensive universities in Australia advocated for less regulation and more trust from the government noting "it is about whether it is appropriate for the government of the day to dictate how universities manage their governance, or whether universities should be trusted to manage their own affairs" (Robson, 2008; cf. Vidovich & Currie, 2011, p. 50).

Avis (2003) suggests that the decline in trust observed in higher education governance between institutions of government and universities is the result of the market competitiveness and the performance driven ethos of globalization that has engulfed higher education. Vidovich and Currie (2011) argue that even in instances when government has relied on financial tools such as "incentives" to support policy implementation in Australian higher education, the approach has been more about coercion than incentives, and this in turn has adverse implications for government-institutional trust. They found, in essence, that the protocols advocated by the government to which universities' compliance was required "represented significant pressure from the external environment of universities to build economic capital for enhanced positioning in the global marketplace, and for university governing bodies to adopt more corporate structures to achieve this end" (p. 54). From a trust perspective, what is important for governance is that these events are major changes and such changes can lead to a reassessment of existing trust relationships, which may lead to a breakdown of bonds and relationships between universities and governments (Tucker, Yeow, & Viki, 2013). As De Boer (2002) notes, the lack of trust also leads to inefficiencies, since increasing accountability and reporting requirements uses resources that could be devoted to other activities. Hence, given the importance of trust to the governance process, major changes would require processes of sense making between parties to safeguard against degrading relationships and ultimately, the diminution of the quality of governance.

GOVERNANCE AND INFORMATION TECHNOLOGY

In this section, we discuss information technology (IT) as an instrument of governance as opposed to governing the technology itself. According to Hashim, Alam, and Siraj (2010), "information technology (IT) helps us to collect, synthesize and analyze a huge amount of open ended and close ended data while maintaining a high level of ethical practice as well as ensuring confidentiality" (p. 384). IT is now fairly widespread and commonplace in higher education institutions and in some cases e-management systems have been developed to support institutional activities such as strategic management and policy, decision-making and planning, and governance and regulatory control (Hashim et al., 2010). Ernst and Young (2012) lists digital technologies and the ways in which they are used to deliver higher education and create value as one of the five key trends impacting higher education globally.

From a governance standpoint, IT plays a critical role in the process of decision-making. It allows information and data that are relied on for decision-making purposes to be routed more efficiently and effectively to users. IT therefore facilitates faster and more efficient decision-making by providing decision-makers with simultaneous access to relevant information and data. Arguably, in this way the governing process benefits from information speed and quality, which are at the heart of regulatory control and planning. For instance, the strategic capacity of universities has been enhanced through an emphasis on business intelligence processes and sophisticated data analysis which allow performance tracking and data trends to be observed in real time (Middlehurst, 2013).

In addition, Middlehurst (2013) notes that some institutions are adapting their collegiality to take advantage of developments in information and communications technology. Thus, one can see how important IT can be to improving efficiency, value-for-money, performance, and responsiveness of higher education institutions and their governance and, ultimately, the higher education sector. The challenge therefore for higher education institutions is to define the balance between having dependable technologies through which information and data are secured, ensuring participation and consultation in the decision-making process and safeguarding ethical and confidential practices.

GOVERNING MULTI-CAMPUS UNIVERSITIES

Multi-campus universities have been in existence for many years. But in more recent times, there has been a proliferation of multi-campus institutions with existing campuses expanding and building new campuses. Some of these new campuses are in different locations within the same national jurisdiction while others are located in different countries as a part of strategic positioning to enhance their global reach. Broadly speaking, there are two types of multi-campus universities: (1) the case in which a university has a main or "mature" campus that has responsibility for the administration and coordination of branch campuses, and (2) a multi-campus arrangement made up of a collection of individual campuses that constitute an overall system.

In the first case, the leadership of the branch campuses is accountable to the leadership of the main campus. The governance arrangements at these campuses are somewhat complex and present a number of issues. For example, Dengerink (2001) believes that issues such as how much autonomy branch campuses have in determining their budgets; the role that faculty at branch campuses play in the senate of the parent campus; how much freedom branch campuses have to conduct independent fund-raising campaigns; whether the branch campuses should be independent regional campuses with different missions and identities from that of the main campus; or how much control deans and departmental chairs at the main campus have over the curriculum. These are governance questions that should be resolved when a new branch campus is being established. A typical example of this type of multi-campus arrangement is the University of Toronto, in Canada. It has a main campus and two branch campuses headed by a vice president who is also the principal, and each has a separate Campus Council that exercises governance oversight of campus-specific matters on behalf of the University's Governing Council.

In the second type, individual campuses have no direct reporting to each other but instead report to the overall system office that in some jurisdictions is headed by a chancellor. A typical example of this structure is the California system in the USA. The University of the West Indies has a similar type of multilevel governance structure in which each of its four campuses reports to the Vice Chancellery. The Vice Chancellery in this case is a higher-level university function with oversight responsibility for the campuses. What is most pertinent about this second type of multi-campus arrangement is that the campuses function autonomously of each other but are held accountable to a higher level body, typically a Chancellery or a Vice Chancellery.

A major consideration in structuring the governance of multi-campus universities is the purpose for which different campuses are established. In some instances, establishing new branch campuses is a way to provide a specific type of service to a defined market, and this could be a metropolitan area where there is a significant amount of commercial activity or it could be an underserved community. Governance issues related to mission and identity come to the fore. Is the campus established as a profit-generating commercial-type entity having a separate identity from the main campus? Or is the campus established to serve its region and is part of the larger system with several identities? Dengerink (2001) suggests that for multi-campus universities to function optimally, the values, roles, and missions must be clearly articulated and the governance structured in such a way that it allows individual campuses to contribute to the overall university mission. However, individual campuses with clearly stated different missions similarly have to be accommodated since these differences also contribute to the university's overall mission.

GOVERNING THE GLONACAL AND TRANSNATIONAL

Marginson and Rhoades (2002) argue that in the analysis of higher education in the context of globalization it is important to recognize that higher education operates along three interrelated and interconnected planes, the global, national, and local (or "glonacal"), and that each plane has its own dimensions and forces. The interconnectedness of the planes suggests that pursuing the international does not necessarily mean reducing emphasis on the local; for example a university might develop a new academic program on global business and new international partnerships to explicitly address local needs. Combining this notion of multiple planes with the concept of agency, Marginson and Rhoades developed a glonacal agency heuristic, an innovative conceptualization for the analysis of higher education in a global context.

Combining the glonacal concept of multiple planes of existence with Clark's (1983) concept of levels of authority, Jones and Oleksiyenko (2011) developed a global higher education matrix as a simple tool for looking at the complex interrelationships in how the local, national, and global dimensions are taken-up within multilevel governance. Focusing on a case study of international research activities at a single university, they note, for example, how certain faculties prioritized activities along the international plane even in the absence of institutional, local, or national government strategy, funding, or incentive systems. The recognition that higher education operates along multiple dimensions (glonacal) and that university governance operates along multiple levels of authority provides the foundation for a matrix view of priorities and policy in the context of multilevel governance.

The global dimension of higher education has become increasingly important for governance as institutions pursue internationalization strategies, including international student recruitment, increasing student and faculty mobility, and developing and strengthening international partnerships. The global competition for international student revenue and international rankings is impacting governance at the system, institutional, and academic unit levels of authority. One broad form of international initiative, transnational higher education, presents a series of complex challenges for university governance.

Transnational higher education (TNHE) refers to "any education delivered by an institution based in one country to students located in another" (Yang, 2008, p. 272). Higher education is being moved across geopolitical borders and THNE therefore represents higher education cross-border market activity.

There are three types of TNHE: the international branch campus which is a "brick-and-mortar" unit of a higher education institution located in another country (Shams & Huisman, 2012), distance and online education, and partner-supported delivery (McBurnie & Ziguras, 2007). These arrangements are either undertaken collaboratively with local universities (in some instances joint degrees are offered), or independently, sometimes in direct competition with local institutions. TNHE raises a number of relatively new governance challenges at the institutional level, as well as challenges at the system level (both for the system with jurisdiction over the institution offering the education program, as well as the jurisdiction in which the student is receiving the education).

In terms of institutional governance, imagine all of the issues and challenges that we discussed in relation to academic self-governance (in chapter 6) and governance processes (in chapter 7) further complicated by operating in two different national environments, with different cultures, languages, academic traditions, stakeholders, regulatory arrangements, and external pressures. A fundamental issue is whether the international campus should be subject to the same academic regulations, standards, and practices as the home campus, or whether it should be governed differently as a special unit with distinct, perhaps more entrepreneurial, objectives. The issue of academic freedom has emerged in several situations where universities have developed campuses in quite different political and cultural environments.

In terms of system governance, the jurisdiction in which the home university is located must ponder the degree to which regulations, quality assurance mechanisms, and accountability requirements should be extended to the transnational education activities of the university or focus only or primarily on domestic activities. Some countries have quality assurance guidelines that their higher education institutions must comply with when engaging in transnational education (Shams & Huisman, 2012). Is transnational education viewed as a legitimate activity for a publicly funded university with a mandate to serve the needs of the jurisdiction, or is it positioned as a revenue-generating auxiliary activity?

Another series of governance issues is associated with the jurisdiction in which the transnational education activity is located, including the basic issue of whether international providers will be allowed to operate. In Malaysia for example, branch campuses of foreign universities can only be established following an invitation from the Ministry of Education or the Ministry of Higher Education (Mok, 2011). Other governance challenges include adequate regulation to ensure a quality educational experience is being offered and transparency to ensure that regulations are being adhered to. The challenges are sometimes augmented because, according to dos Santos (2000), "transnational education [sometimes] falls outside the official framework for higher education and, as a consequence, stays outside the formal supervision of academic standards" (p. 9). In more recent times some countries have implemented legislation to protect higher education consumers, and governments may to some extent control what foreign providers offer. For instance, foreign universities operating in China are subject to detailed legislative stipulations that govern transnational education. Singapore actively regulates transnational higher education including using the practice of selectively inviting overseas partners to set up branch campuses (Mok, 2011). Mok suggests that this practice is a form of market intervention whereby the state decides on which institutional partners will be permitted and determines what they offer—a practice that is related to the country's nation-building agenda.

In some countries in which transnational higher education is part of a national development strategy, governments are enacting or amending legislation to improve governance, reduce bureaucracy, and make higher education more corporate; for example, Malaysia (Mok, 2011). Generally speaking, regulations, according to Shams and Huisman (2012), are of two types: (1) trade regulations which are concerned with import and export of assets, taxation policies, and staff recruitment etc.; and (2) quality assurance, which is about compliance with rules and regulations as they relate to quality. In some cases, universities are subject to the quality assurance requirements associated with both their home jurisdiction as well as the country regulating the international campus or program.

Finally, it is important to note that some countries have made the development of higher education hubs a component part of their higher education and national development strategies (Huang, 2007; Mok, 2012). Asia, Singapore, Malaysia, and Hong Kong have taken steps to promote the development of education hubs (Mok, 2011), though Lee (2014) found that each country was motivated by somewhat different policy objectives. Other examples include initiatives in Dubai (United Arab Emirates) and Qatar. Education hubs represent a strategic form of transnational higher education with complex implications for system-level governance (Knight, 2014).

REGIONALIZATION AND GOVERNANCE

Over the last decade, there has been a noticeable increase in higher education regional level collaboration and reform initiatives (Knight, 2013) or the regionalization of higher education. It is an ongoing phenomenon that represents a harmonization of systems and an incorporation of bilateral and multilateral international efforts and initiatives (Knight, 2013). Knight notes that among these initiatives are the comparability of degrees among member states, regional-based university networks, student mobility programs, regional higher education associations, regional frameworks for quality assurance, and the recognition of degrees along with credits and qualifications from member jurisdictions. This is a very interesting phenomenon in that, in an era of globalization, the regionalization of higher education is gaining significant traction in a number of locations. There is also a growing interest among scholars in exploring its multiple dimensions. Some argue that regional higher education projects have become more influential than their global counterparts because of the scale of strategic importance they have to a region's development.

Two of the most relatively advanced regionalization projects in higher education are the Bologna Process in Europe and MERCOSUR-Educativo in South America. Bologna, a byproduct of the EU supralevel state, is arguably the largest higher education regionalization project in the world. Despite the scale of Bologna and its reach outside of Europe, it serves as a coordinator of member states' policies as opposed to being a mechanism of integration as is the case with trade policies (Verger & Hermo, 2010). Enders and Westerheijden (2011) describe it as "a political process of horizontal integration *[that]* is based on soft governance, where national policies are coordinated by agreement at the European level but national governments try to remain in full control of the decision process, transformation into a national contexts and implementation" (p. 470).

Soft governance relies on soft power and, according to the Nye (2004), it is the power of getting others to want outcomes that you want through a process of co-option rather than coercing them. Hence, rather than adopting a hard command approach, soft power users rely on co-option. Thus, Bologna relies on cooperation with some co-option, is voluntary and not binding on member countries, and does not have the EU conventional processes associated with supranational steering. This is an example of how higher education regionalization projects are governed. There is retention of significant sovereign control of higher education with reliance on soft power to govern member states. Bologna is an example of this type of intergovernmental coordination of higher education across a set of systems in a way that retains the rich diversity of teaching, learning, and higher education cultures (Mok, 2011). In others cases of regionalization, there is what Sasseen (2006) refers to as the denationalization of governance, in which more sovereign authority and control are surrendered to the supralevel state.

Jayasuriya (2008) uses the concept of regulatory regionalism to capture some of these new modes of regional governance occurring outside of national territorial boundaries. Jayasuriya and Robertson (2010) conceptualize regulatory regionalism as an "approach [that] emphasizes the constitution of broad regional regulatory projects within the institutional spaces of the state" (p. 3). In this process, there is regulatory accommodation of diverse patterns of national governments but not an aggregation of national territorial higher education at the supralevel. These new modes, Jayasuriya and Robertson argue, are the result of rescaling higher education institutions and their governance. The extent of the rescaling depends on the extent to which higher education institutions are subject to regulatory governance.

Verger and Hermo (2010) argue that the extent to which regionalization projects such as Bologna or MERCOSUR-Educativo advance and develop depends on their legitimacy, structure, and governance of the regional entity. Regional projects tend to have more legitimacy and this is an important basis on which regionalization projects are accepted (Hettne, 2005). Verger and Hermo (2010) suggest that the legitimacy of regional projects stems from the fact that they are usually started voluntarily by member countries as opposed to being imposed by wealthy countries or international economic organizations such as the OECD. Additionally, because these projects are driven by the interests of member countries, they tend to have domestic structures and function in the best interests of the coalition (Jayasuriya, 2003). The bigger challenge, however, is their governance. Verger and Hermo (2010) demonstrate this point by comparing the institutionalization of governance structures at the suprastate level between Bologna and MERCOSUR-Educativo. They point out that the Bologna process has more deeply entrenched institutionalized governance structures than MERCOSUR-Educativo. They cite, for instance, the low-profile status of the accreditation agencies in South America compared to the European Association for Quality Assurance (ENQA). The ENQA has a General Assembly and Board of Directors and plays a defining role in setting standards and harmonizing policies on an European-wide scale. Hence the institutional robustness and rate of progress are different between these regions, illustrating how the regionalization process can vary significantly by region and how governance can impact progress.

SUMMARY

Our objective in this chapter was to briefly review a number of more recent challenges or practices associated with university governance. Assessing and understanding risk has become an important component of governance practice, as has the development of emergency plans and policies designed to ensure that the institution is prepared for natural hazards and acts of violence. We argue that trust is an important but understudied issue in higher education governance, and note that information technology can be used to strengthen governance processes. There are particular issues and challenges associated with multi-campus governance arrangements. We then turned to look at governance in the context of the glonacal, transnational, and regional dimensions of higher education. There seems little doubt that the global/international dimension of higher education will continue to grow in importance, leading to increasingly complex governance issues and arrangements.

DISCUSSION QUESTIONS

1. Consider a hypothetical higher education system where the government has complete trust in the universities that it funds, and universities have complete trust in government. What do you think the governance arrangements in that system might look like?

2. In an earlier chapter we discussed collegiality and academic self-governance. What are some of the challenges for academic self-governance in an institution that is operating in multiple jurisdictions involving different cultures and traditions? How might these challenges be addressed through governance structures and processes?

3. Information technology is often used to strengthen decision-making and governance processes, but can you imagine ways in which the introduction of information technology could have negative implications for university governance? What are some examples? How might these problems be addressed?

REFERENCES

Avis, J. (2003). Re-thinking trust in a performative culture: The case of education. *Journal of Education Policy, 18*(3), 315–332.

Clark, B.R. (1983). *The higher education system: Academic organization in cross-national perspective.* Berkley, CA: University of California Press.

Clyde-Smith, J. (2014). Utilising enterprise risk management strategies to develop a governance and operations framework for a new research complex: A case study. *Journal of Higher Education Policy and Management, 36*(3), 327–337.

De Boer, H. (2002). Trust, the essence of governance? In A. Amaral, G.A. Jones, & B. Karseth (Eds.), *Governing higher education: National perspectives on institutional governance.* Dordrecht, The Netherlands: Kluwer.

Dengerink, H. A. (2001). Institutional identity and organizational structure in multi-campus universities. *Metropolitan Universities, 12*(2), 20–29.

Dos Santos, M. (2000). *Introduction to the theme of transnational education.* Paper presented at the Conference of the Directors General of Higher Education and the Heads of the Rectors' Conference of the European Union. Retrieved from http://www.fclb.uminho.pt/uploads/artigo36-abr00.pdf

Enders, J., & Westerheijden, D. F. (2011). The Bologna process: From the national to the regional to the global, and back. In R. King, S. Marginson, & R. Naidoo (Eds.), *Handbook on globalization and higher education* (pp. 469–484). Northampton, MA: Edward Elgar.

Ernst and Young. (2012). *University of the future: A thousand year old industry on the cusp of profound change.* Retrieved from http://www.ey.com/Publication/vwLUAssets/University_of_the_future/SFile/

Godegebuure, L., & Hayden, M. (2007). Overview: Governance in higher education—concepts and issues. *Higher Education Research, & Development, 26*(1), 1–11.

Hashim, F., Alam, G. M., & Siraj, S. (2010). Information and communication technology for participatory based decision-making-E-management for administrative efficiency in higher education. *International Journal of Physical Science, 5*(4), 383–392.

Hettne, B. (2005). Beyond the "new" regionalism. *New Political Economy, 10*(4), 543–571.

Higher Education Funding Council for England (HEFCE). (2004). *Guide for members of higher education governing bodies in the UK.* Bristol, England: HEFCE.

Huang, F. (2007). Internationalization of higher education in the developing and emerging countries: A focus on transnational higher education in Asia. *Journal of Studies in International Education, 11*(3–4), 421–432.

Huber, C. (2009). Risks and risk-based regulation in higher education institutions. *Tertiary Education and Management, 15*(2), 83–95.

Ingley, C., & van der Walt, N. (2008). Risk management and board effectiveness. *International Studies of Management. & Organization, 38*(3), 43–70.

Jayasuriya, K. (2003). Introduction: Governing the Asia Pacific: Beyond the "new regionalism." *Third World Quarterly, 24*(2), 199–215.

Jayasuriya, K. (2008). Regionalising the state: Political topography of regulatory regionalism. *Contemporary Politics, 14*(1), 21–35.

Jayasuriya, K., & Robertson, S. (2010). Regulatory regionalism and the governance of higher education. *Globalisation, Societies and Education, 8*(1), 1–6.

Jones, G. A., & Oleksiyenko, A. (2011). The internationalization of Canadian university research: A global higher education matrix analysis of multi-level governance. *Higher Education, 61*(1), 41–57.

Kezar, A. (2004). What is more important to effective governance: Relationships, trust, and leadership, or structures and formal processes? *New Directions for Higher Education* (Special issue) *Restructuring Shared Governance in Higher Education, 127,* 35–46.

Knight, J. (2013). A model for the regionalization of higher education: The role and contribution of Tuning. *Tuning Journal for Higher Education: New Profiles for New Societies, 1,* 105–125.

Knight, J. (Ed.) (2014). *International education hubs: Student, talent, and knowledge-innovation models.* Dordrecht, The Netherlands: Springer.

Korosec, B., & Horvat, R. (2005). Risk reporting in corporate annual reports. *Economic and Business Review for Central and South-Eastern Europe, 7*(3), 217–237.

Lane, C. (1998). Introduction: Theories and issues in the study of trust. In C. Lane & R. Buchmann (Eds.), *Trust within and between organizations: Conceptual issues and empirical applications* (pp. 1–31). Oxford, England: Oxford University Press.

Lee, J. T. (2014). Education hubs and talent development: Policymaking and implementation challenges. *Higher Education, 68*(6), 807–823.

Marginson, S., & Rhoades, G. (2002). Beyond national states, markets and systems of higher education: A glonacal agency heuristic. *Higher Education, 43*(3), 282–309.

McBurnie, G., & Ziguras, C. (2007). *Transnational education: Issues and trends in offshore higher education*. London, England: Routledge Falmer.

Middlehurst, R. (2013). Changing internal governance: Are leadership roles and management structures in the United Kingdom universities fit for the future? *Higher Education Quarterly, 67*(3), 275–294.

Migliore, L. (2012). Leadership, governance, and perceptions of trust in the higher education industry. *Journal of Leadership Studies, 5*(4), 30–40.

Migliore, L. A., & DeClouette, A. H. (2011). Perceptions of trust in the boardroom: A conceptual model. *Journal of Leadership & Organizational Studies, 18*(3), 320–333.

Mok, K. H. (2011). The quest for regional hub of education: Growing heterarchies, organizational hybridization and new governance in Singapore and Malaysia. *Journal of Education Policy, 26*(1), 61–81.

Mok, K. H. (2012). The rise of transnational higher education in Asia: Student mobility and studying experiences in Singapore and Malaysia. *Higher Education Policy, 25*, 225–241.

National Association of College and University Business Officers & PriceWaterhouseCoopers. (2001). *Developing a strategy to manage enterprise-wide risk in higher education*. Washington, DC: National Association of College and University Business Officers.

Nye, J. (2004). *Soft power: The means to success in world politics*. New York, NY: Public Affairs.

Robson, A. (2008). *Go8. on removal of national governance protocols*. Retrieved from http://www.go8. edu.au/index.php?option=com_content&task=view&id=176

Sasseen, S. (2006). *Territory, authority, rights: From medieval to global assemblages*. Princeton, NJ: Princeton University Press.

Shams, F., & Huisman, J. (2012). Managing offshore branch campuses: An analytical framework for institutional strategies. *Journal of Studies in International Education, 16*(2), 106–127. doi. 10.1177/1028315311413470

Subramaniam, N., McManus, L., & Zhang, J. (2009). Corporate governance, firm characteristics and risk management committee formation in Australian companies. *Managerial Auditing Journal, 24*(4), 316–339. doi.10.1108/02686900910948170

Tierney, W. G. (2006). *Trust and the public good: Examining the cultural conditions of academic work*. New York, NY: Peter Lang.

Tucker, D. A., Yeow, P., & Viki, G. T. (2013). Communicating during organizational change using social accounts: The importance of ideological accounts. *Management Communication Quarterly, 27*, 184–209.

University of Pretoria. (2015). *Risk management and internal audit*. [Website]. Retrieved from http://www.up.ac.za/risk-management-and-internal-audit/article/270405/about-the-departmrisk-management-and-internal-auditt

University Risk Management and Insurance Association. (2007). *ERM in higher education*. Bloomington, IN: University Risk Management and Insurance Association.

Verger, A., & Hermo, J. P. (2010). The governance of higher education regionalisation: Comparative analysis of the Bologna Process and MERCOSUR-Educativo. *Globalisation, Societies and Education, 8*(1), 105–120.

Vidovich, L., & Currie, J., (2011). Governance and trust in higher education. *Studies in Higher Education, 36*(1), 43–56.

Yang, R. (2008). Transnational higher education in China: Contexts, characteristics and concerns. *Australian Journal of Education, 52*(3), 272–286.

Zucker, L. G. (1986). Production of trust: Institutional sources of economic structure, 1840–1920. In B. M. Staw & L. L. Cummings (Eds.), *Research in organizational behavior* (Vol. 8, pp. 53–111). Greenwich, CT: JAI.

CHAPTER 10

Concluding Observations and Reflections

Over the last few decades, the governance of higher education has invoked a considerable amount of interest both at the institutional and at the system level. Policy-makers, higher education practitioners, and academics have all been interested in the complex relationships between universities and the state, the internal governance of institutions of higher education, and the impact and implications of reforms. Scholars worldwide have sought to investigate and understand a multiplicity of issues linked to the governance of higher education and to provide some guidance to policy-makers.

In this book we attempted, as much as the literature would allow, to review empirical findings, theories, and practices on governance in higher education. To achieve this, we were global in perspective, theoretical in focus, and policy-oriented. We remained ever mindful that universities are loosely coupled and complex organizations where governance functions at multiple levels. The framework we used attempted to capture governance at multiple levels: the group level within institutions (e.g., faculty and student groups), the institutional level, and the system level. In this regard, we discuss the reflexive interplay between the state, university, academics, and students to illustrate how these levels intersect and the ways in which structures and processes regulate interactions across these levels to govern higher education. Importantly, we showed, through a brief review of governance arrangements and reforms in six countries, how the structure of these interactions varies across national jurisdictions. For instance, in France, senior academics (deans) had a tradition of direct interaction with the state and the academic profession drove developments in the system. This is quite different from the Humboldtian, UK, or USA traditions.

To get a good picture of the interactions across levels, there was a need to locate higher education governance within some historical frame of reference and compare it to contemporary governance. We discussed system-level governance across different national jurisdictions by first referencing the history and tradition of higher education in respective countries. This approach provided a useful baseline from which to understand the changes that are being driven by the desire of some countries, such as China, to modernize. Further, it allowed for a distinction to be drawn between traditional views on governance that were held four decades ago and contemporary thoughts and ideologies such as neoliberalism, new public management, and managerialism. The historical approach also allowed us to illustrate how interactions across levels continue to change over time and in different ways depending on the country and its history, traditions, and specific circumstances. For instance, over time China has moved from a central planning state-centric model to adopting market approaches to governance and, in so doing, has devolved more authority to institutions. Despite the differences by jurisdiction, Musselin (2011) argues that there is some evidence of global convergence between higher education systems occurring through the isomorphic process.

To further help us understand how governance works in the academy and the relationship between the internal and external environment of institutions, we drew on a number of theories. We tried to provide readers with theories that have been applied in governance research, as well as theories that have received relatively little attention in the research literature to date but we believe can contribute significantly to understanding higher education governance. For example, resource-dependence theory has been applied to higher education governance in a number of different studies. Similarly, the structural perspective has been used extensively in research on governance, particularly at the institutional level, but this perspective is devoid of the role of human actors in governance. More recent work by Lane and Kivisto (2008) highlights the importance of applying agency theory, traditionally used in corporate governance research, to higher education governance.

In addition to these individual theories, it is advocated that a multi-theory approach can be quite beneficial to understanding the issues associated with governance. Christopher (2012) shows the usefulness of the multi-theory approach, particularly in assessing the wider influencing forces on higher education governance. This highlights the notion that public universities are subject to the influence of a variety of environmental forces and that a single theory may not always be appropriate. But although scholars in the field have produced a significant body of scholarly research and writings and there has been an increase in the application of theoretical constructs being used to inform these investigations, there remains more work to be done theoretically in ways that explore not only single theory application but also multi-theory usage. The multi-theory approach to governance can combine what may seemingly be at opposite ends of the theory spectrum, for example, agency theory and stewardship theory. Rather than assuming the self-interests of agents, it may be useful to examine empirically the extent of self-interests versus the level of cooperative behaviors of stewards to determine if and when actors switch behaviors as circumstances change.

Another important issue in governance is the role and definition of the state. Mok (2003) suggests that the pressures of globalization have weakened the nation-state and limited its role in the management of the public sector. Simultaneous with the redefinition of the state has been the evolving relationship between the state and universities. While universities are encouraged to become managed entities, the state in many jurisdictions tries to direct the course of higher education. The basic argument for this is that governments are concerned about universities being relevant and delivering the type of education needed in a competitive global knowledge economy. Consequently, universities in some countries have seen an increase in procedural autonomy while governments have taken steps to increase their substantive autonomy over higher education.

The new environment of higher education, some argue, has adversely affected the tradition of collegiality and the practice of shared governance. Traditional governance arrangements are currently being challenged by power shifts within the university and external pressures for more efficient and effective decision-making structures. This has challenged the notion of academic self-governance. A further weakening of academic self-governance occurs with the increase in adjunct and part-time faculty that has become prevalent across universities. Unionization, the level of engagement of faculty in the context of the increasing demands of teaching and research, and the growing adoption of corporate business and governance practices all have implications for collegial processes and academic self-governance. Even how students are viewed in the context of the academy has shifted from the traditional co-producer and guild concept to being customers or clients. The role students play in institutional governance is significantly determined by the institution's conception of its students and the definition of its student-university relationship. Where university students are defined as co-producers, for instance, the model of governance is more cooperative and egalitarian and invokes notions of students as stakeholders with a strong sense of institutional ownership. Where students are viewed as customers or clients, there is a more contractual and customer-rights driven relationship with the institution. Once again, it is important to recognize that the level and nature of these changes vary both by system and institution.

We believe that governance in higher education is process driven and not a set of static institutional arrangements. In the process, there is engagement and consultation with different parties and this is an integral part of the tradition of governance in the academy. Encompassing all of this are power, politics, and conflict. Baldridge (1971) views the political dimension of higher education as germane to understanding governance especially at the institutional level. An important element of this is understanding the role of institutional subgroups and their link to notions of interests, coalitions, and bargaining.

While providing far from an exhaustive review, we have also tried to illuminate a number of more recent challenges and issues for higher education governance. The issue of risk and emergency preparedness, drawn initially from corporate notions of risk management, is receiving increasing attention, as is the role of information technology in furthering evidence-based decision-making and communication within governance processes. The recurring issue of trust in governance raises interesting issues and questions. A complex web of issues and challenges is associated with the increasing international dimension of higher education in the glonacal university, especially issues related to transnational education and regionalism.

FUTURE RESEARCH

Our primary objective for this volume was to create a foundational text designed to introduce many of the basic concepts and theories associated with university governance. As we have noted, while the study of higher education governance is built on a foundation of significant contributions from leading scholars, others are focusing primarily on descriptive analyses of governance at both the institutional and system levels. There is a need for more research on university governance that is grounded in, and will contribute to, theory, and perhaps lead us down new pathways.

While there is a considerable body of comparative scholarship focusing on system-level governance, especially focusing on the impact of system reforms (in response to the Bologna process, for example, or in the former Soviet states), there is a need for more comparative and internationally informed research at the level of the institution and at the level of the academic unit. More theoretically informed research on governance at the level of the faculty and the basic academic unit (the department or institute), perhaps through the lens of multilevel governance, could offer important insight on governance at the "ground level." There may also be important benefits from more directly linking the study of university governance with studies on the academic profession. In addition, the application of cultural and human relations perspectives could yield significant insights into improving the functioning of governance. Further research in these areas is needed, and we are beginning to see glimpses of it. Furthermore, exploring if and how providing interpersonal and leadership training to organizational leaders, departmental leaders, and members of governance committees, such as the senate, could improve the functioning of governing bodies.

We believe that the importance of further research on university governance cannot be overstated. The governance of higher education is, in many ways, the governance of knowledge, since these institutions now play the central role in developing the human resources that are so essential to the economic and social development of the societies in which we live. Universities are key components of national research and innovation systems, and they are the home of the critical scholarship that plays such an important role in furthering our understanding of the world in which we live. Given their central role, it is essential that we take steps to increase our understanding of university governance and contribute to the strengthening of these all important decision-making processes. University governance matters, not just to those of us inside the academy, but to the world.

REFERENCES

Baldridge, J. V. (1971). *Power and conflict in the university: Research in the sociology of complex organizations*. New York, NY: John Wiley.

Christopher, J. (2012). Governance paradigms of public universities: An international comparative study. *Tertiary Education and Management, 18*(4), 335–351.

Lane, J., & Kivisto, J. (2008). Interests, information, and incentives in higher education: Principal-agent theory and its potential applications to the study of higher education governance. In J. C. Smart (Ed.), *Higher education: Handbook of theory and research* (Vol 23, pp. 141–174). Dordrecht, The Netherlands: Springer.

Mok, K. H. (2003). Globalisation and higher education restructuring in Hong Kong, Taiwan and mainland China. *Higher Education Research & Development, 22*(2), 117–128.

Musselin, C. (2011). Convergences and divergences in steering higher education systems. In R. King, S. Marginson, & R. Naidoo (Eds.), *Handbook on globalization and higher education*. Cheltenham, England: Edward Elgar.

Index

Note: Italicized page numbers indicate a figure on the corresponding page.